Faith, Theology, and Psychoanalysis

Princeton Theological Monograph Series

K. C. Hanson, Series Editor

Recent volumes in the series

Faith, Theology, and Psychoanalysis
The Life and Thought of Harry S. Guntrip

Trevor M. Dobbs

Pickwick *Publications*

An imprint of *Wipf and Stock Publishers*
199 West 8th Avenue • Eugene OR 97401

FAITH, THEOLOGY, AND PSYCHOANALYSIS
The Life and Thought of Harry S. Guntrip
Princeton Theological Monograph Series 72

ISBN 10: 1-59752-8463
ISBN 13: 978-1-59752-846-7

Cataloging-in-Publication data

Dobbs, Trevor M.
Faith, theology, and psychoanalysis : the life and thought of Harry S. Guntrip /
Trevor M. Dobbs.

Eugene, Ore.: Pickwick Publications, 2007
Princeton Theological Monograph Series 72

xii + 190 p.; 23 cm.

ISBN 10: 1-59752-846-3   (alk. paper)
ISBN 13: 978-1-59752-846-7

1. Psychoanalysis and religion. 2. Guntrip, Harry. 3. Winnicott, D. W. (Donald Woods), 1896–1971. 4. Macmurray, John, 1891– . 5. Fairbairn, W. Ronald D. (William Ronald Dodds). I. Title. II. Series.

RC438.6 G86 D67 2007

Manufactured in the U.S.A.

Contents

Figures

Acknowledgments

I wish to thank Dr. Judith Kent for mentoring me through my own "regression to dependence" upon her as my supervising analyst in concert with chairing the doctoral dissertation that was the source of this book. Her supervision of my clinical case went beyond theoretical training to that of facilitating my emotional availability to my patient. This experience culminated in giving up my identification with the schizoid resignation of Harry Guntrip who settled for being less than a certified psychoanalyst, as I was tempted to do. She was truly a "facilitating environmental mother figure" for my professional emergence from "my island" into the psychoanalytic community.

I am grateful to Dr. Leslie Rosenstock who was my "Winnicottian" analyst who facilitated my emergence from schizoid intellectual isolation to embracing my own emotional self. Her availability as an emotionally present "holding mother" enabled my interaction with her as the interpreting "object mother" to reconnect my thinking with my feeling. She prepared my heart to be emotionally available for the incredible experience of holding my newborn sons and being moved at a level that I had never experienced before. Thank you Leslie!

I would like to identify Dr. Ray Anderson as my theological mentor who gave deep meaning to the concept that "retreat from the ontic to the ontological is inadmissible by revelation." The parable-like nature of his teaching sowed seeds both in me and my wife, Connie, that bound us together with an intuitive pursuit of a Christian faith that lives in a "religionless" world of the real. His genuine embodiment of that as our pastor-on-call is our hedge against the cynicism that threatens those of us who know the frailty of humanity within church circles only too well.

I want Dr. Bill Erwin to know that he is probably more Winnicottian (to me in my mind) than he knows. Over the years of Psychoanalytic Institute politics and its chaotic family life I have found him to be a "holding presence" as he would intercept my fuming and frustration with a calming response.

I would like to especially thank my "best friend," my wife Connie, that is, Dr. Lillas! In the last twenty five years she has not only provided me with a partner to exercise my mind with as we have "talked shop" ever too much, but has intimately participated with me in our journey of "receiving and holding" all of my "internalized bad objects." (See how we "talk shop" way too much!) But most of all, I literally cannot express the depth of the bond I share with her through our shared connection to our boys, Alex and Niko.

To my boys, Niko and Alex, I give thanks for the miracle of childhood that has evoked from me the depths of my soul that I had not even dreamed of. Their immediacy and spontaneity of emotional responsiveness has been the catalyst that has made the years of personal therapy and analysis a real, rather than an intellectual exercise. They are my point of reference for all the years of psychology that I have studied, and the gift of God along with my wife.

I want to thank Dr. William W. Meissner for his gracious reading of the final manuscript of the book and for offering his support of this project.

Note to the Reader

HARRY Guntrip employed a tradition of italicizing certain words, phrases and entire paragraphs as a way of calling attention to his central points and highlighting his own conclusions. I will continue that tradition, (in addition to quoting Guntrip's own use of such emphasis), in highlighting the statements of *my own thesis* that I am setting forth in this book.

Preface

THE twentieth century has witnessed the secularization of academic disciplines where the departments of science have separated themselves from the humanities, including philosophy, theology, and psychology. During much of the nineteenth century, psychology was still considered a branch of philosophy. In response, modern psychology in western culture has pursued membership in the departments of science, albeit known as a "soft science" in contrast to the "hard sciences" of physics, biology, and other laboratory endeavors. The psychoanalytic tradition has joined this desire for respect from the academic community, to this day commonly referring to psychoanalytic conferences as "scientific meetings."

The famous names of earlier centuries were not so inclined to divide up the understanding of aspects of human life and experience into what have become mutually exclusive categories. The famous philosophers of the western tradition, such as Hegel, Kant, and others, were also theologians. Most strikingly is that the famous mathematicians of the world of science, Descartes, Pascal, and especially Sir Isaac Newton, all wrote of philosophical and theological concerns and viewpoints. To a degree, this is a legacy of the Renaissance centuries earlier and its own famous figures such as da Vinci, where being a "Renaissance Man," (or today, woman), means being versed in multiple disciplines, where art informs science, and visa versa.

The impact of secularization upon the historical tradition of psychoanalysis is best seen in Freud's monograph, *Future of an Illusion*,[1] where he reduces religion to a cultural version of neurotic psychopathology. This has resulted in a common, (although as we shall see, not a complete), adversarial tension between psychology and theology. Harry S. Guntrip, a psychotherapist in the psychoanalytic tradition, is a fascinating example of how these respective traditions in the twentieth century have wrestled with each other, commonly known as the battle between science and religion.

---

[1] Sigmund Freud, *Future of an Illusion* (New York: Norton, 1974).

This is a study that will trace the respective influences on the development of the thought of Harry Guntrip. This includes his personal history of family relationships, membership in various religious organizations, as well as the influence of his academic and professional mentors, both theological and psychoanalytic. A central theme of polarities will be utilized to organize these various influences in Guntrip's life.

The theme of polarities between the classical and romantic worldviews will be outlined as the central feature of the history of psychoanalysis (Chapter 1). The polarities between orthodox rationalism and pietism in the history of philosophy and theology in Europe, and between Calvinism and Revivalism in Britain will show this parallel pattern between these disciplines (Chapters 2 and 3).

The conflictual polarity between psychoanalysis and religion will be examined as a countertransferential phenomenon within psychoanalysis as a form of splitting off and projecting psychoanalysis' own religiosity in Freud's neurotic sense, and the disavowal of its own philosophical/spiritual mindset in its clinical practice. Guntrip's analysis of this dichotomy in Freud of professional rationalism and personal spirituality will also be elaborated.

The development of Guntrip's version of British Object Relations theory in psychoanalysis will be shown to be a derivative of the "personal object relations" between Guntrip and his mentors, Ronald Fairbairn and Donald Winnicott, along with the "Persons in Relation" theological philosophy of John Macmurray as his unifying point of reference (Chapters 4–7).

Polarities in psychoanalysis will be examined as expressed in: (a) Fairbairn's theoretical polarity of libidinal and antilibidinal egos (as a revision of Freud's classical structural theory); (b) Guntrip's central theme of the Schizoid Compromise as a person's desire for human attachment and connection, yet being so frightened of relationships that the person withdraws into psychological "cold storage"; and (c) Winnicott's dialectical holding of polarities in paradoxical tension (Chapter 8).

The paradoxical-dialectical approaches of Donald Winnicott in psychoanalysis, and William W. Meissner's own integration of psychoanalysis and theology will be offered as a perspective of integration for Guntrip's often conflictual tension between the respective polarities (Chapter 9).

In the work of psychoanalysis links are formed with numbers of other mental sciences, the investigation of which promises results of the greatest value: links with mythology and philology, with folklore, with social psychology and the theory of religion.

—Sigmund Freud, *Introductory Lectures on Psychoanalysis*

Introduction

H ARRY S. Guntrip was best known for his affiliation with two famous psychoanalysts from what is known as the British Independent tradition of psychoanalysis in England: Ronald Fairbairn and Donald Winnicott. This book traces the various influences on the development of his clinical and theological thinking in context of the historical tension between religion and psychoanalysis. The central feature of his development will be demonstrated as a series of polarities, both theoretical and personal, conflicts with which he wrestled theologically, psychologically, and interpersonally on the professional level and in his own personal psychoanalyses. A critical evaluation of the outcome of Guntrip's own personal psychoanalyses with Fairbairn and Winnicott will demonstrate the autobiographical nature of his theoretical analysis of schizoid phenomena: a psychological state of self-preoccupation and way of being in the world.

Songwriters Simon and Garfunkel colorfully capture in verse, in "I Am a Rock," what became Guntrip's area of expertise: schizoid states of experience.[1]

In his classic work, *Schizoid Phenomena, Object Relations and the Self,*[2] Guntrip describes with clarity the mindset of the person illustrated by Simon and Garfunkl's popular song. What is not obvious to the reader is that his book is autobiographical to a significant degree, in addition to being a scholarly work informed by clinical experience.

---

[1] Paul Simon and Art Garfunkel, "I am a Rock," in *Greatest Hits* (Los Angeles: Sony Music, 1990).

[2] Guntrip, *Schizoid Phenomena, Object Relations and the Self* (New York: International Universities Press, 1968).

The autobiographical nature of the psychoanalytic tradition itself is, perhaps, best illustrated by Sigmund Freud's book, *The Interpretation of Dreams*,[3] where the dreams that he analyzed and explored where largely his own. Guntrip chronicled his experience of his personal psychoanalyses with two prominent British analysts in a comparative fashion in "My Experience of Analysis with Fairbairn and Winnicott."[4] The focal point in the psychoanalytic literature about his article has been his traumatic emotional attachment to his mother in the context of a number of developmental events in his childhood.

Guntrip's relationship with the pioneering Psychoanalytic Object Relations theorist, Ronald Fairbairn, reflected their shared interest in a psychology that was attachment and relationally oriented, in contrast to the biological drive theory of classical psychoanalysis. Guntrip was drawn to Fairbairn's remaking of Freud's classical model of the person seeking relief from the tensions of psychological drives, into a model where the person seeks attachment to primary caregivers. Both Fairbairn and Guntrip shared a hunger for a "full-blooded" approach to life, characterized by deeply meaningful relationships. Unfortunately for both, to varying degrees, their personal backgrounds had predisposed them to personalities that did not embody in practice what they both wrote about in theory. For example, Guntrip presented his psychoanalytic sessions with Fairbairn as a *classical* psychoanalytic experience that was characterized by Fairbairn's stoic distance and oedipal interpretations. In contrast he presented his analysis with Winnicott as reflecting what has been called the *romantic* vision in psychoanalysis, characterized by the notion of "maternal holding."[5]

In short, I would describe Harry Guntrip as embodying a personal polarity of subscribing to attachment-relationally oriented thinking and theology which conflicted with his personal history of schizoid adaptation: preoccupation with one's own world. My thesis is that this dynamic characterized Harry Guntrip's own life, and is what I propose to demonstrate in this study.

What Guntrip saw as the accomplishment of his psychoanalysis with Winnicott was his recovery of dream images about his relationship with his mother that vividly illustrated his deadening relationship with her, (or traumatic attachment). These dreams were stimulated by the death

---

[3] Sigmund Freud, *The Interpretation of Dreams* (New York: Norton, 1985 [1900]).

[4] Guntrip, "My Experience of Analysis with Fairbairn and Winnicott," *International Review of Psychoanalysis* 2 (1975) 145–56.

[5] Carlo Strenger, "The Classic And The Romantic Vision In Psychoanalysis," *International Journal of Psychoanalysis* 70 (1989) 593.

of Winnicott himself, a tragic loss for Guntrip that evoked unconscious images of a faceless and armless mother who was unable to provide the psychological connection and emotional holding that the schizoid person both lacks and hungers for. His schizoid defenses, exemplified by Guntrip's compulsive intellectualization, prevented him from experiencing his withdrawn and vulnerable self within his sessions with Winnicott. This was the central way for him to keep distance from the overwhelming emotions of loss that he carried inside himself from childhood. This illustrates what can be called the paradox of the schizoid experience: the apparent necessity of the death of his *flesh and blood* relationship with Winnicott in order for him to experience his internalized emotionally dead relationship with his mother. This trauma and loss was carried by his repressed and withdrawn *weak ego*, or vulnerable self. Guntrip's inability to experience the vulnerability of his internalized trauma in a *regression to dependence* upon Winnicott *within the living relationship* reflects the tragic aspect of his personal *schizoid phenomena*.

The Place of the Personal in Psychoanalysis

The stereotype of psychoanalysis in America is probably best represented by the images courtesy of Woody Allen: the detached doctor who silently listened to Allen pontificate about his childhood as he lay on the couch. What is most unfortunate is that this picture of psychoanalysis *has* been characteristic of the American tradition. Bruno Bettelheim, perhaps best known for his writing as a survivor of the Nazi concentration camps of the 1930s, argues in *Freud and Man's Soul*[6] that translations of Freud from German into the English, including Strachey's in The Standard Edition, has "led to erroneous conclusions, not only about Freud the man but also about psychoanalysis."[7] His centerpiece is understanding what Freud's sense of the word "psychoanalysis" itself means. "'Psyche' is the soul—a term full of the richest meaning, endowed with emotion, comprehensively human and unscientific."[8] He is not presenting Freud as religious, but rather as "deeply humane . . . a humanist in the best sense of the word. His greatest concern was with man's innermost being".[9] He goes on to imply that the *Freudian* psychoanalysis of America does not reflect the true Freud at all. Again, in regards to the translations, the "English accent in 'psy-

---

[6] Bruno Bettleheim, *Freud and Man's Soul* (New York: Vintage, 1984).

[7] Ibid., 7.

[8] Ibid., 10–11.

[9] Ibid., 11.

choanalysis' is on 'analysis,' . . . with the German word *Psychoanalyse,* on the other hand, the accent is on the first syllable—on 'psyche,' the soul."[10] From Bettelheim's personal account, the contrast between his experience of psychoanalysis in Vienna to that of the United States is astounding.

> For nearly forty years, I have taught courses in psychoanalysis to American graduate students and to residents in psychiatry. Again and again, I have been made to see how seriously the English translations impede students' efforts to gain a true understanding of Freud and of psychoanalysis. Although most of the bright and dedicated students whom it has been my pleasure to teach were eager to learn what psychoanalysis is all about, they were largely unable to do so. Almost invariably, I have found that psychoanalytic concepts had become for these students a way of looking only at others, from a safe distance—nothing that had any bearing on them. They observed other people through the *spectacles of abstraction,* (emphasis added) tried to comprehend them by means of intellectual concepts, never turning their gaze inward to the soul or their own unconscious. This was true even of the students who were in analysis themselves—it made no appreciable difference. . . . Psychoanalysis as these students perceived it was a purely intellectual system—a clever, exciting game—rather than the acquisition of insights into oneself and one's own behavior which were potentially deeply upsetting. It was always *someone else's* unconscious they analyzed, hardly their own. They did not give enough thought to the fact that Freud, in order to create psychoanalysis and understand the workings of the unconscious, had had to analyze his *own* dreams, understand his *own* slips of the tongue and the reasons *he* forgot things or made various other mistakes.[11]

Harry Guntrip was a champion of the *Personal* in psychoanalysis. His legacy is seen in the naming of his collected papers by his protégé, Hazell, as *Personal Relations Therapy,*[12] a more humanized version of the traditional "Object Relations" language. Guntrip himself was a protégé of John Macmurray, professor of Moral Philosophy at London University, and later at Edinburgh University. Macmurray's Gifford lectures of 1954, *Persons in Relation,*[13] are the capstone of three decades of writing that I will

---

[10]   Ibid., 12.

[11]   Ibid., (emphasis in original) 6–7.

[12]   Jeremy Hazell, ed., *Personal Relations Therapy: The Collected Papers of H. J. S. Guntrip* (Northvale, NJ: Aronson, 1994).

[13]   John Macmurray, *Persons in Relation* (New York: Harper & Brothers, 1954).

show are the principal influence in molding Guntrip's theological-philosophical thinking. Guntrip traces his own development in stating,

> I found my earlier studies in religion and philosophy were by no means irrelevant. I had been thoroughly trained in a "personal relations" school of thought, not only in theology but in the philosophy of Professor J. Macmurray. Such books as J. Oman's *Grace and Personality*, Martin Buber's *I and Thou* and J. Macmurray's *Interpreting the Universe, The Boundaries of Science*, and *Reason and Emotion* had left too deep a mark for me to be able to approach the study of man in any other way than as a "Person."[14]

Guntrip did not approach integration of these influences in his life as a harmonizing of disciplines, which he would have called "an artificial attempt to 'fit them together.'" His *personal* journey led him to his consulting room with patients, where for many years he was in the process of working out this blending of his theology, philosophy, and psychology of the Person. Within the intimacy of the encounters with his patients, and in the form of "the natural emergence of a fully psychodynamic theory of personality within psychoanalysis," he digested and metabolized these various aspects of the human Person.[15] From my perspective, he was practicing a "religionless Christianity in a world come of age," a phrase, ironically, he personally rejected, apparently due to its arrival in Britain via the "Death of God" theologians, without an understanding of its original source, Dietrich Bonhoeffer.[16]

The Religion of Psychoanalysis

In 1992 I was attending a presentation by a British psychoanalyst on John Bowlby, known for both his break with a classical version of Psychoanalysis by Melanie Klein, and his subsequent interest in how human beings attach and form bonds with their caretakers. As I learned that this analyst was familiar with those who knew and respected Guntrip in England, I shared my thoughts and plans for this work on Guntrip. He was surprised at the role that theology played for Guntrip, noting, "I thought all psychoanalysts were atheists" (personal communication). This has been the *orthodox* position of many psychoanalysts, one that has been *religiously* held.

---

[14] Guntrip, *Personality Structure and Human Interaction* (New York: International Universities Press, 1961) 19.

[15] Ibid., 19.

[16] Dietrich Bonhoeffer, *Letters and Papers from Prison*, ed. Eberhard Bethge, trans. Reginald H. Fuller (New York: Macmillan, 1953).

The history of the psychoanalytic movement reads like that of Christian Church history: a record of intolerance where there is a "remarkable history of schisms in psychoanalytic institutes, testifying to the difficulty of containing, much less accepting, theoretical differences within existing organizations."[17] In "The Intolerance of Diversity in Psychoanalytic Institutes," Kenneth Eisold develops this theme of the rampant denominalization of the psychoanalytic movement, including "the more hidden history of factionalism and intellectual intimidation that besets institutional life."[18] While noting the historical nature of these schisms as part of the analytic tradition as reflected in Freud's anxiety over his succession, Eisold presents a dynamic answer to the origin of this phenomena based in "an understanding of the anxieties aroused by the ongoing collective professional activities of psychoanalysts."[19] The isolation of psychoanalytic work, characterized by its immersion in the dyads with the patient as well as with the supervisor, produces an anxiety that "derives from the contradiction between the analyst's need to belong to a particular school and his need to believe that he is fully receptive to the clinical material of his patient." In addition to this is the anxiety generated by the "culture of psychoanalysis" itself which "sees itself apart from the world of social reality."[20] One of the "social defenses" of "intolerance for intellectual differences" that Eisold identifies is turning to the theories that link the analyst "to a community of like-minded practitioners" as a way to manage the "continual assaults on their emotional lives" that come with the territory of practicing psychoanalysis. This is more than an echo of Bettleheim's experience of the intellectualization of psychoanalysis. It is the application of Freud's own thesis in *Future of an Illusion* that "religion" is a set of obsessive-compulsive defenses to anxiety. In short, psychoanalysis is a human phenomenon no less prone to such "adaptations." In fact, it has its own very complex sets of orthodoxies (metapsychology or theory) and rituals (techniques) of practice.

Guntrip makes much of the polarity in Freud between his clinical genius, and his theoretical abstractions that did not faithfully represent his clinical insights.[21] He foreshadows Eisold's thesis in seeing Freud dis-

---

[17]   Kenneth Eishold, "The Intolerance of Diversity in Psychoanalytic Institutes," *International Journal of Psychoanalysis* 75 (1994) 785.

[18]   Ibid., 786.

[19]   Ibid.

[20]   Ibid., 785.

[21]   Guntrip, *Psychoanalytic Theory, Therapy, and the Self* (New York: Basic, 1971).

torting the very personal and subjective nature of analytic work in his theorizing to maintain status within the "scientific" community of his day. (Ironically, Guntrip did not have the insights of Bettleheim who argued that Freud did indeed reflect the human and personal, but that this was lost in translation.) Guntrip acknowledges Freud's identification of "neurotic forms of religion which are an essentially infantile longing for a lost Mummy and Daddy,"[22] yet critiques his reductionism of religion in toto. Guntrip in the later development of his theological thinking, "Religion in Relation to Personal Integration," 1969, ultimately casts religion within his object relational motifs. His psychoanalytic psychology, following Fairbairn, is characterized by the centrality of the splitting of the ego and the schizoid core as the ultimate task for psychoanalysis to address. His theological philosophy joins with "personal integration" as the ultimate task of both therapy and theology.

> *To discuss religion, we must establish some common ground as to what it is, not in terms of doctrines or organizations but facts of experience.* . . . Freud (1927) saw that when he described religion as a regression to infantile dependence, and the projection of the parent image on to the universe. But that only describes neurotic religion. *It is more realistic to see this basically important "personal relations factor" as not in itself infantile, but as the essential permanent factor in our existence at every stage of life, and as itself undergoing a process of maturing that is central to all our development as persons.* . . . I take *"religion"* not as theological doctrine, nor as an intellectual activity, or an organization; . . . I take it as *an overall way of experiencing life, of integration or self-realization through communion with all that is around us, and finally our way of relating to the universe, the total reality, which has, after all, evolved us with the intelligence and motivation to explore this problem: all that is meant by "experience of God"* (emphasis in original).[23]

The Subjective Basis of Metapsychology

Robert Stolorrow argues that the ultimate basis for every metapsychological (or theoretical) model is the subjective experience and orientation of the author. In his classic study of the psychohistories of Sigmund Freud, Carl Jung, Wilhelm Reich, and Otto Rank, *Faces in a Cloud: Subjectivity*

---

[22] Hazell, ed. *Personal Relations Therapy,* 271.

[23] Ibid., 274–75.

in Personality Theory,[24] he traces the contextual influences of each of their respective life histories and how it shaped their psychological theorizing. This is a theme that Guntrip himself champions:

> This leads me to observe that in psychology more than in any other study a writer's judgment is related to his own personal approach to the subject. This in turn arises out of the structure of his own personality and his experience of life. This fact is familiar to us in religious, philosophical and political thinking, where the objective and the subjective most plainly interact. In science it has always been the tradition that thinking is purely objective. This is now realized to be less true than used to be taken for granted, but it is least of all true in psychology. Often, in reading psychoanalytic and psychiatric literature, and trying to form a judgment on its conclusions about human beings, I have wished I knew what sort of person the writer was.[25]

Robert Coles in *The Spiritual Life of Children* addressed what it meant for him to be one who was reared in the psychoanalytic tradition, and how he was impacted by the *person* of his psychoanalytic mentors. During the social unrest of the early 1960s in the American South, he was diverted from his original plans of entering "the profession of psychoanalytic child psychiatry" to that of a "field worker," learning to talk with children not as "patients," but as they were going through their everyday lives. He began a career of thirty years of writing about children, collecting their drawings, paintings, and their various *takes* on life in notebooks and on tape. He reflects upon how he began to organize that material in light of these mentors.

> I had by then gotten to know Erik H. Erikson rather well: I had studied with him and helped teach the course he gave at Harvard. I also came to know, luckily, Anna Freud, first by correspondence and later through meetings in both the United States and England. Those two veteran child psychoanalysts, both wise, thoughtful human beings, were of enormous help to Jane and me as we tried to make sense of what we'd done and tried to figure out where we might next go. In 1978 Anna Freud made a suggestion: "It would be of interest if you went over your earlier work and looked for what you might have missed back then," she said. I remember being somewhat perplexed and amused at the time. I got no leads from her as to what we might discover if we followed her advice;

---

[24] R. Stolorow and G. Atwood, *Faces in a Cloud: Subjectivity in Personality Theory* (New York: Aronson, 1979).

[25] Guntrip, *Personality Structure*, 18.

it was her manner as she made the suggestion which was especially persuasive: a mix of wry detachment and warm-spirited interest (emphasis added). Meanwhile, Erik Erikson had been sharing with Jane and me his experiences in South Africa, where he had gone to deliver an address at the University of Cape Town. "You might want to compare what you've seen in the South with what is happening over there," he remarked one day as the three of us were having lunch. Years later, as we worked in South Africa with black and "colored" and white children, *we often remembered that moment* (emphasis added).[26]

Harry Guntrip's life reflected in his own way what it mean to be influenced by such significant figures within the psychoanalytic tradition. On the one hand he spent much energy and spilt much ink in reaction to Heinz Hartmann's Ego Psychology tradition, as it echoed Anna Freud, Hartmann's close collaborator's thinking. In a theme that spanned his writing career, Guntrip opposed the philosophy of science of the "objective observer" embodied by Hartmann in favor of his own view of the inherent subjectivity of "psychodynamic science." On the other hand, he traced the path of his own growth, both personally and theoretically, under the influence of his two analyses with Fairbairn and Winnicott.[27] In a fascinating third vantage point of this process, Jeremy Hazell describes the transition in the person of Guntrip which he experienced as Guntrip's analysand, (that is, client or patient).[28] During Harry's analysis with Winnicott, Hazell saw Guntrip soften and come to embody the tenets of his personal object relations theory which seemed to be limited to the more intellectual sphere during Guntrip's earlier analysis with Fairbairn. The centrality of Guntrip's own schizoid process, where one's "true self" is kept locked up in "cold storage" and therefore needs evocation, was one that was skillfully theorized with Fairbairn, but only realized with Winnicott. The difference is seen in the personal metapsychology of each analyst: Fairbairn as the brilliant, but himself schizoid, theoretician, and Winnicott as the winsome "court jester of the British Psychoanalytic Society,"[29] who's pre-verbal holding capacity brought Guntrip's inner self more to light.

---

[26] Robert Coles, *The Spiritual Life of Children* (New York: Houghton Mifflin, 1990) xii–xiii.

[27] Hazell, ed., *Personal Relations Therapy*, 351.

[28] Hazell, "Reflections on My Experience of Psychoanalysis with Guntrip," *Contemporary Psychoanalysis* 27 (1991) 153.

[29] Christopher Bollas, *Winnicott Lectures* (cassette recording) (Tustin, CA: Newport Psychoanalytic Institute, 1982).

The Politics of Polarities: Conflict or Complementarity?

Guntrip, in his doctoral dissertation, (later published as *Personality Structure and Human Interaction*), traces the development of psycho-analytical theory as "an unconscious pattern of development of a dialectical type."[30] "The original *European psychobiology* of Freud" is presented as this Hegelian *Thesis*: the classic psycho-analytical teaching. He then presents the *psychosociology* in America, including Karen Horney, Erik Fromm, and Harry Stack Sullivan as the *Antithesis* to the classical stance. Guntrip's *Synthesis* is his British object relational orientation that "comes to correlate the internal and the external object-relationships in which the personality is involved" (emphasis in the original).[31] His approach is his way to interrelate the internal, intrapsychic Freudian emphasis with the external, interpersonal one of the American schools.

Here again, in theory, Guntrip takes an approach that would bring harmony to the divergent trends in psychoanalysis. Yet in practice, Guntrip engaged in career long polemical arguments with Hartmann and the dominant ego psychological school on the one hand, and Behaviorism as represented by Hans Eysenck on the other. Although he was analyzed by two prominent analysts from the British Independent school, Fairbairn and Winnicott, he did not receive formal training as a psychoanalyst and was never a member of the British Psychoanalytic Society. In 1956 he was therefore "ineligible to attend the centenary celebrations" of the birth of Sigmund Freud, "but with typical crusading spirit, he published 'Centenary Reflections on the Work of Freud'. . . . Guntrip continued his argument against the depersonalizing methods of Eysenck and the behaviourists, who, in their desire for scientific status, showed a tendency to reduce the patient to an oversimplified mechanism."[32] Guntrip's professional battles with Hartmann and Eysenck, his external objects, seem to have mirrored his internal object world of internalized early relationships which are tense and obsessive, where he was never really at peace, either internally or externally. He carried with him the internal psychological object of his unavailable and unattachable mother. His professional world seemed to follow in suit. As Hazell notes, "One can perhaps detect in these arguments [of Guntrip for a personal growth viewpoint] the struggles of a nonmedical psychoanalytic psychotherapist working daily in academic departments of psychiatry and psychology, with their strongly organic and

---

[30] Guntrip, *Personality Structure*, 50.

[31] Ibid., 51.

[32] Hazell, ed., *Personal Relations Therapy*, 9.

behavioral influence."[33] This dynamic, again, echoes the autobiographical influences upon Guntrip's theoretical and clinical writings.

[33] Ibid.

PART ONE

The Nature of Theology and Philosophy in Relation to Psychoanalysis

THE first two chapters will introduce the dynamics inherent in the first polarity of this study: theological philosophy in dynamic tension with psychoanalysis. Chapter one will identify the philosophical and theological traditions that underlie the psychoanalytic tradition. This chapter will analyze the history of the development of psychoanalytic theory according to a spectrum embodied by two polar opposites: the *classic* and the *romantic* views. The ideal type of the *classic vision* is represented by the stoic and rationalistic Freudian tradition, while the ideal type of the *romantic vision* is represented by the spontaneous and optimistic Kohutian tradition. The parallel representative versions of the *classic* Kleinian and the *romantic* Winnicottian traditions within British psychoanalysis will be delineated. The philosophical traditions that underlie each of these psychoanalytic viewpoints will be articulated.

Chapter two will examine the opposite side of the coin identifying the psychological traditions that underlie the *classic* and *romantic* theological traditions of England and Europe, as well as the *theopathology* of these traditions from a psychoanalytic viewpoint.

The first polarity within the psychoanalytic tradition that I will examine is between what Guntrip called the rational and mechanistic theories in contrast to the dynamic and personal points of view. I shall begin with polarity within Freud himself.

1

The Philosophy and Theology of Psychoanalysis

The Polarity within Psychoanalysis between the Classic and Romantic Philosophical Worldviews

The Polarity within Freud

PETER Gay, in his biography of Freud, details Freud's ambivalence about philosophy by highlighting Freud's theoretical denial that psychoanalysis is a worldview, or *Weltanschauung*. Freud disassociated himself from philosophy in an attempt to establish credibility for psychoanalysis within the "scientific" community. Freud steeped himself in literature and history, describing himself as one who "'found my way back to my earliest path,' which was to 'understand something of the riddles of the world in which we live and perhaps even to contribute something to their solution.' In a word, he was returning to philosophy at last."[1] Yet Freud sought to reflect, if not identify with, the worldview of the Cartesian and positivistic philosophy of the scientific community of his day. René Descartes, famous for his dictum, *I think, therefore I am*, reflected this rationalistic and reductionistic thinking of the Enlightenment of the eighteenth century. His counterpart, Blasé Pascal, also a philosopher and mathematician of that period, embodied the intuitive response in his: *The heart has its reasons of which Reason knows not*. Gay frames this analysis of the philosophy (and thereby the theology) of psychoanalysis by identifying this ambivalence within Freud: consciously a rationalist, yet a philosopher, which is to say, a *lover of wisdom (philo-sophia)* at heart, the unconscious *romantic*.

Guntrip himself framed this ambivalence within Freud, citing a bifurcation of his theory into two main groups: "(1) the id-plus-ego-con-

[1] Peter Gay, *Freud: A Life For Our Time* (New York: Norton, 1988) xvii–xx.

15

trol apparatus, and (2) the Oedipus complex of family object relationship situations with their reappearance in treatment as transference and resistance."[2] He cites Heinz Hartmann, the central figure of American Ego Psychology, as the one who developed this line in Freud, where the picture of the psyche is a mechanism for maintaining homeostatic organization: "the autonomous system-ego and its apparatuses." Guntrip sees Melanie Klein in England picking up the other line of Freud's thought where the superego that "enshrines the fact of personal object-relations" is the "starting point of all of her new developments."[3] Guntrip saw Freud "trying to ride two horses at once, that of mechanistic theory with his economic and topographical points of view, and that of personal theory in his dynamic point of view worked out on the basis of psychogenetic processes in the medium of family relationships."[4]

The Classic and Romantic Visions in Psychoanalysis

In his historical survey of the development of psychoanalytic theory, *Personality Structure and Human Interaction*,[5] Guntrip employed a Hegelian dialectic in summing up object relations theory as the *synthesis* between Freudian instinct theory and the American Interpersonal-Cultural theory of Sullivan and Horney. Guntrip saw these two traditions as reductionistic in opposite directions, with the Freudian *thesis* trapped within a deterministic intrapsychic world, and the Interpersonalist *antithesis* limited to the environment of external interactions. Guntrip offered object relations theory as the *synthesizing* bridge between the two. Carlo Strenger makes a similar argument that a dialectical tension characteristic of psychoanalytic thought has existed since the 1920s.

Strenger himself is trained as both a philosopher and a psychoanalytic psychotherapist, teaching in the graduate program for history and philosophy of science at Hebrew University in Jerusalem. In his ponderous work, *Between Hermeneutics and Science*, he initially set out to answer the philosophical critiques by Grunbaum that psychoanalysis is a non-scientific discipline. He describes his own process of taking an intellectual and rational stance that would logically dispatch the critics of psychoanalysis "on

---

[2] Guntrip, *Psychoanalytic Theory, Therapy, and the Self* (New York: Basic Books, 1971) 28.

[3] Ibid., 28–29.

[4] Ibid., 31.

[5] Guntrip, *Personality Structure and Human Interaction* (New York: International Universities Press, 1961).

a relatively high level of abstraction,"[6] a position that he would refer to in another context as the stoic and intellectualized "classic vision" in philosophy.[7] Yet the experience of his own analysis as well as working with his own patients brought this lofty effort down to earth.

> I saw patients in psychoanalytic therapy and I went through my own analysis. The movement between daily clinical work and my own experience as an analysand on the one hand, and theoretical reflection about what I was doing and experiencing on the other, were both fruitful and at times difficult. If one writes purely about theoretical issues, one is less bothered by reality, so to speak. The sheer inner coherence of one's ideas is what counts. It is more difficult to come to grips with and make sense of one's own experience as it is lived and yet maintain a sense of direction about the theoretical view one wants to propound.[8]

Strenger here is describing the strong temptation within himself to retreat into "the sheer inner coherence of one's ideas," what Guntrip would call a *Schizoid phenomena,* rather than "come to grips with and make sense of one's own experience as it is lived." He asserts that "none of the philosophical models of what scientific knowledge is has turned out to be very useful in understanding what we actually do," referring to *both* scientists and psychoanalysts. On the one hand, psychoanalysts have felt that the criticisms leveled against the discipline were based on a misconception of what they actually do. On the other, Strenger notes that psychoanalysts have not been open to criticism from the outside to be able to make use of it "in sharpening our understanding of what psychoanalytic thinking is all about."[9] His contribution to this gap is to offer his own model that attempts to bridge this distance between abstracted ideas and lived experience. "By integrating my clinical experience with a more philosophical level of abstraction, I have tried to give an account of psychoanalytic clinical thought which is neither disjoined from experience nor insensitive to recent critiques of psychoanalysis."[10]

---

[6] Carlo Strenger, *Between Hermeneutics and Science: An Essay on the Epistemology of Psychoanalysis* (New York: International Universities Press, 1991) x.

[7] Strenger, "The Classic and the Romantic Vision in Psychoanalysis," *International Journal of Psychoanalysis* 70 (1989) 593.

[8] Strenger, *Between Hermeneutics and Science: An Essay on the Epistemology of Psychoanalysis* (New York: International Universities Press, 1991) x.

[9] Ibid., x.

[10] Ibid., x.

In his journal article of 1989, "The Classic and the Romantic Vision in Psychoanalysis," Strenger addresses this same kind of tension between intellect and lived experience *within* psychoanalysis itself. He notes that this tension essentially has existed implicitly, not often discussed, yet "unmistakably there." His metaphor of "vision" undergirds his philosophical critique of the psychoanalytic movement, identifying the various "worldviews" (*Weltanschauung)* from which different psychoanalysts view their patients (and themselves). Strenger illustrates his position "by creating ideal types in order to demonstrate the salient features of each of the visions."[11] He does so by quoting T. E. Hulme's classic paper, *Romanticism and Classicism.*

> Put shortly, these are the two views, then. One, that man is intrinsically good, spoilt by circumstance; and the other that he is intrinsically limited, but disciplined by order and tradition to something fairly decent. To the one party man's nature is like a well, to the other like a bucket. The view which regards man as a well, a reservoir full of possibilities I call the romantic; the one which regards him as a very finite and fixed creature, I call the classical.[12]

Strenger illustrates these "ideal types" with a number of pairings of polarized personalities. He cites Freud himself as the embodiment of the classic attitude, while presenting Heinz Kohut as the "most typical representative of the romantic stance." He traces the developments of the classic vision through both American ego psychology represented by Hartmann, Kris, and Lowenstein, as well as through the work of Melanie Klein in Britain. He contrasts this with the romantic roots as found in Sandor Ferenczi and taken up by Michael Balint whom Strenger attributes as the one who first recognized and commented on the classic/romantic vision of psychoanalytic cure in 1935, ("The Final Goal of Psychoanalytic Treatment," in *Primary Love and Psychoanalytic Technique).* This was further developed within British object relations as reflected in the work of Donald Winnicott. Strenger chose the Viennese trained émigré to Chicago, Heinz Kohut, as his ideal counterpoint to the classic Freud in light of Kohut's "theoretical and therapeutic approach as explicitly trying to change the central outlook of psychoanalysis."[13]

Strenger emphasizes the *Weltanschauung* nature of this dynamic as these respective psychoanalytic systems reflect "the value-laden traits of a

---

[11] Strenger, "The Classic and the Romantic," 593.

[12] T. E. Hulme, 1924. *Romanticism and Classicism* 1924, in ibid.

[13] Ibid., 594.

manner of experiencing and interpreting reality."[14] He then traces the great philosophical systems of the western world as the "paradigmatic embodiments of such visions." He places this philosophical dialectic historically within the eighteenth century conflict between the rationalistic streak of the Enlightenment and the romantic reaction against it. He pits Kant against Rousseau.

Classical	*Romantic*
Kant	Rousseau

Immanuel Kant's maxim is to strive toward autonomy as characterized by the reign of reason, where reason is the capacity to know the general and lawful in reality. "The fully rational man is able to submit his more idiosyncratic, subjective side to the voice of reason. If he succeeds in doing so, he will turn from being driven by his animal nature into a fully autonomous person." The egotistic and antisocial nature of emotions, as Kant sees them, require *constraints* imposed by reason in order for humans to be truly free. Being self-directed calls for the imposition of *categorical imperatives* in the ethical domain, that is, cognitive use of one's will to act according to principles, or categories, as well as providing human freedom in the form of "the ability to transcend the individual and idiosyncratic by applying reason."

The Romantic View: Spontaneous and Optimistic

The Romantic view, as developed by Rousseau, which flourished in the works of Goethe, saw the supreme value as the development of the individual. The unique self of each person with a unique perspective on the world is characterized by true spontaneity, and by the richness of subjective experience. Ideals provide the motive force for life and are fueled by the awareness that "they express his own personality in its concrete, unique individuality."[15]

> Rousseau saw the foundations of ethics not in reason but in an emotion which he believed to be intrinsic to human nature: compassion. Identifying with the other and feeling his suffering and sorrow is as natural to man as sexual desire and hunger. Not only did Rousseau therefore not see the need for constraints on human nature; he thought that human nature unadulterated was intrinsically good. Whatever has gone wrong with man is a function of

[14] Ibid., 595.

[15] Ibid.

distortions on human nature which have been imposed artificially by society.[16]

Classical	*Romantic*
Hegel	**Kierkegaard**

Strenger cites the great representatives of these respective positions in the nineteenth century as Hegel and Kierkegaard. On the one hand, they shared a value in common, that of autonomy. Hegel's classic vision of this was "the individual's recognition that he is but an aspect of the general structure of reality and the submission to the laws of the whole." This was in contrast to Kierkegaard's romantic version which "considers autonomy in the individual's ability to attain his own subjective truth."[17]

Classical	*Romantic*
Freud	**Ferenczi**
Klein	**Winnicott**
Hartmann	**Kohut**

As noted above, Strenger historically traces the psychoanalytic version of this dialectic or polarity of worldviews with the original European dance partners as Freud and Ferenczi, with Klein and Winnicott squaring off in England, while the Viennese emegrés Hartmann and Kohut came to represent the tension within American Psychoanalysis, the traditional figureheads of Ego Psychology and Self Psychology, respectively. Strenger contrasts the stoic championing of the reality principle over the pleasure principle, and secondary process over primary process as Freud's classic dichotomizing, where the former is the developmental achievement over the latter. In contrast, the characteristics of a spontaneous id and the *illusions* of the wish seeking pleasure principle are the romantic's examples of the freedom of being alive and the capacity for creativity itself. These are considered *infantile* and *regressive* by classic psychoanalysis.

> In analysis the patient wants to enact his wishes, but Freud demands of him that he must understand and verbalize instead. Where the patient wants to make insight into an intellectual, one-time event, Freud patiently forces him to work through the manifold manifestations of his infantile wishes and fantasies. Where whole cultures want to perpetuate illusions, Freud exhorts them to achieve maturity and renounce the comforting distortions of reality. Ultimately

---

[16] Ibid., 595–96.

[17] Ibid., 596.

the whole setting of classical psychoanalysis is an expression of this attitude. The patient lies down and hence cannot discharge tension through motility. He must say everything which comes to mind, but no wish—except for that of being understood—should be gratified by the analyst. *Nothing but the truth can cure, since the essence of neurosis is the avoidance of reality* (emphasis added).[18]

The Classic View: Stoic and Pessimistic

The Freudian paradigm, according to Strenger, is culturally pessimistic, where such community is in the service of teaching people how to master their inner nature. The stoic vision is that of achieving the virtue of mastering one's own passions, where Freud's own measure of success for the hysteric patient was that of "transforming your hysterical misery into common unhappiness."[19]

Strenger develops this theme in a direction which will have crucial importance for how Harry Guntrip wrestled both with his psychoanalytic psychology as well as his theological philosophy. Strenger notes Philip Rieff's classic study of Freud as having *The Mind of a Moralist*.[20] He emphasizes that the type of morality involved is that of "maturity and dignity," which reflects a long road toward mental health that has no shortcuts, and again is characterized by surrendering "the dreams of childhood" and its seductions in favor of "true adulthood." Guntrip went on to organize his central thesis that the contribution of "a true object relations theory of the personality" as was first theorized by Ronald Fairbairn as *pre-moral,* in contrast to the *moral* concern of the management of aggression reflected in the classical psychoanalytic concerns around depressive states. The *pre-moral* developmental motif is Guntrip's jumping off point for his seminal work, *Schizoid Phenomena, Object Relations and the Self,* 1968.

Not to leave a *distortion* in the mind of the reader in terms of the complexity of Freud's own thinking, Strenger notes that Freud "has his romantic moments as well," yet, nevertheless, Strenger sees Freud's classic stance as the core. Guntrip will, as noted above, cast Freud as "riding two horses" as an embodiment of the spectrum from classic to romantic. To change the metaphor a bit, I would offer that Freud carried aspects of the two traditions in a way that can be illustrated as an *isomorphic polarity.* This has been described by Henry Dicks in his object relational description of

[18] Ibid.

[19] Sigmund Freud, *Studies on Hysteria,* 1895; in ibid., 597.

[20] Philip Rieff, *The Mind of a Moralist.* 1959; in ibid.

the psychodynamics of couples, (1963). This is where one partner *enacts externally* what the other carries as an *unconscious internal object*, forming an unconscious tie between them. This is theologically represented in the Genesis creation account of *Eve* being apprehended by *Adam* as a lost-but-now found aspect of himself: "Bone of my bone and flesh of my flesh," the rib *taken out of him* in the creation of his partner. I would offer that Freud *enacted* a classic and rationalistic *external* presentation of psychoanalysis, embodied by his metapsychology, while his "romantic moments" can be understood as an "unconscious internal object" which formed his interpersonal ties with such *mystical* and romantic personalities as Fliess and Jung.

Guntrip's approach was to describe a theoretical-clinical polarity within Freud himself which characterized Freud's theory as a concession to the mechanistic scientific zeitgeist which would fall within the classic vision, while his clinical writings and case examples betray Freud's intuitive genius, reflecting the romantic vision of the person.[21]

Kohut's Self Psychology: The Romantic Ideal

Heinz Kohut is Strenger's choice as the *ideal type* to represent the romantic vision in psychoanalysis. In essence, he recasts the Freudian dichotomy between pleasure and reality principle in seeing the newborn infant as *not* being a "pure pleasure ego," where the essence of mind is not to seek pleasure, but rather to "achieve a sense of oneness, cohesiveness and purposefulness." Kohut's developmental steps toward this goal predicate the acquisition of a "sense of the unity of his body, then a sense of being at the center of his own volitions." Upon this foundation senses of industry and competence that are characteristic of the classic vision of Ego Psychology are acquired. Yet then, the highest stage of development is "the cohesive self" as a structure composed of "ideals which are experienced as intrinsically valuable and the ambition, the belief of the individual in his ability to realize his ideals."[22] This "cohesive self" is dependent upon the "care and love of his parents" in order to develop a sense of self that is positive. In contrast to the classical view that idealization is a defense against aggression, Kohut sees it as essential to the development of the capacity to hold something as intrinsically valuable, worth striving for, and therefore meaningful. The cohesive self is a bi-polar structure: both the experience of self as lovable, worthy and capable, and also the holding of values which

---

[21] Guntrip, *Psychoanalytic Theory.*

[22] Carlo Strenger, "The Classic and the Romantic," 599.

give direction and meaning. This self is also, again, interpersonally dependent upon parental figures whose term of "self-object" given by Kohut reflects this dependency on the environmental caretaking. The "function" provided by the self-object is also two-fold: communicating to the child its own sense of worth "by enjoying the child's existence in all of its aspects." The second is the inclusion of the child in the parent's activities in a way that "enables the child to admire the parent." This is often referred to as the "transmuting internalization" of the parent, which is Self Psychology's version of what the object relations people call "internalizing" the good object.

The Romantic Vision in England: The Independent Tradition

This American version of the romantic vision is essentially a late development for what was a central emphasis in the *Independent* school of British object relations thinking for decades before. As early as the 1930s and 40s Ronald Fairbairn was developing his revision of Freudian metapsychology to that of seeing humans as *object seeking* as opposed to pleasure seeking. In concert with this was Donald Winnicott's emphasis on the centrality of the *Facilitating Environment* as promoting the *Maturational Processes* in infants, as well as his popularization of the notion of the development of one's *True Self*, in contrast to the *False Self* adaptation to environmental expectations. This was the British romantic vision in which Harry Guntrip would come to steep himself, and these were the two principal figures with whom he would experience his own two psychoanalyses.

Classical	Romantic
Anna Freud ↔ Klein	Fairbairn/Winnicott

The tension between the two visions in Guntrip's Britain reflect the history of the British Psychoanalytic society itself. On the one hand, there was an open battle between the camps of Melanie Klein and Anna Freud who represented two variants of classical psychoanalysis. While they both pledged allegiance to Freudian instinct theory and saw the path of development as the taming and housebreaking of the dual drives of sex and aggression, they clashed over the control of psychoanalytic orthodoxy. Anna's camp continued the more rationalistic and stoic tradition of her father in their approach to both theory and clinical practice, essentially detailing the child's adaptation to the environment. Klein and her cohorts, on the other hand, brought a phenomenological and existentialist apprehension of the unconscious and its processes, with a strong emphasis on death instinct and the phenomenology of *phantasy*. The war between these two champions of instinctual psychoanalysis resulted in a partitioned society, essentially a Beirut of British psychoanalysis. Their respective interest in aggression as instinct was practiced in their relationships with each other.

Guntrip's circle, with Fairbairn, Winnicott, and others, was spoken of as the "Middle Group" between these two warring factions. Yet Strenger's philosophical polarity and dialectic better represents what they would ultimately insist on as their identity: those *Independent* of theoretical orthodoxy and the fundamentalist practice of clinical technique, their official title since 1962.[23] Perhaps the *Independents* provided a kind of transitional space between the two other polarized groups; they were needed to be thought of as in the "middle."

The Classical Vision in England: The Kleinians

Klein's theory of development "assumes that ultimately it is the congenital balance between love and hate, envy and gratitude which makes all the difference between mental health and mental illness."[24] Her approach is a clear embodiment of the classic vision in its emphasis on analysis of the patient's distortions as manifest in the primitive defensive handling of envy and hate through projection into others. Winnicott, who for years had an appreciation Klein's description of the *experience* of children and adults who manifest such conditions of rage, eventually opposed her adamantly in regards to the genesis of it, as with envy. For Klein, envy was from the patient's instinctual core; for Winnicott, it was an artifact of the child's experience of the *tantalizing* mother who offered nurture and then withdrew it prematurely. It has been said, *For Klein, there is no such thing as a bad mother. For Winnicott, there is no such thing as a bad baby.* These two figures, then, provide ideal types for Strenger's presentation of his thesis. They are essentially representative of this polarity within the theory of British object relations. Strenger's own synthesis of these philosophical dialectics foreshadows the paradoxical holding of such tensions made popular by Winnicott. In prefacing this, he offers a concise summary of each view:

---

[23] Guntrip, "My Experience of Analysis with Fairbairn and Winnicott," *International Journal of Psychoanalysis* 77 (1996) 739.

[24] Strenger, "The Classic and the Romantic," 601.

The *classic* view sees man as governed by the pleasure principle and the development towards maturity is that towards the predominance of the reality principle. Neurosis is the result of the covert influence of the pleasure principle. The analyst's attitude towards the patient is a combination of respect and suspicion and the analyst takes the side of the reality principle. The ethic is stoic: maturity and mental health depend on the extent to which a person can acknowledge reality as it is and be rational and wise.

The *romantic* view sees man as striving towards becoming a cohesive self. Development aims at a self which consists of a continuous flow from ambitions to ideals, from a sense of vitality towards goals which are experienced as intrinsically valuable. Mental suffering is the result of the failure of the environment to fulfill the self-object function and the patient's symptoms are the desperate attempt to fill the vacuum in his depleted self. The analyst's attitude towards the patient is one of trust in his humanity and the analyst takes the side of joy and vitality. The ethic is romantic: maturity and mental health consist in the ability to sustain enthusiasm and a sense of meaning. (601).

Strenger's resolution of the tension ultimately is to allow it to exist, which means to allow both visions to exist together inside oneself as a dialectic, rather than exclude one or the other through the polarization of *good or bad*, or, *true or false*, or, *right or wrong*. He believes most analytic therapists already do this to one degree or another, albeit striking this kind of balance intuitively. Yet he does not present this as a kind of "golden mean," but a differential emphasis on either the classic or romantic attitude as being called for depending on the particular patient and the particular circumstance. His final casting of the issue is to see the dialectic as characteristic of the human condition itself, and as ultimately unresolvable.

> The essence of the tension between the classic and the romantic attitude is ultimately the *tension between identification with one's own perspective and the detachment from it*. It is the expression of the fact that *as human beings we have the ability to experience ourselves from within and to reflect about ourselves from without*. On the one hand we can ask ourselves: "is this *really* valuable?" or we can reflect "is

this *really* what I want or am I fooling myself?" Such questions are the expression of our ability for self-reflection, and this ability is essential to our humanity . . . and this ontological split within ourselves cannot be closed (emphasis in the original).[25]

I would propose, in harmony with Strenger, that the ultimate integration of conflictual polarity is to be realized in the form of dialectical paradox that is mutually enriching.

The Religiosity of Psychoanalysis

Psychoanalysis as Religion

When religion is defined psychoanalytically as a human phenomenon, as a way of organizing experience and providing meaning, then ritual can be either be "neurotic" or a growth enhancing transitional phenomena. Psychoanalysis can be seen as reflecting the typical stereotype of religion: rituals of lying on the couch, (psychoanalytic genuflecting), the (American) tradition of the patient needing to have a minimum of four sessions per week to be "truly psychoanalysis," (which has become a debate within institutes about the psychoanalytic orthodoxy of determining *what is* "truly psychoanalysis"); traditions of psychoanalytic "neutrality," "anonymity," and other acts of "holiness" to preserve the "sanctity" of the "psychoanalytic situation," (vs. "contaminating the analytic field"). Psychoanalysis in Los Angeles, as well as around the world, reflects the "denominalization" of the movement into various groups who feel they are the "true expression" of psychoanalysis: Kleinians, Kohutians, Subjectivists, Freudians, Ego Psychologists, Independents, et al. Each group or collection of groups has split off and formed its own "seminary," (training institute), to pass on its own particular brand of psychoanalysis, including orthodoxy and practice. Victoria Hamilton has published the results of her research on the schools of psychoanalysis representing these "denominational" differences as *The Analyst's Preconscious*,[26] the respective belief system that every psychoanalyst holds. Two of the groups, the Kleinians and the Kohutians, or Self Psychology practitioners, she describes as the most similar in that they demonstrate the most consistency between their stated beliefs and their practice, and essentially reflect a "unity of opposites,"[27] where they have essentially opposite philosophical anthropologies and yet are so similar in

[25] Ibid., 607.

[26] Victoria Hamilton, *The Analyst's Preconscious* (Hillsdale, NJ: Analytic Press, 1996).

[27] Paul Watzlawick, *The Language of Change* (New York: Basic Books, 1978) 108–13.

character. As we will examine in greater detail later, the Kleinian theology is *Calvinistic* in cast, that is, pessimistic and deterministic. The Kohutian ethos in contrast is *Revivalistic:* optimistic yet schismatic as it has "broken the old wineskins" of Freudian orthodoxy and historically has moved out of the orthodox psychoanalytic church or synagogue into its own confines. The formation of the Southern California Psychoanalytic Institute was a splitting off of a group of the followers of Franz Alexander and his emphasis on "corrective emotional experience"[28] in psychoanalysis as curative, (a very *revivalist* notion), leaving behind the classical Freudians of the Los Angeles Psychoanalytic Institute. The Kohutians and Intersubjectivists repeated this pattern a generation later as the Institute for Contemporary Psychoanalysis was the fruit of their revival as they split off from the Southern California Institute. In short, psychoanalysts are *human beings,* people who practice these stereotyped notions of religion as part of the human experience.

In response to Peter Gay's critique of *those who would critique psychoanalysis* as religious in nature or form,[29] I would like to propose the following arguments. First, we must clarify the ambivalent or paradoxical nature of the matter as Gay critiqued Freud in regard to philosophy. Just as Gay rejects Freud's conscious and official position that psychoanalysis was independent of having a belief system or worldview, so psychoanalysis itself reflects the religiosity inherent in human groups. Secondly, I think that it is important to normalize defensive "religiosity" as well as the pursuit of (spiritual-subjective) meaning as endemic to the human condition, a normal part of the countertransference to be taken up. Within psychoanalysis there is a contrast between classical psychoanalysis and ego psychology's emphasis on the minimization and avoidance of countertransference in managing clinical practice, versus seeing it as inevitable and helpful by making use of it, initially presented by Paula Heimann in the British Independent Tradition.[30]

My own conclusion is that when psychoanalysis can accept its inherent religiosity, then as a movement it can integrate these historically disavowed and split-off parts of itself. This is a process that has already begun with certain members within psychoanalysis itself, such as William Meissner. This approach will be more fully developed in Chapter 9.

---

[28] Franz Alexander, *Psychoanalytic Therapy: Principles and Applications* (New York: Ronald, 1946).

[29] Gay, *Freud,* xxvi–xxix.

[30] Paul Heimann, "Counter-transference," *British Journal of Medical Psychology* 33 (1960) 9–15.

Rapprochement between Religion and Psychoanalysis: William Meissner, M.D., S.J.

William Meissner holds a unique place within the psychoanalytic community, being trained as a Jesuit Catholic priest as well as being a supervising and training psychoanalyst from the Boston Psychoanalytic Society and Institute. He is probably best known for his works on the *Borderline Spectrum*[31] as well as being a well respected author about the *Paranoid Process*[32]. In his classic work, *Psychoanalysis and Religious Experience*, he pursued bringing about a *rapprochement* between psychoanalysis and religious thinking. He, perhaps, is the American Catholic version of the English Protestant Guntrip in reflecting a personal identification with, and scholarly interest in, bringing integration between psychoanalysis and religion.

I will address two principal areas of Dr. Meissner's contribution: firstly, his critique of Freud's anti-religious position in light of Freud's personal dynamics that colored his view; and secondly, in chapter nine I will take up Meissner's own proposition that religious experience is a form of *transitional phenomena* in normal human development, drawing upon Winnicott's concept of *the area of faith*.

A central critique of the psychoanalytic tradition that I am putting forth in this study, one taken up by Guntrip himself, is that traditional psychoanalytic thinking has been unable to think very developmentally about religious phenomena, (especially from the view of the classic vision), and as a consequence the psychoanalytic movement itself in its own developmental history has played out this lack of perspective as a countertransference enactment. As noted above in Eishold's work, psychoanalysis has been a very *religious* community with schisms, battles over the *orthodoxy* of which is the *true* psychoanalytic metapsychology, the questioning of psychoanalytic techniques, (which are the *rituals* of psychoanalytic practice), and regularly raising the question of psychoanalytic *orthodoxy: Is this really psychoanalysis, or merely psychotherapy?* The psychoanalytic movement, therefore, by and large, has been unable to master its own countertransference of *religiosity* and instead critiques this internal object through a projective identification with traditional religion.

Meissner approaches this issue through an analysis of Freud's own *unanalyzed* religious developmental history.

---

[31]   William W. Meissner, *The Borderline Spectrum* (Northvale, NJ: Aronson, 1984).

[32]   Meissner, *The Paranoid Process* (Northvale, NJ: Aronson, 1978).

Behind the Freudian argument about religion stands Freud the man, and behind Freud the man, with his prejudices, beliefs, and convictions, lurks the shadow of Freud the child. A basic psychoanalytic insight says that the nature and content of any thinker's or creative artist's work reflect essential aspects of the dynamic configurations and conflicts embedded in the individual's personality structure. Freud is no exception, and his religious thinking unveils these inner conflicts and unresolved ambivalences more tellingly than any other aspect of his work.[33]

On the other hand, Meissner also takes up Freud's argument of *The Future of an Illusion* "on its own ground and in its own terms," so as not to reduce this traditional Freudian view of religion merely to its psychological determinants in Freud, but also to differentiate the valid aspects of Freud's critique. Meissner acknowledges the primitive psychological functioning present in many religious adherents, where

> the most primitive levels of infantile fusion and narcissistic omnipotence can be found in the religious delusions of psychotics. A caricature of religion, which Freud himself employed as an analogy to obsessional states, is not infrequently found among religious people in whom blind adherence to ritual and scrupulous conscientiousness, as well as conscience, dominate religious life. In fact, we can safely say that the great mass of believers lend credence to Freud's formulations.[34]

Meissner commends Freud's bringing us to "the interface of man's religious life with his psychological life."[35]

RECONSTRUCTION OF "MYTHOLOGY" IN BOTH THEOLOGY AND FREUD

As Freud wrote *Moses and Monotheism* (1934–1938) at the end of his own life, Meissner points to Freud's identification with the eighty-year-old Moses as the founder of a movement whose issues and ambivalences reflect "the early infantile strata of Freud's psychic life" which emerge in the conflictual efforts of Moses "who has never been able to reach the promised land and who stands on the threshold of death."[36] Meissner traces the Hegelian tradition of Biblical scholarship which was the basis for Freud's

---

[33] Meissner, *Psychoanalysis and Religious Experience* (New Haven: Yale University Press, 1984) vii.

[34] Ibid., 15.

[35] Ibid., viii.

[36] Ibid., x.

psychological *exegesis* of the biblical accounts, (the critical study of texts to ascertain their meaning). He cites the monumental German scholar of the Old Testament in the tradition of historical source criticism, (establishing the sources used by the author), Julius Wellhausen, as *reconstructing* the evolution of Israelite religion according to the popular Hegelian dialectical model of the *thesis* of the absolute monarchy of the Near East with its absolute subjection of the individual; the *antithesis* of classical Greek and Rome as revolt against political absolutism; and the *synthesis* of "the triumph of Germanic culture, in which man would become conscious of his freedom yet freely will the submergence of the individual in the universal idea."[37]

Meissner describes Freud's own use of Wellhausian reconstruction of the texts along the line of movement from "primitive naturalism to lofty ethical monotheism" as fitting with the dominant scientific culture of his day's use of higher criticism, (investigating the origins of a text). It is ironic that one of Freud's favorite hobbies was that of collecting archeological artifacts, which became a basic metaphor for the psychoanalytic process, as it was the archeological discoveries in the 1920s that launched the biblical archeology movement which challenged the historical-critical approaches of Wellhausen from the nineteenth century. Led b William F. Allbright of Johns Hopkins University, this approach to biblical scholarship argued for the general historical accuracy of the biblical texts in contrast to the more historically pessimistic paradigm of higher criticism. In the same manner that Freud abandoned his "seduction hypothesis" which supposed a traumatic historical event as the source of hysterical symptomotology, and replaced it with the dominance of infantile sexual fantasy as the organizing principle, Meissner chronicles how the historicity of the biblical accounts were "demythologized" according to the Hegelian assumption of the historical unreliability of the "primitive mind."[38] In essence, the biblical texts were considered neurotic adaptations or hysterical fantasies which were in need of analysis and reconstruction. Meissner in his own way is painting the *classic vision* of the German biblical scholars, including that of Freud himself.

---

[37] Ibid., 107.
[38] Ibid.

Freud's Religiosity and Mystical "Best Friends": Theological Bad Objects

Meissner goes on to *excavate* Freud's own religion as the paradox of one who was a "self-professed agnostic" and a "Godless Jew" who had religion as one of his predominant preoccupations.[39] Freud's household was characterized by his father Jakob's membership in the Haskala, "a movement that saw Judaism as the epitome of rational and philosophic enlightenment," while on the whole "the family was undoubtedly Jewish, but nonreligious." Yet the Freud family followed "some of the religious practices, and there is evidence that Freud received lessons in Hebrew."[40]

The most striking study of Freud by Meissner is that of his superstitious nature and the parade of best-friends who held extremely spiritual worldviews in contrast to Freud's professed rationalistic scientism. "For the hardheaded agnostic and objective scientist that Freud professed to be, he was an uncommonly superstitious man."[41] Ernest Jones in his biography of Freud noted his tendency to "unrestrained imagination," while Jung observed the "mystical side of himself that Freud seemed to have denied."[42] Jones recounted Freud's lifelong preoccupation with superstition, such his application of numerology to the number seventeen which he drew as a boy in a lottery, purportedly to reveal one's character. Freud told his wife, Martha, of the numerological application which yielded its meaning as "constancy," which he applied to the seventeenth day of the month upon which they were engaged. In reflecting upon his own free associative use of "the numbers . . . so freely at the disposal of my unconscious thinking," he noted that he has "a tendency to superstition, whose origin for long remained unknown to me." Freud continues in noting his "friend in Berlin [who] has made the periods of human life the subject of his calculations, which are based on biological units, must have acted as a determinate of this unconscious juggling."[43] This reference which Meissner notes as undoubtedly to his friend, Wilhelm Fliess, was later omitted from the 1907 and all subsequent editions of this passage. The most striking example of Freud's numerological superstitions was his preoccupation with the date of his own death. What the Freud scholars note is "his well-known *Todesangst,*

---

[39] Meissner, *Psychoanalysis and Religious Experience,* 23.

[40] Ibid., 24–25.

[41] Ibid., 26.

[42] Ernest Jones, 1957, *The Life and Work of Sigmund Freud,* vol. 3, in Meissner, *Psychoanalysis and Religious Experience* (New Haven: Yale University Press, 1984) 26.

[43] Sigmund Freud, 1901, in Meissner, ibid., 27.

or fear of death."[44] Through a number of letters to Fliess, at that time his friend, Freud analyzes the manifestation of this in his own dreams, reflecting the death of significant figures, including his mentor Fleischl as well as his own father in the late 1890s. This material would eventually surface in his classic self-analysis, *The Interpretation of Dreams*. This friendship with Fliess would eventually deteriorate, with Fliess being the object of medical malpractice in the pursuit of his non-traditional theory of female sexuality being found in the nasal bones; a botched surgery on a woman that greatly embarrassed Freud. As with the editing out of his above reference to Fliess from 1907 on in the editions of *Psychopathology of everyday life*, Freud edited his medical quack friend from his life as well.

Freud's next significant and telling friendship was that with Carl Jung, whose own predilection for the mystical and the occult was well known. Meissner quotes the famous account of Jung citing the "so-called catalytic exteriorization phenomena" where, after Jung had experienced strange feelings in his chest, a loud noise from the bookcase in Freud's study sounded out not once, but twice. Later Freud would write Jung about "the poltergeist business," essentially rationalizing the experience as a manifestation of "the magic of [Jung's] personal presence," citing this as an example of Freud's own suggestibility. Meissner's point is that of Freud's lifelong ambivalence about such matters, where Ernest Jones also commented on Freud's "tall tales" of "uncanny experiences with patients" and their more mysterious aspects. Jones in his biography (1957), along with Shur (1972), both point out that "Fliess served as a transference object who allowed Freud to personify his own mystical trends by way of externalization. The same projective device undoubtedly came into play in relation to Jung later on."[45] I would put forward, in this light, that Freud's spirituality and religious identity was largely kept as a split-off, internal object, which he would projectively identify with his intimate relationships in the likes of Fliess and Jung. One might say that Freud was *classical at head*, but a *romantic at heart*, as the *return of the repressed* that manifested through his ambivalent expressions of his own spirituality surfaced in these relationships, yet were quickly put to flight again. Yet the most telling friendship for Freud was one of the few that was actually lifelong: that with Oskar Pfister, the Lutheran pastor from Zurich.

---

[44] Ibid., 27.
[45] Ibid., 39.

Freud's Theological Good Object

Oskar Pfister maintained a warm, yet dialectical relationship with Freud that "spanned nearly three decades of unbroken and mutual respect and friendship."[46] Anna Freud would describe his presence in the Freud household in her preface to the Freud-Pfister correspondence:

> In the totally non-religious Freud household, Pfister, in his clerical garb and with the manners and behaviour of a pastor, was like a visitor from another planet. In him there was nothing of the almost passionately impatient enthusiasm for science which caused other pioneers of analysis to regard time spent at the family table only as an unwelcome interruption of their theoretical and clinical discussions. On the contrary, his human warmth and enthusiasm, his capacity for taking a lively part in the minor events of the day, enchanted the children of the household, and made him at times a most welcome guest, a uniquely human figure in this way. To them, as Freud remarked, he was not a holy man, but a kind of Pied Piper of Hamelin, who had only to play on his pipe to gather a whole host of willing young followers behind him.[47]

Freud maintained his emphasis on the differences between psychoanalysis and religion throughout his correspondence and relationship with Pfister. Yet, as his daughter Anna noted above, he clearly recognized a healthy presence in the form of this religious pastor and essentially cast Pfister's religion within an object relations motif. Freud noted "that the young people with whom Pfister worked were drawn to him by a personal attraction and could thereby be influenced by religion as a form of sublimation. The vehicle of success is the same as that in analysis, an erotic transference to the influencing figure." Freud essentially recast what he actually experienced in his relationship with the person of Pfister as essentially a good or helpful psychoanalytic relationship, and in contrast to his standard view, cast religion in the positive category of sublimation. In embracing the person of Pfister into his life, Freud essentially embraced a religion that is ultimately *incarnational:* that which exists within the flesh and blood, *I-Thou* relationship between two human beings. He describes this in one of his letters to Pfister:

> But you are in the fortunate position of being able to lead them to God and bringing about what in this one respect was the happy

---

[46] Ibid., 74.

[47] H. Meng, and E. L. Freud, eds. *Psychoanalysis and Faith: The letters of Sigmund Freud and Oskar Pfister* (New York: Basic Books,1963); in Meissner, ibid., 76.

state of earlier times when religious faith stifled the neuroses. For us, this way of disposing of the matter does not exist. . . . *Thus our patients have to find in humanity what we are unable to promise them from above and are unable to supply them with ourselves.* Things are therefore much more difficult for us, and in the resolution of the transference many of our successes come to grief.[48]

Freud seems to reflect his *classic* self at this point, where the *humanity* within which "the happy state" is to be found does not come from the analyst, invoking the ultimate autonomy of the patient which is facilitated and maintained by the analyst's technical neutrality: the withholding of the giving of values or direction except that of describing the reality of the patient's psychic situation. Meissner put it as "the analytic method cannot influence the course of therapy by either granting or refusing an illusory emotional satisfaction. . . . At the same time, Freud observes in a moment of concession, the analyst might make a technical mistake if he gave the impression of belittling this emotional demand for illusory satisfaction. He cannot require everyone to overcome a piece of infantilism; only a few may be capable of doing so."[49] In essence, Freud seems to begrudgingly grant some room for the *romantic* use of illusion while characteristically categorizing it as infantile. With his own superstitions and mystical interests hanging in the background, Freud seems to have found in Pfister a person who is a stable and apparently healthy external version of the *romantic* object whose spirituality provides a point of unconscious resonance for his own internal object version.

Indeed, Freud's writing of *The Future of an Illusion* was done within the heart of his relationship with Pfister, where Freud anticipated and welcomed his friend's rejoinder to his pamphlet. In poetic and dialectic fashion, Pfister's written response was entitled, *The Illusion of the Future* which was, among other things, a critique of the *classic* vision that sees faith in science and its technology as the hope of the future as being reductionistic. Pfister writes his critique with the optimism and warmth of the theological romantic:

I have been using the rest chiefly to write my friendly criticism of you. I have been doing so with the greater pleasure because I do battle for a cause that is dear to me with an opponent who is the same. . . . And yet I turn decisively against your judgment on religion. I do so with the opposition that suits a disciple, but also with

---

[48] Ibid., 77, emphasis added.
[49] Ibid.

the sense of joy with which one defends a holy and beloved matter, and with the earnest seeking for the truth that your teaching demands. But I do so also with the hope that many who have been frightened away from psychoanalysis by your denial of religious belief can be drawn back again through the insight gained from a methodological summary of experience. And so, I would prefer to write not against you but for you, since whoever takes a stand for psychoanalysis fights for you. I am also fighting on your side since you are devoted, as I am, to the conquering of illusion through truth. Whether you come closer to the ideal with your *Future of an Illusion* or I with my "Illusion of the Future" will be decided by a higher tribunal.[50]

Meissner describes in detail the dialectic of personalities between Freud's pessimism and Pfister's optimism; Freud emphasized the gulf between psychoanalysis and religion and therefore between himself and his pastor-friend, while Pfister minimized the differences, emphasizing his debt to Freud in his own application of psychoanalysis to the pastoral setting. Freud's *classic* pessimism about human nature will be a theme of the English Calvinism that is the backdrop for Guntrip's theological roots, as we will examine later in detail in the history of the *Independent* tradition. Again, in dialogue with his more optimistic friend, Freud writes:

I do not break my head very much about good and evil, but I have found little that is "good" about human beings on the whole. In my experience most of them are trash, no matter whether they publicly subscribe to this or that ethical doctrine or to none at all. That is something that you cannot say aloud, or perhaps even think, though your experience of life can hardly have been different from mine. If we are to talk of ethics, I subscribe to a high ideal from which most of the human beings I have come across depart most lamentably.[51]

Freud's own characterization of the contrast between the two visions expresses his resignation as well as a sense of envy. "Thus to me my pessimism seems a conclusion, while the optimism of my opponents seems an *a priori* assumption. I might also say that I have concluded a marriage of reason with my gloomy theories, while others live with theirs in a love-match. I hope they will gain greater happiness from this than I."[52]

---

[50] Ibid., 79–80.

[51] Ibid., 80.

[52] Ibid., 81.

Pfister practiced his psychoanalytic-pastoral ministry for over thirty-seven years in Zurich, enduring difficulties with his ecclesiastical superiors due to his espousal of psychoanalysis with the turmoil surrounding Freud's sexual theories. He remained Freud's friend to the end, noting in a letter to Freud's wife on the occasion of Freud's death in 1939 that "your husband's letters are among my most cherished possessions."[53] Their relationship remains a striking portrait of the *classical-romantic* and the *psychoanalytic-religious* polarities integrated into the dialectical paradox that is stable and mutually enriching.

In the spirit of Meissner's recognition of the validity of Freud's critique of religion in its neurotic manifestations, I shall now turn to an analysis of the polarities and pathologies within philosophy and theology.

---

[53] Ibid., 103.

2

The Psychoanalysis
of Theology and Philosophy

The Dialectic Tension within Western Theology:
Calvinism and Revivalism

Historical Theology in Europe and England

THE history of theology in the western tradition since the Reformation also reflects the parallel traditions of the *classical* and *romantic* philosophical viewpoints as was discussed in regards to psychoanalysis.

Classical	*Romantic*
Orthodox Rationalism	Pietism

On the *classical* side is the tradition of *Orthodox Rationalism* which is characterized by a cognitively biased emphasis on the correctness of doctrine and systems of belief. On the *romantic* side are what have been called the *Pietists*, those who say to "know about God" in merely an intellectual fashion is inadequate to a life of faith that requires one to "know God" in a personal, existential, and subjective sense. While the *Orthodox Rationalists* through the centuries insisted on maintaining adherence to the orthodox or approved body of teaching, the *Pietists* insisted on practicing a devotional life of prayer and meditative reflection that at a certain point, and within certain circles, entered into mystical experience. Over the centuries from the 1500s on, each vision would vie for control over the departments of theology and philosophy of the major universities of Europe (which were not as bifurcated as they are today in the "secularized" twentieth century).

Psychoanalytic Critique of Theology:
The Classical Psychoanalytic Spectrum

There has been a movement within psychoanalysis in the last three decades that holds the tension between validating a patient's "healthy religiosity" while attempting to distinguish it from psychopathology. A foray into this arena is represented by a number of articles contained in the volume, *Psychotherapy of the Religious Patient.*[1] The clinical challenge that is reflected in these writings is the movement from the classical position that religion and faith is neurotic per se, to that of encountering patients "whose religious beliefs and practices are deeply enmeshed in their core psychological and interpersonal conflicts."[2] In essence this viewpoint reflects a *dimensional* approach to personality theory and psychopathology, rather than the *categorical.*[3] The categorical way of thinking is best represented by the medical model thinking of the DSM series of the American Psychiatric Association, *The Diagnostic and Statistical Manual of Mental Disorders.*[4] This is an *either/or* style of thinking where a patient is either ill or well, and the diagnostic system uses a decision tree methodology to determine which "box" or category the patient best fits. While acknowledging the capacity to have a *dual diagnosis,* the mentality is Cartesian, reductionistic, and *classical.*

The dimensional approach sees personality, and therefore psychopathology, on a spectrum, where one condition blends into another, and the mixture of colors is theoretically infinite, although characteristic hues and shades do exist. The psychopathology of a given person is seen as a manifestation of one's healthy personality, a kind of distortion or twisting of what is normal.[5] Therefore, the blending together of creativity and destructiveness, substance and shadow, is the normal dilemma of human existential being. This *romantic* approach is much messier than the Cartesian-classical one, as most artists in the midst of a creative moment could attest; yet it is not without order.

---

[1] Moshe Halevi Spero, ed., *Psychotherapy of the Religious Patient* (New York: Aronson, 1996).

[2] Ibid., 5.

[3] Barbara Engler, *Personality Theories* (Boston: Houghton Mifflin, 1993).

[4] American Psychiatric Association, *Diagnostic and Statistical Manual of Mental Disorders,* 4th ed. (Washington, DC: APA Press, 1994).

[5] John Oldham and Lois Morris, *The New Personality Self-Portrait* (New York: Bantam, 1995).

Psychoanalysis has historically embraced both models, depending upon the theorist or even upon "which Freud" that one is reading, the "riding two horses" that Guntrip pointed out above. The classic *categories* of *obsessive-compulsive* and *hysteria* can be seen as such a spectrum, and have been represented as such by non-psychoanalytic personality research-ers, including, ironically, one of Guntrip's polemical opponents, the be-haviorist, Hans Eysenck.[6]

Obsessive Compulsive	Hysteria
Classic	Romantic

Obsessiveness and the Classical

As discussed above, the respective psychoanalytic visions reflect a pro-pensity toward a "shadow self" that errs towards certain characteristics. The stoic and autonomous *classic* vision often reflects a way of being in the world that borders on, if not resides in the area of the *obsessive* and the *compulsive*. Laplanche and Pontalis define obsessional thinking and compulsive behaving according to the traditional categories. *Obsessional neurosis* is

> identified by Freud [as] constituting one of the major frames of reference of clinical psycho-analytic practice. . . . The psychical conflict is expressed through symptoms which are described as compulsive-obsessive ideas, compulsions towards undesirable acts, struggles against these thoughts and tendencies, exorcistic ritu-als, etc. and through a mode of thinking which is characterized in particular by rumination, doubt and scruples, and which leads to inhibitions of thought and action.[7]

The basic mechanism employed is the displacement of the affect onto ideas. The old cliché for this is: *Obsessives don't want to feel.* The condition reflects a "cruel superego" where hostility is turned inward in a masochistic fashion, reflecting the classical developmental analogy of *anal retentive.* The utilization of "reaction-formations" as defenses where the person does the opposite of what they really feel emphasizes the ego-dystonic nature of their own emotions, particularly those of the aggressive variety. Over time, the theoretical development within psychoanalysis was a movement

---

[6] Christopher F. Monte, *Beneath the Mask: An Introduction to Theories of Personality*, 4th ed. (New York: Holt, Rinehart & Winston, 1991) 809–10.

[7] J. Laplanche and J.-B. Pontalis, *The Language of Psychoanalysis* (New York: Norton, 1967) 281.

from focusing on this as a symptomatic condition to that of a personality structure.[8]

The classic description of this character style fits well with the stoic management of "the irrational id forces" characteristic of the *classical* psychoanalytic vision.

Hysteria and the Romantic

On the other side of the spectrum are the *hysterics*, traditionally a "class of neuroses presenting a great diversity of clinical pictures," principal of which are *conversion hysteria* and *anxiety hysteria*. In the former, psychic conflict is expressed through somatic symptomotology such as "emotional crises accompanied by theatricality or more long lasting anaesthesias, hysterical paralyses, 'lumps in the throat', etc." In the latter, "the anxiety is attached in more or less stable fashion to a specific external object" such as in the phobias. The major mechanism and defense is the traditional *repression*, where unwelcome psychic knowledge must be kept out of conscious awareness, and thereby is repressed and displaced onto the above symptomotology. The psychoanalytic cliché is: *Hysterics don't want to know.*[9]

"Following Freud, psycho-analysts have consistently looked upon hysterical neurosis and obsessional neurosis as the two major divisions of the field of the neuroses," hence our spectrum of psychopathology. The *romantic* tradition would find its shadow self in the hysteric camp, with its affectively felt embrace of human potential, at a certain point, fending off knowledge of one's own human capriciousness and ego-centric destructiveness.[10] Each vision's strength ultimately becomes its own weakness, and each is the alter-ego to the other.

The Psychopathology of Theology: Obsessive-Compulsivism and Hysteria

In the sphere of religion, there are also theologies that reflect this spectrum and range of psychological predispositions. Each has a "character" that drives its particular orthodoxy and practice.

---

[8] Ibid., 281–82.

[9] Ibid., 194.

[10] Ibid., 195.

Obsessive Compulsive	**Hysteria**
Orthodox Rationalism	Pietism
Calvinism	Revivalism
Fundamentalism	Pentecostalism

Obsessional Theology

As noted above, the tradition of Orthodox Rationalism champions "right thinking," finds its theological security in the coherency of well ordered doctrines, and ultimately banishes anything from its orthodoxy that smacks of "irrationality" such as the miraculous and mystical. This shadow side is the obsessive compulsive religion critiqued by Freud and others. The history of the tradition has its various incarnations such as English Calvinism (to be detailed below) and American Calvinism, with its twentieth century version best know as Fundamentalism. All share this particular psychological bent toward a "cognitive Christianity" with its propensity toward obsessional *theopathology*.

Hysterical Theology

The tradition of *Pietism* initially reflected a "quietism" and devotional subjectivity, and found its hysterical manifestation in the cyclical periodicity of revivalism and its rejection of orthodox rationalism's intellectually detached form of faith. The renewal and revival movements in Guntrip's England, which will also be detailed below, manifest profoundly in the Wesleyan Methodism of Donald Winnicott's heritage, and were the counterpoint to the Calvinism of Ronald Fairbairn. The American incarnation of the twentieth century is the Pentecostalism of miraculous "signs and wonders" and the ecstatic spirituality of "speaking with other tongues." The hysterical qualities are highly visible in this latter example.

Theopathology

Guntrip himself critiqued theology that is reductionistic and prejudiced toward psychotherapy (as Freud was toward religion). In his response to Professor J. C. McKensie's article "Limitations of Psychotherapy" in the *British Weekly* of March 6, 1958, he critiques McKensie's "seriously erroneous description of psychotherapy" as unable to "supply the love the patient needs," where "all that the psychotherapist can do is to lay bare what is hindering (the patient's) needs from being fulfilled," . . . and "to help the patient repress the guilt." Guntrip challenges this as a theological reductionism of psychotherapy to "the most arid days of Freudian orthodox and scientifically impersonal technique." He addresses McKensie's position that "The only thing that can dissolve guilt feelings is the forgiveness of God" as ignoring "the difference between pathological and real guilt. Furthermore, an experienced psychotherapist does not help the patient to repress anything at all, whether pathological or real, but rather helps him to remain conscious of as much as he can of his mental life and deal with it with full awareness: only so can genuine maturing of personality occur."[11] Theological reductionism is ultimately as defensive as psychoanalytic reductionism.

In contrast, the standard for respectable theological study, for example, involves extensive study of the historical background within which a text is written. Fleshing out the *Sitz im Leben*, or the "setting in life" in which the author is contextualized, is standard practice in the theological disciplines of exegesis and hermeneutics: the technical study of a text in order to determine the meaning of the author within its historical and social context. The *Sitz im Leben* is essentially the object relational matrix of the author, and to that task of *exegeting* the psychoanalytic psychology and the theological philosophy of Harry Guntrip we will now turn.

---

[11] Guntrip, "Can the Therapist Love The Patient?" in *Personal Relations Therapy: The Collected Papers of H.J.S. Guntrip*, ed. Jeremy Hazell (Northvale, NJ: Aronson, 1994 [1958]) 399.

PART TWO

Historical Contexts of Guntrip's Psychology and Theology

THE next five chapters will identify and articulate the principal influences upon Guntrip's thinking. Chapters 4, 5, and 6 will sketch a biography and theoretical synopsis of his most influential mentors: philosopher John Macmurray and psychoanalysts Ronald Fairbairn and Donald Winnicott. Chapter 7 will be a preliminary examination of Guntrip's autobiographical account of his personal analyses with Fairbairn and Winnicott, along with the critical assessment of this account by other psychoanalysts. This will be compared and contrasted with themes drawn from a biographical sketch of Guntrip's own life experiences. I will delineate the connections between the influence of Guntrip's family history and childhood themes with the development of his object relational theorizing on the one hand, and his experience of his personal analyses on the other.

To lay the groundwork for these inquires, however, requires an exposition of the historical context within which each of Guntrip's mentors were shaped and formed themselves. So now I will turn to the *Sitz im Leben*, the "setting in life" of the Independent tradition in England.

3

History of the British
Independent Tradition in England

Harry Guntrip grew up in two professional cultures that converged under the heading of "British Independent." Both his training and personal affiliations within the British Psychoanalytic Society were with those who were known from the outside as the "Middle Group," those between the Kleinians on the one side and the Anna Freudians on the other. They, however, saw themselves as *Independent*, drawing from many resources which included the other two camps, but *not* as some middle ground between them. This *Independent* spirit has a history and tradition in England that goes back over three centuries. This, on the one hand, is the history of the Congregational Church in England, the community of Guntrip's theological, philosophical, and ministerial rearing. It is also, on the other, the culture out of which the *Independents* of the Psychoanalytic movement in England and Scotland emerged. Fairbairn's Presbyterian and Winnicott's Methodist family roots are also echoed in this church history. In order to place not only Guntrip, but the *Independents* of British Psychoanalysis as well, a survey of this mindset follows. As this ecclesiastical history became an "internal object" for the British Psychoanalytic Society, I will parallel its three centuries of historical development with its manifestations in the history of the British Society in the twentieth century.

Congregationalism: Guntrip's Theological Tradition

"The 'Congregational way' emerged as a distinctive and powerful expression of the Christian faith in England and Wales in the tempestuous years that followed 1640." So begins the history of *Congregationalism in*

England: 1662–1962, by R. Tudor Jones.[1] The name of the publisher itself, the *Independent Press LTD*, bespeaks the identity of nonconformity to state religion. The name "Congregational" refers to what is known as "gathered churches," a group of people who come together out of their own choice and personal interest to form a congregation or community of shared faith and interest. "Unlike those forms of Protestantism that were the fruit of co-operation between theologians and statesmen, it was a spontaneous growth whose origins are all but lost in the obscurity which envelops early Elizabethan nonconformity" of the sixteenth century. This "Separatism" reflected a kind of "monastic ideal of a holy society knit together in a godly discipline" as was characteristic of the Puritan movement in England, as well as New England in America.[2]

Perhaps the most famous Puritan in England was Oliver Cromwell. He led a consortium of groups under the Parliamentary banner which included a variety of Nonconformists such as Presbyterians, Baptists, Congregationalists, and others. During the English Civil War of the 1640s, he led the Parliamentary army in a war of Independence from Royal domination. Within the Independent camp itself were its own divisions, as the Parliamentary majority's "scheme for a thoroughly Presbyterian national church on the Scottish pattern" was opposed by the "Dissenting Brethren" within the group who resisted any kind of hierarchical approach, Anglican or Presbyterian.

The "Church History" of Psychoanalytic Figures

Here already can be seen a dynamic that emerged between Guntrip and his respective analysts, Fairbairn and Winnicott. The Presbyterian Fairbairn conducted his analysis of Guntrip sitting behind his desk, symbolizing the distance and authority of the hierarchical model.[3] Winnicott, on the other hand, in true Methodist spirit and temperament, offered cups of tea and hospitality to Guntrip that would have perhaps left Charles Wesley, Methodism's founder, "strangely warmed;" (Wesley's term for his spiritual experience that inspired the launching of his revival movement within the Church of England).

---

[1] R. Tudor Jones, *Congregationalism in England: 1662–1962* (Boston: Independent, 1962) 13.

[2] Ibid., 13.

[3] Guntrip, "My Experience of Analysis with Fairbairn and Winnicott," *International Review of Psychoanalysis* 2 (1975) 145–56.

The Brief Political Reign of the Independent Church Tradition: Commonwealth

In the English Civil War, Cromwell and his fellow-Independents eventually won the day.

> The Parliamentary victory over the Cavaliers, the ousting of the Presbyterians, the curbing of the Levellers and the execution of the King were the steps that led to the establishment of the Commonwealth. In the Commonwealth the Independents and their friends enjoyed a pre-eminence they had hardly dreamed of ten years previously. More than any other party, they had the ear of "the great Independent," Oliver Cromwell himself. Influential posts in church, court, and universities fell to them and they could gain the ear of the highest in the land. Their leading men were appointed to positions of power and responsibility at the very seat of government.[4]

The reign of Cromwell, the Puritan "Lord Protector," lasted eighteen years. In a case of "identification with the aggressor," the "whole experiment was threatened by the failure" of implementing a broad constitutional basis for rule, with power ultimately still in the hands of a small minority. The "independence" of the *Independents* was their ultimate undoing as schisms within the larger group, a lack of common policy, and lack of vision emerged at Cromwell's death and the loss of his strong hand.[5] Victoria Hamilton's study of the Psychoanalytic schools echoes this quality in her reference to the British Independents of Psychoanalysis as not even being a group per se, but a number of individuals who are similar in that they practice psychoanalysis in personal and idiosyncratic ways.[6] The chaos of 1659 eventuated in the restoration of Charles II, and returned the *Independents* to the status and identity of "Nonconformists and Dissenters" as they are until this day.

Dissension within the British Psychoanalytic Society

The "Controversial Discussions" within the British Psychoanalytic Society during the 1940s is a modern version of this struggle. As with the death of Cromwell in 1659, the death of Sigmund Freud in 1939 created a power vacuum in psychoanalysis. "Without an omniscient leader who could im-

---

[4] Jones, *Congregationalism,* 30.

[5] Ibid., 34.

[6] Victoria Hamilton, *The Analyst's Preconscious* (Hillsdale, NJ: Analytic Press, 1996).

pose his opinion on us," noted James Strachey at the time, a climate was produced where such "difficulties were bound to reoccur periodically."[7] The two camps vying for control over the training of psychoanalytic candidates, the Kleinians and the Anna Freudians, reflected the hierarchical (royal and Episcopal) aspirations of these groups to dictate policy and exercise control. Strachey described the attitudes of the opposing factions in this way:

> Your views are so *defective* that you are incompetent to carry out a training analysis or for the matter of that any analysis at all," says one protagonist. "Your views are so *false* that you are incompetent to carry out a training analysis or for the matter of that any analysis at all," says the other protagonist.[8]

John Bowlby was at one time a supervisee of Klein and eventually left the British Society and pursued his ethnological research on attachment in response to such infighting. He saw Klein and Anna Freud as "mirror images of each other—stubborn women who refused to open up their minds to the ideas of others. . . . Anna Freud worshipped at the shrine of St. Sigmund, and Klein at the Shrine of St. Melanie."[9] Another example of the rhetoric was that "Psychoanalysis was not the private game preserve of the Freud family," an allusion to the rejection of aristocratic and royal privilege.[10]

From Commonwealth Back to Uniformity

Once back in power in 1660, the response of the royalists was to press for uniformity of religion in England in the passing of "The Act of Uniformity," described as "a distillation of the hatred and bitterness with which the Cavalier politicians viewed the Puritan religious bodies."[11] Its goal was to "eject" the nonconforming Puritans from the Church of England, demanding that all ministers use the Book of Common Prayer, revised to assure loyalty to the crown and the Episcopal, hierarchical power structure of the Anglican Church. Not only ministers, but also schoolmasters and teachers in colleges and universities were "brought within the net of uni-

---

[7] Phyllis Grosskurth, *Melanie Klein: Her World and Her Work* (New York: Knopf, 1986) 334–35.

[8] Ibid., 335.

[9] Ibid., 325.

[10] Ibid., 341.

[11] Jones, *Congregationalism*, 58.

formity. Not a corner was left in which a nonconformist could hide. So, modern Nonconformity was born in England and Wales. The long battle, which had lasted for a century, to include in the Established Church people of varying views was over."[12] St. Bartholomew's Day was the deadline for these declarations of loyalty. Among Dissenters this came to be known as "Black Bartholomew," with its name printed in their books in heavy Gothic type, the suggestion of mourning.[13]

During this quarter century of 1662 to 1688 the State attempted to uproot Nonconformity, forcing it underground, having to hold its secret meetings with the threat of being spied upon by informants. It has been described as the "Golden Age of Independency," where their minds turned to the pursuit of refining their thinking, as evidenced in the writings of John Milton such as *Paradise Lost* and *Paradise Regain'd* in 1667 and 1672.[14] Thus, a turning inward was part and parcel of leaving *concerns-politic* behind.

The Independents of the British Psychoanalytic Society

The Independent Analysts in a sense left power-politics to the Kleinians and Freudians. Fairbairn was essentially sequestered in Scotland, and made his impact through his writings, much as in the British Independent church tradition of the writing of tracts to debate the controversial issues. He took on the Freudians in his major revision of the classical structural model of *Id–Ego–Superego* into his Object Relational scheme of *Libidinal–Central–Antilibidinal Egos*. He challenged Melanie Klein herself to reassess the "Paranoid Position" of her own metapsychology to include "schizoid" as a central feature. Fairbairn was something of the evangelist here as she actually did amend her model to the "Paranoid-Schizoid Position," although she dismissed the larger impact of his work. In her biography of Klein, Phyllis Grosskurth describes the controversies between the Klein camp and Fairbairn.

> It is difficult to understand their strong objection to Fairbairn, particularly since he had prefaced his remarks by saying that in his opinion 'the explanatory concept of "phantasy" has now been rendered obsolete by the concepts of "physical reality" and "internal objects" which the work of Mrs. Klein and her followers has

---

[12] Ibid., 59.

[13] Ibid., 62.

[14] Ibid., 64.

done so much to develop." Fairbairn seemed to be taking Kleinian theories to their logical conclusion.[15]

Grosskurth postulated that Klein's identity as extending Freud's theories in her own were in conflict with Fairbairn's which were spoken of as leaving Freud's theories behind as "outworn preconceptions." Her other explanation for Klein's hostility to Fairbairn was that "Klein was undoubtedly resentful that Fairbairn—who had never even been analyzed!—was developing concepts similar to her own, yet was not beholden to her."[16]

Winnicott, on the other hand, was much more true to the "Middle Group" rendering of the Independents. He criticized Fairbairn for attempting to "knock over Freud" in his revision of the structural model, and was profoundly influenced by Melanie Klein in her early writings on children's mental states. Referred to as "the court jester of the British Psychoanalytic Society" by Christopher Bollas,[17] Winnicott respected both Freud and Klein, pursuing an integration that ultimately "rewrote what he read by the time he got to the bottom of the page" to be made use of by his own creative and paradoxical mind.[18]

Tolerance of Dissent

King James II ultimately failed in his attempts to bring Dissenters into conformity. The open resistance by clergy culminated in the trial of the bishops and their acquittal on June 29, 1688 amid scenes of frenzied excitement [that] sealed the King's fate. His son-in-law, William Henry, Prince of Orange, protector of the *Independents* who had fled to Holland, was invited to England the next day.

> At two o'clock on the morning of 11 December, so Roger Morrice was told, King James II 'carrying a wax candle in his hand to give him light to go down the stairs by' as he began his journey into exile. Nonconformists might well appreciate Morrice's care in preserving such a morsel of gossip. For them that flickering candle was the promise of a better dawn.[19]

---

[15] Grosskurth, *Melanie Klein,* 325.

[16] Ibid., 325.

[17] Christopher Bollas, *Winnicott Lectures* (cassette recording) (Tustin, CA: Newport Psychoanalytic Institute, 1982).

[18] Dodi Goldman, *In Search of the Real: The Origins and Originality of D. W. Winnicott* (New York: Aronson, 1993).

[19] Jones, *Congregationalism,* 104.

The Prince of Orange set out "to endeavor a good Agreement between the Church of England, and all Protestant Dissenters."[20] Yet again there were differences of opinion within the Nonconformist ranks in response to this overture.

> It was still true that the Independents were like a man "who smells the smoaking snuff of a candle, as soon as he comes into the room" while the Presbyterians were like "a man who cannot smell it, untill it be clapt close to his nose." This explains why the Independents preferred to stay in the background when the Presbyterians were showing great enthusiasm for the new monarch.[21]

Many Congregationalists, in fact, did not want the Presbyterians united to the Church of England, not wanting to shrink the ranks of those who would stay outside the circle of the state church, "that the toleration would be best maintained when great numbers should need it."[22] The Toleration Act of 1689 was passed that excused Nonconformists from the worship and discipline of the Church of England on the condition that they accepted its doctrine.

Denominational Partitioning between the Psychoanalysts of England

The culmination of the "Controversial Discussions" within the British Psychoanalytic Society was known as the "Gentleman's agreement" of 1944. This in itself was rather a misnomer as it is the twentieth century version of the Toleration Act that brought a negotiated settlement between the rivalry over the "religious instruction," (that is, psychoanalytic training), between the "Warring Women" of the British Psychoanalytic Society: Anna Freud and Melanie Klein. They devised two tracks of psychoanalytic training to pursue affiliation with one or the other group. When this became the eventual solution to avoid "official splitting in the Society," the then president of the Society, Edward Glover, tendered his resignation from the Society on January 24, 1944. He reflected on the situation years later in an interview in 1965: "Training systems had by then developed into a form of power politics thinly disguised by the rationalizations that however unsatisfactory eclectic politics had proved in general psychother-

---

[20] Ibid., 105.

[21] Ibid., 106.

[22] Ibid., 106.

apy they had somehow acquired virtue when they developed as teaching systems."[23]

Polarity in Thought:
The Intellectual Debates of the 1700s

After the establishment of the Toleration Act in 1689, a period of vigorous intellectual debate ensued. Prior to the *secularization* of philosophy which culminated in the twentieth century, the majority of the famous philosophers were at one time also theologians. Figures such as Kant, Hegel, and Kierkegaard wrote theological treatises as one aspect of their philosophical thinking, and visa versa. This was also true of the famous scientists such as Galileo, who did not see his own discoveries as antithetical to God as the still medieval thinking church did, as well as Isaac Newton. So when Newton published his *Principia* in 1687, there began a paradigm shift in thinking to understanding the universe through mechanistic explanations that would therefore not only impact science and philosophy, but theology as well. Modern philosophy and science was loosening the hold of the late Middle Ages and the Reformation. Deism was in its "heyday" during this period, a theological worldview that reflected this Newtonian upsurge of science.

> Physical science provided not only specific conclusions but also an atmosphere of thought. By means of a rational method it had achieved the picture of a universe whose parts were harmoniously interrelated, and whose laws were universal, objective and simple. The "mystery" of nature was penetrated and dissolved. Alexander Pope gave voice to a common mood: *Nature and Nature's law lay hid in night. God said: "Let Newton be," and all was light.*[24]

The Age of Enlightenment

This was the British version of the "Age of Enlightenment" in Europe. A number of cultural contexts colored the rise of science. The British empire itself had brought an influx of new cultures and viewpoints. The simple and "noble savage" was idealized as "unruined by the artificialities of civilization."[25] Chinese religion was seen as one of the purest forms of natural religion, where the "sacred history" of Western Christianity was giving way

---

[23] Grosskurth, *Melanie Klein,* 343.

[24] E. Graham Waring, editor, *Deism and Natural Religion* (New York: Ungar, 1967) v–vi.

[25] Ibid., vii.

to a universalism based on rational principles. The quest was for common denominators among all religions which were "reasonable" and "natural."

Another central feature of this Enlightenment climate was the rejection of authorities. Interestingly, this had been a central characteristic of the Nonconformists all along. Parallel to the political upheavals that eventuated in the American and French revolutions was an intellectual one. "Ideas and institutions which represented a traditional authority were increasingly called into question in the name of 'reason.'"[26] On the Continent, the secularization of science began, symbolized in Galileo's conflict with the Roman Catholic church, leading the way for similar revolutions in political and economic theory, philosophy and psychology. Yet at the same time in England most parties retained a conviction of the existence of God. The Newtonian view postulated the world-machine as an orderly, intricate mechanism that implied an intelligent designer. Indeed, Newton himself was one of many prominent scientists who saw their ideas as essentially religious in nature, creating the new mindset of "scientific theism." What grew in proportion was the distance between the "Divine Designer" of the world-machine and the daily affairs of human beings.

> Theologically, "God" became increasingly transcendent; psychologically, "God" became increasingly abstract. God was seen as the author of the natural law (in both the scientific and the moral senses of the term). But as the author of the law which describes the regular, orderly inter-relations of things, "God receded" behind the battery of secondary causes with which men have daily to do. And to speak of "God" as the author of the moral law of nature was often to do little more than bestow an honorific on man's ability to make autonomous rational calculations in matters of personal and social morality.[27]

Guntrip would ultimately pick up on this distancing between the "subjectivity of faith" and the "objectivity of science" as detached observer in his polemics against Hartmann's version of Ego psychology. It would be the next scientific revolution of Einstein's relativity that would provide a basis for the reintegration of the use of the subjective in Guntrip's *Psychodynamic Science.*[28]

---

[26] Ibid., viii.

[27] Ibid., xii–xiii.

[28] Guntrip, *Psychoanalytic Theory, Therapy, and the Self* (New York: Basic Books, 1971).

Theological Splitting:
Calvinist Determinism and Deist "Ego Psychology"

Guntrip's Congregational church during this period was experiencing a split between the traditional Calvinist theology and the Deist Rationalists. The division was described in the classical, historical controversy between the deterministic Calvinism of the Puritans on the one hand, and the free-will wielding "Arminians" on the other. The rationalism of the Deists was the latest incarnation of the Arminian theological view of humans as exercising determinative personal choice in their own destiny, what Hartmann would later call the ego's capacity to observe, analyze and adapt to the environment (creation).[29]

> The shaking of the theological foundations was felt widely in the churches. By 1742, the defection of younger ministers was forcing some to ask whether Dissent was a cause worth serving and in the West Country the retreat from orthodoxy was grave indeed. Splits and successions began to sap the vitality of the churches.[30]

The Evangelical Revivals: 1760–1815

Out of the polarity of the Calvinist-Deist split of the first half of the century arose a "movement of spirit" that cut across all church affiliations: Anglicans, Baptists, Quakers, and Independents. Theology again became personal and salvation a dramatic event. The vanguards of the movements were notables such as George Whitfield and the famous Charles Wesley, whose *methods* of devotion and spiritual discipline coined the term, "Methodism." It was a kind of parallel to the movement within the North American psychoanalysis of Self Psychology. Indeed, Christopher Bollas spoke of Self Psychology's founder, Heinz Kohut, as a kind of "missionary" to American psychoanalysis for articulating theory to represent empathy, "affective attunement," and an emphasis on *the personal* in the analytic relationship. He notes that good analysts in the United States had implicitly practiced such personal concern and responsiveness for their patients all along, but this was never reflected in the "orthodoxy" of the clinical theory of Freudian Ego psychology. Bollas adds that analysts in Britain never thought much of "the Kohutians" as it was considered a rediscovery of the basic teaching of Donald W. Winnicott about the "true self," (along

---

[29] Heinz Hartmann, *Ego Psychology and the Problem of Adaptation* (New York: International Universities Press, 1958 [1939]).

[30] Jones, *Congregationalism,* 139.

with derivations through Fairbairn and Guntrip), thus the missionary analogy of bringing an existing "good news" to a new land.[31] It is striking, I think, that most within the Self psychology "revival" were trained in the psychoanalysis of classical Freudian and Kleinian determinism, as well as the rationalistic, structural thinking of American Ego psychology. In my own exposure to those within the Self-Psychology movement in Los Angeles psychoanalytic circles, I experienced a consistent theme of resentment toward the rigidity, impersonality, and dogmatism of their previous psychoanalytic training. This hearkens back to the sentiment borne by those who left their Calvinism behind in 1745. "*Almost all the Calvinists I have known are narrow, sour, and wrathful*; not to be with them *alone*, is to be against them.'"[32]

Revivalism in Psychoanalysis

Self psychology's emphasis on the affective and subjective experience of the individual patient seems very similar to the eighteenth century revival. Bernard Brandshaft, in a sense, describes his "conversion" experience from the determinative, hierarchical and interpretive emphasis in his Kleinian training to the affectively empathic milieu of Self psychology.[33] Charles Wesley, for his part, described his conversion from his previous (Anglican) orthodoxy as his "heart being strangely warmed."

Another strain within the English revival was an existential theme that was familiar to Guntrip in the drama of Kleinian interpretation.

> It was part of the genius of the Revival that it made personal salvation a dramatic event. It forced thousands of people in an age when rationalism, classicism and indifferentism were in the ascendant to see that their own personal destiny was the one great issue. The rhetoric of the preachers was dedicated to bringing men to a point of decision. To do this, absolute choices were presented in highly emotive language. Men had to choose between light and darkness, between life and death. The similes, metaphors and illustrations of the preachers were dramatic in substance and existential

---

[31]   Bollas, *Winnicott Lectures*.

[32]   Jones, *Congregationalism*, 139.

[33]   Bernard Brandshaft, "The Negativism of the Negative Therapeutic Reaction and the Psychology of the Self," in *The Future of Psychoanalysis*, edited by A. Goldberg (New York: International Universities Press, 1983) 327–59.

in intention. They were aimed at producing a decision rather than
to illustrate a point.[34]

"This fundamental defense against the death instinct Freud attributed to the organism," wrote Melanie Klein in *Envy and Gratitude* in
1957, "whereas I regard this process as the *prime activity of the ego.* There
are other primal activities of the ego which, in my view, derive from the
imperative need to deal with the *struggle between life and death instincts*"
(emphasis added). A characteristic of the Kleinian genre of psychoanalytic
interpretation, in my own experience as well as references in the literature,
has readily reflected this dramatic style and the use of bodily metaphors of
polarity. Klein continues. "I have, for many years, attributed great importance to one particular process of splitting: the division of the breast into a
good and a bad object. I took this to be an expression of the innate conflict
between love and hate and of the ensuing anxieties."[35]

The Congregationalists were ambivalent toward the Wesleyan revivalists as are the British Independent analysts toward the revivalists of
American Self Psychology. While the revivalist George Whitfield had an
open system approach toward his converts where he did not care where
they went to church, just so they went somewhere, Wesley used his superb
gift of organization to weld his followers into a denomination. In response
to a defection of a one-time Wesleyan preacher, Charles Skelton, to becoming a Congregational minister, John Wesley was quoted as caustically
saying, "Did God design that this light should be hid under a bushel? In a
little, obscure, Dissenting Meeting-house?"[36]

*I have encountered a similar attitude from some of those in the Self
Psychology movement who have told me that they have "moved beyond
Freud, and gone through Object Relations to reach the level of Contemporary
Psychoanalysis," (that is, Self-Psychology); apparently the pinnacle that towers
above the rest.* Kenneth Eishold chronicles the splitting of psychoanalysis
into factions, or "denominations," as seen in the Psychoanalytic Institutes
of Los Angeles. The "revivalist" analysts of the Southern California Institute
who were identified with Franz Alexander's "corrective emotional experience" approach split off from the Freudians (Calvinist-determinists) of the
original Los Angeles Institute in the 1970s. In the 1990s the next generation of revivalists from the Southern California Psychoanalytic Institute
split off to form the Institute of Contemporary Psychoanalysis with its

---

[34] Jones, *Congregationalism,* 146.

[35] Melanie Klein, *Envy and Gratitude* (London: Tavistock, 1957) 190.

[36] Jones, *Congregationalism,* 151.

dominant representation of Kohutian and Intersubjective Self Psychology adherents. On the other side of the psychoanalytic spectrum, the Kleinian psychoanalysts formed their own "denominational" Institute that specializes in the study of "primitive mental states" at the Psychoanalytic Center of California in this same city.

The impact of the Revival on the Congregational churches in particular was the abandonment of their original Calvinism in a move toward the characteristic affectively- expressive forms of preaching and worship. The contrast can be seen in the British Psychoanalytic Society between the Anna Freudian technique of "keeping equidistant from Id, Ego, and Superego," and that of the Kleinian technique of "cutting to the depths" of the unconscious with dramatic interpretations.[37]

Not all in Congregationalism were happy with the impact of the Revival on their churches, and exhibited a critical attitude toward Methodism. "Their reasons were that they could not approve of preaching which was not subject to the discipline of the church and which 'tended to great irregularity in gathering separate societies out of formed churches'"[38] The Calvinist-Puritan spirit of form and order raised a voice in protest of the "unhappy *Divisions* almost in all the Congregations in the Kingdom chiefly occasion'd by *Methodistical Delusions.*"[39] The split between the Freudian tradition and Self Psychology is articulated in differences over *method* in treatment, that is, psychoanalytic technique. The Freudian tradition emphasizes the kind of distance that the Puritans would be proud of in the classical rules of the analyst's anonymity, neutrality, and emphasis on cognitive interpretation of the patient's material. The Self-Psychological tradition's championing "affective attunement" and empathy for the patient's subjective experience is a *methodology* often seen by classical analysts as "not psychoanalysis," with a traditional fear that "wild analysis" would be an inherent danger with the loss of the traditional affective and interpersonal distance of the classical analyst. The British Independents seem to reflect a "middle school" where Guntrip himself argues strongly for "subjectivity" as a base for "Psychodynamic science" on the one hand, yet he develops Fairbairn's revision of Freudian structural theory clearly as an "ego psychology" that does not partake of the reductionistic phenomenology of the Self-Psychology camp, where seeing the psyche as having

---

[37] Donald Meltzer, *The Kleinian Development, Part II: Richard Week by Week* (London: Clunie, 1989) 4.

[38] Jones, *Congregationalism*, 160.

[39] Ibid.

"structures" has been replaced by the notion of phenomenological "organizing principles." The "divisions" within the Congregationalists between the Puritan structural metapsychology with its accompanying interpersonal distance and cognitive bent, and the impact of the Revival showed both the tension within the Independents, and the development of their temperament.

> The carefully prepared and copiously sub-headed sermon of 1700 had been transformed into the daring existentialism of the imitators of Whitfield. The cool, impersonal tones of the earlier preachers gave way to the shouting that grated so on the ears of Philip David. . . . Now the sermons were accompanied by groans and sobs. The Romantic Age of Religion had arrived.[40]

The Romantic Age of Psychoanalysis

The Romantic Age of Psychoanalysis as expressed by *The Independent Mind in British Psychoanalysis* is described by Eric Rayner. He traces the rise of *philosophical romanticism* as originating in France, developing through the English romantic poets like Keats, Shelley and Byron, yet cites it as predominately neither French nor English but German. Rayner argues that the London psychoanalysts saw themselves firstly as Europeans, as most early analysts went to Vienna, Berlin or Budapest for their training analyses. The philosophic thread that ran through much of European, and therefore, psychoanalytic intellectual culture, was this romanticism that was represented in the work of Immanuel Kant. Woven into this intellectual fabric was a

> metaphysical doctrine that reality is derived from a living Spirit or the Absolute. This is essentially creative so that the ultimate foundation for all things is the urge to self-expression. Nature is one manifestation of Spirit, man another. Essential knowledge must be emotional and intuitive, there must be depth of feeling if reality is to be understood. Reason, being artificial and analytic, is inadequate to the task of comprehending the Absolute. The idealist tradition, stemming from romanticism and led by Fichte, Schopenhauer and Nietzsche, emphasized mind, soul, spirit and life.[41]

---

[40] Ibid., 162.

[41] Eric Rayner, *The Independent Mind in British Psychoanalysis* (New York: Aronson, 1991).

The competing philosophical tradition was that of empiricism. Echoing the "Glorious" Revolution of 1688 that ousted James II and his authoritarianism, as well as "the tyrannies of enthusiastic ideologies" (such as the Puritans), the British as a culture came to distrust closed systems of theory and thought. "There was a public ideal of quiet debate and civilized discourse that would inevitably lead to compromise, justice and fair play. It was essential that there be no fanaticism."[42] The philosophers Locke, Berkeley and Hume saw knowledge as drawn from perception and experience, not innate ideas. Conflicting perceptions would be sorted out by discussion and compromise. Trial and error was the welcome road of learning, where "error is as valuable as truth, and doubt can be enjoyed."[43]

While romanticism emphasized values, teleology (goals), and the intuitive, empiricism championed the spatial, corporeal (flesh and blood), sensuous, factual, and mechanistic. The scientific attitude of modern times sides with the latter rather than the romantics. Guntrip debated Eysenck among the behaviorists,[44] and critiqued Hartmann among the Freudian Ego Psychologists in promoting the romantic view in psychology and psychoanalysis, respectively. He described Freud as split between the two traditions where Freud's clinical papers reflected his intuitive brilliance, yet he capitulated with the zeitgeist of scientific empiricism in presenting his theory in the forms of drive theory and mechanistic structure. As Guntrip described Freud as "riding two horses," Rayner also notes that Freud was born into the heart of both traditions.

Winnicott as Romantic and Revivalist

Dodi Goldman describes how Donald Winnicott fit within these two traditions. On the one hand, Winnicott seemed to view himself much along the lines of the pragmatism and open-systems thinking of the Empiricists. He sought open-minded and playful discussion rather than polemical debate, in contrast to Guntrip's continued polemical wranglings with Hartmann and others. He reflected Hume's "moderate skepticism" in seeing ideas as always tentative and mistakes as informative and curative as successes.

---

[42] Dodi Goldman, *In Search of The Real: The Origins and Originality of D. W. Winnicott* (New York: Aronson, 1993) 90.

[43] Ibid., 91.

[44] Jeremy Hazell, ed. "Response to Eysenck," in *Personal Relations Therapy: The Collected Papers of H. J. S. Guntrip* (Northvale, NJ: Jason Aronson, 1994) 413–17.

On the other hand, Winnicott was "far more intuitive than he cared to admit."[45] He rejected many of the empiricist notions, seeing the mind as endowed with primary creativity rather than as a *tabula rasa* or blank slate. If the mind merely "discovers" reality, "reality does not 'feel real.'" Creative apperception must accompany passive perception. An experiencing self—a notion more akin to existentialism than empiricism—is central to Winnicott's worldview."[46] He also differed from the empiricist notion of self-knowledge through introspection as being basic to understanding since his was a two-person psychology, seen in his proverbial "there is no such thing as a baby" [without a mother]. In contrast to the intellectual and rationalist style of the Continental psychoanalysts, Winnicott was seen as "typically British and totally beyond the comprehension of the Teutonic Hartmann style of theorist" due to his being "too much of an intuitive Englishman."[47]

Consolidation within the Congregational Church: 1815–1850

Early in the nineteenth century the British dispatched Napoleon at Waterloo to end the long period of skirmishes, potential threats, and political insecurities. At the same time the Independents posted a similar victory over the state ecclesiastical hierarchy with the passage of *An Act to repeal certain Acts, and amend other Acts relating to Religious Worship and Assemblies* in July 1812. Not quite a Waterloo, the legislation, nicknamed "The Little Toleration Act," stated that anyone who "molests a religious meeting commits an offense."[48] With the end of the Napoleonic wars in 1815, peace ensued where Congregationalists were far more numerous, energetic, and optimistic than ever before. Powerful social and economic forces that would shape the Victorian century were to change the life of the churches in significant ways. It was a time of harvesting the fruits of the Revival during the long peace that lasted to the Crimean War in 1850.

> The dynamic of the Evangelical Revival was transformed in the period that lay between the Battle of Waterloo and the Great Exhibition into the activism of Victorian Nonconformity. The

---

[45] Dodi Goldman, *In Search of The Real: The Origins and Originality of D. W. Winnicott* (New York: Aronson, 1993) 92.

[46] Ibid.

[47] Ibid., 87.

[48] Jones, *Congregationalism,* 186.

quiet and diffident Independency of the eighteenth century adopted militant Liberalism that had as its spearhead a Nonconformist variation of Christian Radicalism. The second-class citizens of the era of Toleration resolved to play their full part as first-class citizens in the life of the State and of the nation. In a word, consolidating the gains of the Evangelical Revival was to mean an all-round attack on remaining disabilities, both social and political.[49]

Creativity and Conflict during the Psychoanalytic Golden Age

The "Gentleman's Agreement" between the warring camps of the Kleinians and Anna Freudians coincided with the end of the World War in the mid 1940s. A period of growth and development ensued for psychoanalysis in general, with a significant impact upon western society, both British and American. On the one hand, since during the war resources were stretched in England and the Kleinians were better entrenched than those of the Viennese camp, many of the emegrés from the Continent were "encouraged" to move on to America as a final stop. The Freud family and certain Viennese remained in London where Anna established her domain embodied in the Hampstead clinic. Yet the majority of the Continental analysts went to New York, embodied perhaps by Heinz Hartmann and the shaping of American psychoanalysis after the mindset of Ego Psychology. Edith Jacobson, Margaret Mahler, and a long list of notable psychoanalysts from both the Viennese circle and Budapest spread outward from New York to make Ego Psychological psychoanalytic thinking the dominant force in American psychiatry for the next two decades. At one point, the head of almost every psychiatric residency in the United States was a psychoanalyst.[50]

In England, during the war, the analysts of the British society were scattered across the country in service of the war effort, and broadened the influence of psychoanalysis as they treated patients for the effects of the war in a multitude of settings. Wilford Bion became known for psychoanalytic therapy in groups.[51] The Tavistock clinic, with its Kleinian-Independent Object Relations mix, became a significant site for the pro-

---

[49] Ibid., 187.

[50] Nathan G. Hale, *The Rise and Crisis of Psychoanalysis in the United States* (New York: Oxford University Press, 1995).

[51] John Sutherland. *Fairbairn's Journey into the Interior* (London: Free Association Books, 1989) 122.

liferation of psychoanalytic thinking in the larger mental health arena for England. Ronald Fairbairn's two papers in his collected writings, *The War Neuroses—Their Nature and Significance* and *The Repression and the Return of Bad Objects*, in *Psychoanalytic Studies of the Personality*, 1952, illustrates how the psychoanalytic treatment of the vast number of combat veterans for "shell shock" helped put psychoanalysis more clearly on the map in England. "His understanding of these conditions had also the importance of contributing to an urgent national problem."[52]

This became also, perhaps, the *Romantic Age* of psychoanalysis where the social ills of society could now be addressed in a prophylactic manner through influencing the rearing of children and the school systems. This optimism was perhaps more characteristic of the American scene where the utilitarian character of the "Psychology of Adaptation" fit easily with the culture of American pragmatism. England retained a version of Calvinism where the Kleinian emphasis on envy and the death instinct came to be referred to in the British Psychoanalytic Society as "believing in original sin," as noted by D.W. Winnicott in a letter to Joan Riviere.[53] The Independents came more clearly to differentiate themselves *from* the Kleinians during this period through a series of formal breaks, both with allegiances to the more growth oriented humanistic spirit of the time as seen in Winnicott, as well in the Darwinian genre with John Bolby's ethnology research that would form the basis for his Attachment Theory.

Winnicott had been appreciative of Klein for many years, and was considered by many as a kind of protégé of hers; (apparently those who did not know Winnicott's maverick self that well). Yet in 1957, in response to her paper on envy as a normative expression of the death instinct, Winnicott, with personal distress, challenged her position and argued for the relational breakdown between mother and child as the source of envy. Rather than the deterministic (Calvinistic) position of inherited destructiveness, he cited the *tantalizing* mother who offers the "breast," (care, attentiveness), and then pulls away before the child is sufficiently fed as the stimulus for a response of envy. In criticizing Klein's minimization of the impact of the mother on the infant, Winnicott described the experience of trying to make this point to Klein as "speaking of color to the color-blind."[54]

---

[52] Ibid., 120.

[53] F. Robert Rodman, editor, *The Spontaneous Gesture* (Cambridge: Harvard University Press, 1987) 95.

[54] Ibid., 96.

John Bowlby described his experience of presenting a child analysis case to Klein for supervision. At a certain point the distress and depression in the mother of the child led to an interruption in the child's treatment, to which Bowlby reported Klein's reaction as frustration about her disrupting the analysis. Bowlby was appalled at Klein's apparent disregard for the well-being of the mother herself and especially about her ignoring the dynamics going on currently between mother and child as she took a predominantly intrapsychic approach.[55] Bowlby eventually left the British Society entirely and became known for his attachment research and authored his classic volumes on attachment and loss. A true *nonconformist*, he is an example of an Independent who "left the church" of psychoanalysis entirely.

During this period Guntrip did the majority of his own creative work. This was his "Fairbairn period" where he collaborated with Fairbairn on theoretical issues and was his analysand. After Fairbairn's failing health precipitated the end of his analysis with him, Guntrip produced a number of papers during this time before he began his analysis with Winnicott. He capped off his creativity with his post Winnicott analysis reflection in his account of his analyses with both men.

Perplexity and Progress within Congregationalism: 1850–1890

The Victorian era was known by those who lived it as "an age of transition. They were conscious of great changes taking place not only in the fabric of their society but in the texture of their minds."[56] Jones describes the religious climate as one of experiment, in contrast to the twentieth century view of it as "the Age of Faith." It was a time of defending the faith and giving reason for it. Theologically this was a pinnacle of rationalism with the "de-supernaturalification" of the biblical accounts where "Jesus now becomes a mythical expression of general ideas."[57]

The younger Congregational ministers were profoundly influenced by what traditionalists called "German speculation," since the classic liberal scholars, such as David Friedrich Strauss, were German. As what was known as the "New Theology" crossed the English channel, the "hallmarks of this liberalism were an unreadiness to assert the unique inspiration of

---

[55] Grosskurth, *Melanie Klein,* 402.

[56] Jones, *Congregationalism,* 245.

[57] Ibid., 252.

the Bible and a positive desire to assert the Fatherhood of God rather than eternal torment and double predestination," which is the orthodox Calvinist doctrine that God pre-determines both who will be "saved" and who will be "lost."[58] These two issues, the authority of the Bible and traditional Calvinism, were central concerns to the Congregationalists of this period.

The Authority of the Bible

The second half of the nineteenth century saw a reevaluation of the nature and infallibility of the Bible. What was known as "higher criticism" of the Bible was the application of the current tools and assumptions of scholarly literary criticism to areas of authorship, date of writing, and historicity of events in the biblical accounts. The general trend of this German scholarship was to reject supernatural events as mythology, irrational projections of the primitive mind. Freud himself went through this same transition just decades later when he renounced his original "Seduction Theory" of historically valid events of sexual trauma as the source for hysterical symptomotology.[59] He substituted and developed his ideas of "Infantile Sexual Fantasy" in its place. Many of his critics have argued that he was capitulating to the "spirit of the age." Alice Miller and a host of others have raised this cry in recent years of Psychoanalysis's abandonment of the historicity of such trauma.[60]

The Beginning of Sorrows: 1890–1930

Rarely in its long history has organized Christianity in England been called upon to face such a series of reversals and disappointments as "those which tested its spiritual powers in the forty years that separated 1890 from 1930. . . . The interest of the general public in religion began to wane. The retreat from Christianity gathered momentum." Radical social changes disorganized the life of many churches and the accompanying discontent created political tensions which divided Christian people.[61]

> The Boar War left the political life of the country in confusion, and for another thing, it did untold damage to the nation's moral

---

[58] Ibid., 253.

[59] Peter Gay, *The Freud Reader* (New York: Norton, 1989) xx.

[60] Alice Miller, *Banished Knowledge: Facing Childhood Injuries* (New York: Doubleday, 1990).

[61] Jones, *Congregationalism,* 314.

life. It coarsened the moral fiber by releasing jingoistic passions
for which the conflict in South Africa offered no justification. . . .
the outbreak of war "was a terrible blow" and the "unreason, and
violence, and passion" were . . . a heartbreaking opening to the
twentieth century.[62]

Above all the 1914–1918 War shook life to its foundations. It was little wonder that Christians should begin to ask searching questions about
the validity of the Gospel by which their fathers had stood.[63]

Gay describes this period in the life of Sigmund Freud in terms of
changes in his own personal outlook due to the impact of the horrific impact of the "Great War" on his view of society and his personal tragedies
soon thereafter. The Influenza of 1920 took the life of his daughter, Sophie
Halberstadt, his beloved "Sunday child."[64] In 1923 he was diagnosed with,
and had the first of many surgeries for cancer of the jaw. That same year
Heinz Halberstadt, "Freud's cherished little grandson, dies of miliary tu-
berculosis, a loss he finds hard to recover from."[65] Gay notes the pessimistic turn in his metapsychological and clinical interests during this period
away from the recovery of repressed traumata to wrestling with *Mourning
& Melancholia* (1917), and his work on anxiety, *Inhibitions, Symptoms,
and Anxiety* (1926). In his above noted letter to Pfister, his comment that
"most people are trash" echoed the pessimism that was already extant within his deterministic views. Freud's focus on *thanatos*, the "death instinct,"
was in some ways a philosophical exercise that was part of the "speculations" that Freud considered part and parcel of the scientific enterprise.
The developmental line in metapsychology that went through Vienna did
not echo this concept as it did that of anxiety and its vicissitudes. The
carnage of the First World War and the decimated Austrian empire that
was left in its wake was to influence Freud's theorizing along the lines of
those who live with the specter of death and must endure the anxieties of
living without its finality. His cancer was a constant reminder of the death
he carried around within himself, but without the relief of "returning to
the dust of the earth." This rendering of Freud's view of *thanatos* carried
more of the tone of "rest in peace," rather than an expression of predatory
aggression in the human psyche.

---

[62] Ibid., 335.

[63] Ibid., 315.

[64] Gay, *Freud Reader*, xlii.

[65] Ibid., xliii.

Melanie Klein championed "death instinct" as the innate aggression that made sense of human destructiveness. In her first book, *The Psycho-Analysis of Children*, she first expressly took up Freud's notion of the life and death instincts. These two instincts, a dialectical structure of opposites, reflected her rendering of love and hate that were to form the basis for her later metapsychology of paranoid-schizoid and depressive positions. She presented her view as based on Freud and Abraham's psycho-sexual stages, yet her concept of anxiety related to them was essentially her own. Freud had clarified his own position in a discussion with Einstein where "death instinct" is directed against the self and "destructive instinct," derived from the death instinct, is directed outwards.[66]

The Liberal Age of Congregationalism

In 1900 Congregationalism found itself face-to-face with several difficult theological and intellectual questions. Biblical criticism had been accepted by the majority of the intellectual leaders of the denomination. A Liberal Modernist theology was following in its wake which many of the younger ministers and laymen found more satisfying than the theology of their fathers. It was becoming increasingly fashionable to emphasize experience at the expense of doctrine; to exalt morality and social action; to disparage private piety and worship as matter of quite secondary importance to religion; to magnify the Fatherhood of God at the price of minimizing his righteousness and holiness. Consistently with this type of approach, the authority accorded to the Bible by the Protestant tradition was felt to be excessive. The authoritative element in Scripture is the character and teaching of the Jesus who really lived in Palestine. The "quest for the historical Jesus" began with the suspicion that the apostles, with Paul in particular, had distorted the original image of Jesus by wrapping Him in garments woven by their own convictions about him. Therefore, if the true historical figure was to emerge, these garments must be stripped off him. That would present us with the grand simplicity of the essential story and it would be seen that the complexities of theology could be resolved into the simple gospel message that men are all brothers and God is their Father. By thus re-molding traditional Christianity, it was hoped to gather modern man into the fold of the faith. But first, the new gospel had to be tested to try its veracity.[67]

---

[66] Grosskurth, *Melanie Klein*, 191.

[67] Jones, *Congregationalism*, 347.

The publication in England in 1901 of Adolf Harnack's *What Is Christianity?* crystallized with brilliant directness and clarity the vague feeling that many possessed that the only unique thing about Christianity was the teaching of its Founder about the Fatherhood of God and the Brotherhood of Man. The pervasive influence of Hegelian Idealism taught men to look for similarities rather than contrasts. Sharp distinctions between God and man, between Christianity and paganism, between the Bible and other books, between the Church and society, between Heaven and Hell were unwelcome. Any theology that could give expression to this mood was bound to attract attention and that is precisely what happened with the proclamation of the "New Theology."

> The starting-point of the New Theology "is a re-emphasis of the Christian belief in the Divine immanence in the universe and in mankind." The scientist, the poet and the religious man are all in different ways answering the call of "the un-caused Cause of all existence" which is God. . . . Fundamentally, therefore, the whole human race is a unity because God pervades it. Evil is but a negation; it is a necessary concomitant of our knowledge of good, and sin is but a wrong way of seeking life, for it concentrates on the self and not on the whole. . . . For the New Theology, "Deity," "Divinity" and "humanity" are "fundamentally and essentially one. Humanity is Divinity viewed from below, Divinity is humanity viewed from above" (from *The New Theology*, Reginald John Campbell, 1907).[68]

This is the theological milieu that Guntrip referred to as the "Modernism" through which he passed as part of his theological training and heritage. At this point in European Protestant thought, theology had become anthropology; transcendence, (God as other), had been supplanted by immanence, (God as Self). The rationalism of René Descartes from two centuries previous, "I Think, therefore I am," had crystallized in a way that tended toward, if not embodied, a self-contained "I."

The Liberal Ethos in Psychoanalysis

This spirit is represented in Freud's *Interpretation of Dreams* in that his insightful work is the fruit of his own *self-analysis*. It also resonates with his view of religion in *The Future of an Illusion* as the projection onto the heavens of the wish for an ideal father. Christopher Bollas, in discussing the varied notions and nuances of the "object" in Psychoanalysis,

[68] Ibid., 349.

cites Freud as thinking in terms of a *Cartesian object*, as above. Bollas sees Klein as representing the *phenomenological object* of the internal world of phantasy that reflects the existential milieu that mushroomed after the First World War. He then described Winnicott as embodying the *corporeal object* of the flesh and blood mother who incarnates psychological presence in bodily form, corresponding to the baby's primal development as a *psyche-soma*.[69] Guntrip ultimately found the theological reductionism of modernism unsatisfactory as he did classical Freudianism. For Guntrip, along with Fairbairn, the self-contained "I" would become the centerpiece in articulating "Schizoid Phenomena" as the central core of psychopathology. He would go on to describe his indebtedness to Klein for articulating "internal objects" as the starting point for understanding the internal world of schizoid experience, but would ultimately, along with Winnicott and Fairbairn, part company with her over her reductionism to instinctually based, and intrapsychically defined phantasy objects. He built upon Fairbairn's foundation of the schizoid starting point and went on to develop in more detail his own concept of "ego weakness" as the place of despair which must be worked through in order to have a solid sense of self. Following Winnicott, this working through requires a "regression to dependence" upon another that is impossible within the self-contained "I" of Modernist theology and classical psychoanalysis.

Guntrip's first mentor in his journey down the path of his theoretical development was John Macmurray, professor of moral philosophy during Guntrip's days at University College at London University. In the next chapter I will describe the object relational themes within Macmurray's philosophical teaching that were to have a profound influence on Guntrip.

---

[69] Bollas, *Winnicott Lectures.*

4

The Psychology and Theology of John Macmurray

Guntrip's Transitional Object from Religion to Object Relations

H ARRY Guntrip cited John Macmurray as the philosopher who had "thoroughly" trained him in the "personal relations" school of thought. Professor of Moral Philosophy at University College in London in the 1930s, and eventually at the University of Edinburgh in Scotland by the 1950s, Macmurray's teaching and writings in the 1930s came to provide Guntrip with a transitional space between what he referred to as his traditional, conservative Salvation Army heritage, and the liberal modern theology of the twentieth century, both of which Guntrip found wanting. Macmurray was addressing the philosophical development of the twentieth century western mind, with a particular focus on the respective characters of science and religion, and the relationship between the two. This he set out in a rather technical way in his *Interpreting the Universe* in 1933, and in a much more compelling fashion in his book published in 1935, *Reason and Emotion*. A summary of his basic arguments from this latter work will lay out his principal philosophical viewpoint that shaped Guntrip's own thought and worldview.

In a series of what were originally lectures, Macmurray lays out his philosophical metapsychology under the rubric of "Reason in the Emotional Life, I, II, and III," with what then would be considered his theory of technique, "Education of the Emotions." In the latter part of the book he takes up directly the topic of what we might call "Religion and its vicissitudes," as he develops his theological philosophy that would so strongly impact Guntrip. He explores the nature and meaning of religion through its various comparisons with science, reason, reality, and his view of its maturity in contrast to the religious "superstition" so commonly practiced.

Reason in the Emotional Life

His basic premise in these writings is that Reason should not be reduced to the intellectual enterprise, as is common in western Rationalism since the Enlightenment of the 1700s. He argues for what he calls "emotional reason," the basis for the experience of "aliveness," in contrast to the utilitarian striving towards achieving "ends" characterized by mechanical functioning. This thread that runs through the book is his critique of twentieth century European culture. Although he never uses the title "Existentialism," and would differentiate himself from its formal philosophical tradition, his emphasis on "experience" smacks of the philosophical dueling between the rationalists and the existentialists. His remake of the "Age of Reason" we might ultimately see as a complementarity between the two, with his emphasis as a corrective to the dominant intellectualized and utilitarian culture.

He begins with a critique of the individualism and ego-centrism of the dominant intellectualized culture, positing that "we are all enmeshed in that network of relation that binds us together to make up human society," like it or not.[1] He goes on to develop this theme that Winnicott would echo in his musing that "there is no such thing as a baby [without a mother]." Macmurray's version is that "we have no existence and no significance merely in ourselves."[2]

"What is emotional reason?" Macmurray asks. It is that which has been dissociated from the popular notion of reason as "thinking and planning, scheming and calculating," losing its connection to "music and laughter and love."[3]

> We associate reason with *a state of mind which is cold, detached and unemotional.* When our emotions are stirred we feel that reason is left behind and we enter another world—more colourful, more full of warmth and delight, but also more *dangerous.* If we become *ego-centric,* if we forget that we are parts of one small part of the development of human life, *we shall be apt to imagine* that this has always been so and always must be so; that reason is just thinking; that emotion is just feeling; and that these two aspects of our life

[1] John Macmurray, *Reason and Emotion* (London: Faber & Faber, 1935) 14.

[2] Ibid., 15.

[3] Ibid.

are in the eternal nature of things distinct and opposite; *very apt to come into conflict and requiring to be kept sternly apart.* We shall be in danger of slipping back into a way of thinking from which we had begun to emerge; of thinking that emotion belongs to the animal nature in us, and reason to the divine; that our emotions are unruly and fleshly, the source of evil and disaster, while reason belongs to the divine essence of the thinking mind which raises us above the level of the brutes into communion with the eternal (emphasis added).[4]

What was it that captured Guntrip's interest that he would identify Macmurray as playing such a central role in the development of his own thinking? Macmurray's style of writing is one which Guntrip himself would eventually emulate: a colorful and engaging prose that artfully communicates concepts that are normally discussed with abstract and mind-numbing technical language in their respective fields, philosophy and psychoanalysis. Yet I would offer that the stronger appeal was very personal as Macmurray essentially describes the Schizoid landscape of western culture that Guntrip wrestled with as his own psychological self-experience. Guntrip, I believe, found in Macmurray the hope of transcending the qualities of *the cold, detached and unemotional* schizoid adaptation: the *ego-centrism* of the withdrawn ego that engages in the use of the splitting of the ego to manage the internal conflict between good and bad objects by *keeping them sternly apart.* What Guntrip would later jointly pursue with Fairbairn in the remaking of Freudian metapsychology was the redemption of the emotional "id" experience as *unruly* and portending *disaster* to that of a hungering after attachment to the object which was the experience of meaningful aliveness.

Macmurray continues his own treatise that would foreshadow Guntrip. He describes reason "in general," (both the intellectual and emotional dynamics), as that which differentiates humans from the rest of organic life, as reflected in the common notions of speech, the invention and use of tools, and the organization of social life. "Behind all these there lies the capacity to make a choice of purposes and to discover and apply the means of realizing our chosen ends."[5] Here he foreshadows his later work in *The Self as Agent* (1953), which in scholarly-philosophical style he challenges the Cartesian "thinking 'I'" as intellectualized and narcissistic. "Against the assumption that the Self is an isolated individual, I have set the view that the Self is a *person,* and that personal existence is *constituted*

---

[4] Ibid., 16.

[5] Ibid., 18.

by the relation of persons."[6] The "capacity to make a choice" has the ring of existentialism to it, yet Macmurray will hold out for the language of the "practical." He sums up this enterprise of the 1950s, read by Guntrip, in his introduction: "All meaningful knowledge is for the sake of action, and all meaningful action for the sake of friendship."[7] This line, penned two decades after *Reason and Emotion*, is a distillation of his earlier writings. Yet, let us continue with our exposition of the latter as it coincides with Guntrip's seminal development.

In his complementary fashion, Macmurray cites science, art, and religion as the central expressions of reason in man, with science reflecting its intellectual nature and art and religion that of the emotional. Here he develops what is essentially his philosophical basis for object relations. "Reason is the capacity to behave in terms of the nature of the object, that is to say, objectively. Reason is thus our capacity for objectivity."[8] Macmurray critiques the one-person psychology that looks for "something in the inner constitution of the human being to explain the peculiar nature of his behavior."[9] He defines reason as the capacity to behave in terms of knowledge of the outside world, rather than merely as a reflex. Science, as that which gathers data about the object, reflects the intellectual side of the coin of Reason. Yet science itself has its own form of countertransference, the "desire to retain beliefs to which we are emotionally attached to for some reason or other. It is the tendency to make the wish father to the thought. Science itself, therefore, is emotionally conditioned."[10] Macmurray essentially describes the projective process "where we colour the world with our own illusions," to which the intellectual enterprise is as susceptible as the emotional.[11] Thinking is as subjective as feeling. In gaining knowledge of the outside world, of the nature of the object, the painful process of *disillusionment* applies to thinking as well as feeling. The central problem is that of the tendency toward ego-centrism which prefers the illusion of self-sufficiency over the painful awareness of one's need for connectedness to the outside world. Again, this echoes the Schizoid dilemma of a desire for connection and the fear of engaging in it. Fairbairn would later take the dependency of the infantile state and rather than make it

---

[6] John Macmurray, *The Self as Agent* (New York: Harper & Brothers, 1953) 12.

[7] Ibid., 15.

[8] John Macmurray, *Reason and Emotion*, 19.

[9] Ibid., 20.

[10] Ibid., 21.

[11] Ibid., 22.

something to be outgrown, dependency becomes that which one matures into, an echo of Macmurray's basic premise.

Macmurray goes on to develop this parallelism between thought and feeling as both striving toward an objectivity that allows one to behave in light of the nature of the object. It is interesting that during this same decade Heinz Hartmann was developing his own version of this theme of *adaptation to the environment,* yet in the rationalistic manner to which Guntrip would take such exception for many years. What would be the difference? Macmurray makes the process of observation of the outside world, the external object, one based on action, whose motives are ultimately emotional. He cites that he follows Plato in his *Republic* and *Philebus,* that not only thoughts but also feelings could be true or false. It is a false dichotomy that thoughts are *rational* and that feelings are *irrational,* secondary and subordinate to cognitions. Macmurray ultimately takes a stance of embodiment toward the nature of reason. "For if reason is the capacity to *act* in terms of the nature of the object, it is emotion which stands directly behind activity determining its substance and direction, while thought is related to action indirectly and through emotion, determining only its form, and that only partially."[12] Thought ultimately becomes a form of reflection on the existential act which arises from one's (e)motives.

Macmurray turns to the issue of psychoanalysis directly, citing its contribution in revealing the extent to which our emotional life is unconscious. He takes a rather Winnicottian tack at this point, noting that "psychoanalysis has only extended and developed a knowledge which we all possess."[13] In the same way Winnicott saw that all mothers knew intuitively what it meant to hold and care for their child.[14] Macmurray presents this same sort of intuitive approach toward the functioning of the emotional life. Bringing this intuitive, emotional world into awareness is the daunting task undertaken by psychoanalysis, but common to all for emotional development to occur. He draws out his thread of *ego-centrism* as the confounding variable to development, which affects both thinking and feeling. This essentially is the narcissism of the *paranoid-schizoid* position of British Object Relations, where one *assimilates* one's experience of the outside world and reshapes it fit one's internal world. Here the nature of the outside object is distorted to spare one the pain of the *disillusionment*

[12] Ibid., 26.

[13] Ibid., 27.

[14] Donald Winnicott, *Babies and Their Mothers* (Reading, PA: Addison-Wesley, 1987).

of realizing where it is different from one's internal object representation. "The real problem of the development of emotional reason is to shift the center of feeling from the self to the world outside. We can only begin to grow up into rationality when we begin to see our own emotional life not as the center of things but as part of the development of humanity."[15] The process of emotional development is that of *accommodating* our current model of the world to the nature of the outside object in order to act toward it based upon its actual nature, rather than our projection upon it. Macmurray is essentially describing the development of the capacity for empathy, which he illustrates as learning to "appreciate" art as expressions of the artist's essential being, rather than evoking some form of aesthetic "pleasure" that narcissistically leaves us in an isolated state. He concludes with making a differentiation between notions of "love" that are essentially experiencing a pleasurable emotion that is stimulated by the other person, and that of "appreciating" the person for who he/she is in his/her own right. "Is he an instrument for keeping me pleased with myself, or do I feel his existence and his reality to be important in themselves? The difference between these two kinds of love is the ultimate difference between organic and personal life. It is the difference between rational and irrational emotion. The capacity to love objectively is the capacity which makes us persons."[16]

Education of the Emotional Life

Macmurray addresses what is essentially the clinical application of his thesis in the context of education. He seems to take a page from what Bion would later call *Learning from Experience,*[17] as he uses the organic senses as his schoolhouse for the education of the emotional life. He takes pains to develop the idea of *sensuality* as the perceptual gathering of data from the outside world, much in the same way that Carl Jung described it in his *Psychological Types.*[18] Jung's category of *perception* entails the dominant use of one or other side of a psychological polarity, apprehending the (external) object world with either *Intuition* or *Sensing.* Intuition is the perceptual process of apprehending the "bigger picture" through mental mapping, while Sensing is the perceptual process of ascertaining "facts" through sen-

---

[15] Macmurray, *Reason and Emotion,* 30.

[16] Ibid., 32.

[17] Wilfred Bion, *Learning From Experience* (London: Heinemann, 1962; Karnac, 1984).

[18] C. G. Jung, *Psychological Types,* The Collected Works of C.G. Jung 6 (Princeton: Princeton University Press, 1971 [1921]).

sory input.[19] Ironically, Macmurray earlier described a rather intuitive process of apprehending the emotional life in general, yet his methodology is patently empirical. On the one hand he substitutes the word *sensibility* for *sensuality* in order specifically to avoid the popular shameful connotations of the latter, but his choice of *sensibility* seems to me to reflect his integrative style of thinking where *sensing* takes on a rather *intuitive* character. Here again I see the appeal to a Guntrip whose interest in integration of polarities would resonate with Macmurray.

Macmurray notes that the normal sensibility of Europeans is "underdeveloped and irrational because of the way we have treated it," that is, the ego-centric focus on satisfaction of the senses, rather than using the senses as "the avenues along which we move into contact with the world around us."[20] He champions sense-life as the fundamental source to fullness and richness in life, providing "the material out of which the inner life is built."[21] Here the object relations theme of Guntrip's use of both Fairbairn and Winnicott stand out in bold relief. Guntrip's basic stance that all psychological roads lead to schizoid phenomena and the earliest oral experiences of "swallowing" up life can be seen in Macmurray's version of the introjection process. That the human is primarily object-seeking rather than pleasure-seeking is central to Macmurray's whole enterprise. The sensual experience of the infant with the mother was even better illustrated through Winnicott's descriptions as his development of the idea of "body ego" echoes Macmurray's sensibilities. Indeed, Macmurray waxes very "Winnicottian" in his own language as he develops this theme. Rather than employing utilitarian motives of applying "awareness" of the world for purposeful striving, Macmurray argues for sense awareness "for the sake of awareness itself," so as to "use them in a different and fuller way."

> We look at things not because we want to use them but because we want to see them. We touch things because we want to feel them. Sensitive awareness becomes then a life in itself with an intrinsic value of its own which we maintain and develop for its own sake, because it is a way of living, perhaps the essence of all living. When we use our senses in this way, we come alive in them, as it were, and this opens up a whole new world of possibility. We see and hear and feel things that we never noticed before, and find ourselves taking delight in their existence. We find ourselves living in

---

[19] David Kiersey and Marilyn Bates, *Please Understand Me: Character and Temperament Types* (Corona Del Mar, CA: Prometheus Nemesis, 1978).

[20] Macmurray, *Reason and Emotion*, 39.

[21] Ibid., 40.

our senses for love's sake, because the essence of love lies in this. . . . You don't want merely to know about the object; often you don't want to know about it at all. What you do want is to know *it*. Intellectual knowledge tells us about the world. It gives us knowledge *about* things, not knowledge *of* them. It does not reveal the world as it is. Only emotional knowledge can do that.[22]

The complement to the immediacy of sensuous perception is that of spontaneous expression, "activities which are spontaneities of emotion, activities which are performed for their own sake, and not for any end beyond them."[23] These are words which Winnicott could have written himself. In his own turn of phrase, Winnicott coined the term "spontaneous gesture" of the infant and essentially of the person as that which expressed one's "true self." This seems very reminiscent of Macmurray's view of emotional life and the sensual apparatus through which such aliveness emanates.

Macmurray also offers a theological illustration of his treatise on the "sense-life" in a New Testament quote. "'I am come', said Jesus, 'that they might have life, and that they might have it more abundantly.' The abundance of our life depends primarily on the abundance of our sensuous experience of the world around us. If we are to be full of life and fully alive, it is the increase in our capacity to be aware of the world through our senses which has first to be achieved."[24] This sounds rather similar to the words that Fairbairn wrote in his diary entry during his college days, his own lobbying for a "full blooded Christianity." We shall now turn to Macmurray's specific description of "religion" and how it reflects the emotional rationality of humans.

Science and Religion

"For centuries, until relatively recent time, the pride and prejudice of religion tyrannized over the minds and consciences and even the bodies of men." So begins Macmurray's treatment of religion. He goes on to chronicle essentially the development of what he calls "religious imperialism, under the pseudonym of Christianity."[25] He describes the tradition of Jesus as having flowed into the vast organization of the Roman Empire, mixed with Stoicism, and ultimately adopting the Roman tradition of empire in

[22] Ibid., 42–43.
[23] Ibid., 73.
[24] Ibid., 40.
[25] Ibid., 171.

pursuing "universal domination over the spirit of civilized humanity."[26] The medieval spirit was the culmination of the suppression of personal freedom, whose limits were reached in the Renaissance and Reformation. "The rediscovery of the art of Greece awakened the medieval spirit to the artistic spontaneity of the Renaissance, which in turn led to the rediscovery of the religious spontaneity of Jesus in the Reformation."[27] The "vast tissue of prejudice" that was Christianity was set on a course of disintegration, with the "continuous disruption of Protestantism into sectarian fragments" burning up like a meteor on reentry to the atmosphere of the earth. Macmurray cites science as the one creative achievement of the Reformation, "the one proper, positive expression of Christianity that the world has yet seen. The rest of modern culture—its art, morality, and religion—is simply the disrupted remnants of the pseudo-Christianity of the Medieval world. That is why the newly awakened pagan world clutches at our science while scorning our culture."[28] He describes an ongoing competition between the Roman and Protestant camps as the aftermath of the disruptive force of the Reformation, each competing for the re-establishment of the old autocracy. Control over the "inner springs of human life" was the "nut" over which the two sides have battled, with science, as the Reformation's child, being neglected by both. ". . . when science, come of age, entered upon the stage as arbiter of the dispute, it was only to crack the nut, give either party half of the shell and keep the kernel for himself."[29] Macmurray further illustrates his disgust for authoritarian structures in describing the religious system's attempt at rigid control over philosophy and science, and describes its ultimate demise and arrival at a form of impotence, the turning point being the loss of the battle over evolution, religion's "Waterloo" as it were. By the end of the nineteenth century, science was supreme, triumphing over the jealousy, fear, and superstition bred by medieval religion. "But it is difficult to fight an enemy who uses such underground methods without learning to use them oneself."[30] In the same way that Anna Freud was to describe the child who is abused as one who will "identify with the aggressor" as part of its survival, the same is said to have happened to this child of the Reformation.

---

[26] Ibid.

[27] Ibid., 172.

[28] Ibid.

[29] Ibid., 173.

[30] Ibid., 174.

> In the hour of its triumph science has become as full of pride and
> prejudice as ever religion was. . . . There is nothing like pride for
> blinding us to our own limitations, driving us to assert as truth
> what is only our own speculative opinion, . . . Modern science is
> very liable to superstition, and tends to breed superstition in its
> devotees. The visionary dream of the medieval church of a univer-
> sal empire over the hearts of mankind, purified by obedience and
> submission, was not so madly irrational as the modern dream of
> a world made peaceful and happy by obedience to the dictates of
> scientific thought."[31]

Macmurray gives a number of examples of this parallelism between
science and religion, citing "pride and prejudice" as the ultimate culprits
and the "parents of superstition." Macmurray's theme of *narcissism* seems
the unifying one here, differentiating both science and religion in essence
from their popular manifestations as authoritarian institutions. Macmurray
fits so very well with the spirit of the *Independents* in England.

His discussion echoes the one cited earlier between Freud and his
friend the pastor, Oscar Pfister, where Freud critiqued "religion" as simple
obsessional neurosis in *The Future of an Illusion*. Pfister's friendly rejoinder
in *The Illusion of the Future* presented essentially the same counterpoint as
Macmurray, that faith in technology and science, even psychoanalytic science, as promising a brighter future was a neurotic illusion about the nature of being human. Macmurray's ultimate goal is to root out the superstition that he has already defined as irrational ego-centrism. "Superstition
is not religion because it masquerades in the cloak of religion; neither is it
science because it masks itself in scientific terminology."[32]

Macmurray rejects a harmonization between science and religion by
assigning them separate spheres. "Science and religion are not logical defi-
nitions. They are forces in the world of men, and in the minds of men. The
struggle between science and religion goes on in us, and it is a real struggle,
a dramatic struggle, often a tragic struggle. . . . It is a deep seated *schism* in
the personal life of every intelligent modern man who wishes to be honest
and sincere with himself."[33] He goes on at length in describing the tension
between the two, where choosing one over the other is another example
of "pride and prejudice," and to want to look at problems from both sides
merely restates the problem and does not solve it. "It is as difficult a problem as the combination of the Wave theory of light with the Quantum

---

[31]   Ibid., 174–75.

[32]   Ibid., 176.

[33]   Ibid., 177–78.

theory of energy."[34] Here Macmurray cites the classic paradox of the twentieth century where two "truths" of a common phenomenon cannot be reduced down to a common denominator or synthesis, an unreconcilable polarity of the modern world. Ironically as one who has philosophically championed Plato to a degree, (as have Donald Meltzer and many in the Bion psychoanalytic tradition), Macmurray opposes the common neoplatonist dualism so characteristic of western culture that separates the "spiritual" and the "material." "Both meet in the mind of man, and demand to be related. . . . Science and religion are not concerned with two different worlds but with one and the same world—the only world there is."[35] His ultimate common denominator for the two is to see them both as truth seekers. "All honest religion necessarily involves a strenuous effort to know the supreme reality, and the knowledge of God must involve all knowledge in its scope."[36]

Macmurray applies a form of analysis: breaking down condensations into elemental parts; a form of theological form criticism: finding the "nut" within the "shell." His goal is to compare "essential religion" with "essential science." One the one hand, he sees science ultimately as "fragmentary," a collection of specializations whose methodology is to "analyze and classify" in abstract terms in order to identify general laws. On the other hand, religion is unitary or one, (like philosophy), seeking an at-one-ment with one God, through a methodology of the "concrete" that examines the wholeness of the individual, and is meant to be "always personal."[37] Of particular note is the relationship to reality itself.

> Science, though it may know everything in general, can know nothing in particular, and reality is always something in particular. It follows that science is not knowledge of reality. Is that startling? It is a commonplace of much philosophy, from Plato to the present day. . . . Science is descriptive, not explanatory. . . . Knowledge is by definition the apprehension of the real—not the description of it. . . . I do not say that it is not cognition, but simply that it is not knowledge in the full sense. For example, you cannot know anybody, your father or your friend, by science.[38]

---

[34] Ibid., 179.

[35] Ibid., 180.

[36] Ibid., 183.

[37] Ibid., 185–86.

[38] Ibid., 187–88.

For Macmurray, knowledge is ultimately *personal* and must apprehend far more than the data of organic existence, but must embrace all that goes into making up a *person*, which ultimately involves that which is *unseen*, that which technically speaking is *spiritual*, (the Greek word for spirit, *pneuma*, literally means "wind" or "air").[39] The classic theological illustration of this personal knowledge is the Hebrew rendering from Genesis that "Adam *knew* (*yada*) his wife," and she conceived. Macmurray's concept of *knowing* is intimate and personal, and therefore requires the *religious viewpoint* as he defines it.

Reason and Religion

Macmurray continues his development of his object relations philosophy. Religion is one of the three general expressions of rationality, along with art and science, where rationality is defined as "objective consciousness" through the perceptive methodology of sensory apprehension as delineated above. This is only possible, he writes, "in beings who stand in conscious relationship to objects which they know and which are not themselves."[40] Macmurray essentially presupposes a developmental level that reflects at least a basic self-other differentiation, what Winnicott would later call "the first Not-Me possession" of the external object. He describes three general fields or types of external objects: "material objects, living creatures, or persons like ourselves."[41] These correspond to his threefold expression of rationality. "Science grows out of our rationality in relation to material things. Art grows out of our relation to living beings. Religion grows out of our relation to persons."[42] Religious institutions and beliefs in themselves may be required to be swept away in the interest of religion itself which is inherent in the human situation. He sees religion as the fuller expression of rationality as it subsumes all three of the fields. The relation of a person to a person also includes the relation of a body to a body and of living creature to living creature. This position would follow in light of Macmurray's use of the sensual (body) as the apprehension of the object, and his focus on wholeness requiring a living creature rather

---

[39] Walter Bauer et al., *A Greek-English Lexicon of the New Testament and Other Early Christian Literature*, 3d ed., revised by Frederick William Danker (Chicago: University of Chicago, 2000).

[40] Macmurray, *Reason and Emotion*, 195.

[41] Ibid.

[42] Ibid., 196.

than a dissected one. He is careful to point out that he does not mean "more rational," just more inclusive or "fuller."

He describes the appropriate use of science: to relate ourselves "properly to matter, and use it as our material and our instrument. Science is the sign that we have learned not to pretend that matter is what we would like it to be, . . . that we have learned that a patient effort to discover its real nature and to deal with it in terms of its real nature will give us power to use it as our instrument. Through science we relate ourselves *really*, as material bodies, to the material world."[43]

Art is the medium through which we would relate ourselves to the organic world with "a pressure toward balance and rhythm and harmony, toward functional relationship," a rationality of the instinctual and emotional life.[44]

The religious field of personal relationships has the drive "to achieve equality and fellowship in the relations of persons."[45] Macmurray purposely defines religion without any reference to God. "The idea of God can have no fixed meaning of its own which is not related to our experience of human relationships; and it is the significance of the term to the persons who use it that matters."[46] Macmurray essentially goes on to critique the "God-talk" of society who "has crystallized a conception of God which is false, [where] the professed atheist may be more truly religious than the theist."[47] He invokes Kant as an ally in this endeavor to differentiate "false self" representations of religion from its essential enactment in genuine human interaction. "Kant is a milestone in the development of rational thought, and a giant among the intellectuals; yet he announced his great work as '*destroying reason to make room for faith*', and dubbed the process of reason '*a dialectic of illusion*'" (emphasis in original).[48] Macmurray here summons support for his own attack on "the arid speculations of the rationalists" in favor of the "experimental empiricism" of science which he touts as "the secret of its own superb rationality."[49] In short, Macmurray ends up with a form of natural religion, where one finds God on the planet rather than looking to the heavens. Yet, he does not appear to don the

---

43 Ibid., 202–3.

44 Ibid., 204.

45 Ibid., 205.

46 Ibid., 207.

47 Ibid.

48 Ibid., 208.

49 Ibid.

apparel of the more popular natural religion of the Enlightenment which saw God's fingerprints on the structure and design of the natural order. He seems to relegate that to the scientific and aesthetic realms without disputing their forms of rationality. Macmurray ultimately comes down on the side of a form of *incarnational* thinking, where it is within the particularly human sphere of interactions between persons that God shows his face. "In particular the really religious man will define the nature of God, not in terms of analysis of ideas or of transcendental beliefs, but in terms of his empirical knowledge of human relationships. So Jesus is reported to have said: 'He that hath seen me hath seen the Father, and how sayest thou, then, show us the Father.'"[50]

The Maturity of Religion

The "Maturity of Religion" was a theme of Macmurray's that was to make a significant impact on another member of the British school of psychoanalysis: Neville Symington. In his *Emotion and Spirit: Questioning the Claims of Psychoanalysis and Religion*, (1994), Symington gives his own account of the movement of religion from *primitive* to *mature*, taking a rather eastern slant in championing the detachment model of the *Upanishads* as his organizing principle. He described Macmurray's "natural religion" as a "Socratic religion in the context of our contemporary world."[51] He essentially is referring to the Socrates "we meet in the dialogues of Plato."[52] He sees Socrates as a co-confrontor along with the Buddha and Jesus as challengers of primitive religion which Symington describes as the "projection of the self as agent—the representational self—into the natural world or the imagined natural world."[53] Driven by the Darwinian survival instinct, and paralleled by the Kleinian vision of the *paranoid position* as defined by the same process, he contrasts this with *mature religion*, the anthropological change which is marked by "burying ones dead," characterizing "the birth of the *representational self*, . . . [where] a being in its own right has died, not just a fragment of the tribe."[54] Symington reflects the Kleinian-Winnicottian development shift from the *paranoid position* to the *depressive position*, or in Winnicott's turn of phrase, developing the *capacity for*

[50] Ibid., 210.

[51] Neville Symington, *Emotion and Spirit: Questioning the Claims of Psychoanalysis and Religion* (New York: Palgrave Macmillan, 1994) 43.

[52] Ibid., 37.

[53] Ibid., 7.

[54] Ibid., 10.

concern, where one becomes aware of one's own agency, power to make an impact on the world, and the capacity to mourn loss rather than fear attack as coming always from the outside. Symington joins Macmurray in critiquing "rites, sacrifices and votive offerings," whether Buddhist or Christian, as essentially a primitive religion of placating the gods "out there" from a paranoid developmental stance.[55] Symington's version of mature religion parts company to a degree with Macmurray, however, as his emphasis is on a much more mystical detachment from narcissism, citing that the Christian mystics were "more spiritual men than Jesus," in contrast to Macmurray's patently interpersonal view.[56] Symington sees Macmurray as Socratic in that the "religion of Socrates differs from that of the Buddha and Jesus in that it resulted from a process of reasoning."[57] This would reflect Macmurray's organizing principle of rationality. Symington makes the greatest use of Macmurray in the movement from use of the object for self-gratification, to that of valuing the other to the point of recognizing that the human world has a claim upon us because each of us has a value which demands recognition. Macmurray says,

"The primary fact is that part of the world of common experience for each of us is the rest of us. We are forced to value one another, and the valuation is reciprocal. The recognition that the 'other' has a claim on me is the religious attitude of mind, and the inner signal of this claim is conscience."[58]

"Socrates said this claim is exerted upon me by the good. Macmurray puts this into a modern perspective by stating that the good is in the other, or that the good is immanent in other human beings, and that this has a claim upon my actions," with God symbolizing this claim. Symington prefers the notion of "Ultimate Reality as comprehended in the Upanishads, which is in me as well as the other."[59] This would appear to fit better with the dual intrapsychic *and* interpersonal view of object relations. He then makes his application to psychoanalysis as the field of concern with "that emotional activity of which we are unaware," that which occurs between people as well as "within the frontiers of the self." Psychoanalysis' aim is

---

[55] Ibid., 12.

[56] Ibid., 14.

[57] Ibid., 37.

[58] Ibid., 43.

[59] Ibid., 44.

to "transform activity which is invisible and destructive into that which is constructive."[60]

In sum, Macmurray facilitated in Guntrip the articulation of a new direction in his pursuit of freedom from the imprisonment within his intellectualized-schizoid, personal world, one that was given theological structure and reinforcement during his days in the Salvation Army. The promise of "aliveness" spoken of by Macmurray was one that he also did not find within the modernist theology of his Congregational ministry training per se, as it also suffered from a different form of Hegelian "imprisonment in the 'I'." Macmurray's passionate philosophy of personal relations freed him up "intellectually" to continue his pursuit of apprehending this aliveness in his own person. Guntrip next turned to Ronald Fairbairn to find an "other" who might move him further along this path.

[60] Ibid., 44.

5

Fairbairn's Theological Roots and Impact on Guntrip

JOHN D. Sutherland chronicled Ronald Fairbairn's personal, professional, and theological development in his psychobiography of 1989: *Fairbairn's Journey into the Interior*. A fellow Scotsman and protégé of Fairbairn, Sutherland taught at Edinburgh University and was a central figure at the Tavistock Clinic, acting as its Medical Director from 1947 to 1968. He, in the 1930s, like Guntrip later on, had a personal analysis with Fairbairn of five years as Sutherland "became drawn to the kind of work he did" and decided to become a psychoanalyst himself.[1] In his moving account of Fairbairn's life, he draws upon his personal knowledge of him, as well as important private documents, "to bring about a close integration between Fairbairn's life and ideas, on the one hand, and his fraught inner world and symptoms, on the other."[2] The impetus for its writing Sutherland found in his relationship with Guntrip who requested a biographical chapter for a book that Guntrip was planning to write on Fairbairn's work, one incomplete at Guntrip's death.

In the spirit of the psychobiography that he was writing, Sutherland begins with his own professional history and how their lives wove in and out of contact with each other. Early on, he expresses his admiration of the man in his characterization of Fairbairn as a "disciplined, critical mind in a gentleman scholar whose aim was to advance our knowledge of man as a person." He quickly notes the dialectical theme of science and religion. "To my mind, there has been in the psychoanalytic movement an excessive persistence of what can rightly be termed an idolatrous worship of Freud and his work. The profoundest appreciation of any thinker's ideas is surely to explore where they lead. Fairbairn never thought of himself in

[1] John Sutherland, *Fairbairn's Journey into the Interior* (London: Free Association, 1989) xi.
[2] Ibid.

any other way than as a diligent student groping forward with his assimilation of the unique contributions Freud had made" (Sutherland, 1989, p. x). Fairbairn's reworking of Freudian metapsychology, therefore, according to Sutherland, was in the spirit of the critical thinking scientist who would challenge the religious establishment of Freudian orthodoxy. At the same time the *critical thinking scientist* suffers from a certain schizoid orientation that *cuts off* with scientific detachment in the process of *cutting up* and analyzing the data in order to understand. I would propose that the central impetus for understanding schizoid states reflected Fairbairn's personal struggle to create a metapsychology that came to grips with such "splitting of the ego" with his own goal of being a whole person. Sutherland notes that "the emergence of some of Fairbairn's ideas clearly stemmed from the dynamics of his own inner world."[3] This is a bit of foreshadowing of what he would develop in the rest of the book: Fairbairn's painful struggles with the schizoid character of his Father's strict Scottish Calvinism on the one hand, and his mother's repressive Victorian Anglicanism on the other. In psychoanalysis he found an avenue to understand such repression and to confront it, eventually leaving the Scottish Presbyterian church. Yet, on the other hand, it was not spiritual or theological concerns that he left, but repressive religion that "split off" sexuality and other manifestations of "aliveness" that are characteristic of the schizoid way of withdrawing from *felt* experience. Indeed, through his professional life he was on a journey through which he sought to liberate himself from the "frozen chosen" in pursuit of becoming a "hot Scott." This is a theme that would reverberate through his own writings and become central to Guntrip's as well.

His professional challenging of the orthodox status quo reinforced his "outsider" status, both as a psychoanalyst in the anti-psychoanalytic departments of psychology in Edinburgh, and as the *neither Freud nor Klein* Independent, isolated from the main psychoanalytic community in London.

Sutherland describes how in his own relationship with Fairbairn he was able to bridge the distance that Fairbairn seemed to experience in his own personal world. Even when he was in London and Fairbairn in Scotland for twenty-six years, Sutherland would meet with Fairbairn several times a year. In addition, Sutherland was the editor of the *British Journal of Medical Psychology* in which Fairbairn published many of his articles, affording another avenue of contact and collaboration. Sutherland notes,

---

[3] Ibid., ix.

Although separated geographically, I always felt I was in fairly close touch with what he was thinking, and with his personal and family life in general. These contacts were increased when Guntrip began to publish his papers on Fairbairn's views. I then became involved in a triangle which, I think, was much enjoyed by all of us."[4]

One dialectic that is interesting to trace in Fairbairn's development is that of the schizoid nature of his family environment as it was represented by theological and church tradition. Sutherland signposts its atmosphere as "pervaded by the contradictions of devoted loving care combined with oppressive strictness."[5] The only child of these successful middle-class parents of the late Victorian age, Ronald grew up with the usual complement of professional staff of the period, maids and his own nurse or nanny. "Within this highly formalized and controlling background, the young Ronald received a great deal of attentive care," echoing again this concoction of rigidity and attention, even though seemingly provided by the hired help.[6] His parents' liberal quality was that of providing for the development of his talents, and a social life that included a circle of friends and relatives from all over the country. A particular dialectic of the schizoid orientation is the development of the internal world of intellectual talents to the nth degree, while at least maintaining a certain affable presence with others in social settings. The external presence often masks the internal rage that parallels the intellectual prowess. Sutherland makes a strong point about Fairbairn being "extremely friendly," and gives considerable focus to the other side, his repressed rage or anger.

Fairbairn's father is described as "staunchly Presbyterian," married to an English Episcopalian, perhaps, Sutherland muses, as "a latent need on his part to mitigate the harshness of the Calvinistic tradition."[7] Yet Thomas Fairbairn was seen as a friendly man, to those who knew him, "fond of entertaining and interested in his society as he saw it. The wife he chose, Cecilia Leefe, seemed to end up being the harsher of the two, "strict to the point of being a martinet in bringing her son up to conform to the formalities of their class, religious and otherwise."[8]

Sutherland saw Ronald's "freer relationship with his nanny" as a kind of compensation for the restrictive aspects of his parents. It "was thus in-

[4] Ibid., xi–xii.

[5] Ibid., 1.

[6] Ibid., 3.

[7] Ibid., 2.

[8] Ibid.

evitable that the little boy was thrown rather much into his inner world. He had an active fantasy life with systematized creations such as a country of which he evolved the features in great detail."[9] Sutherland does not make clear the connection between Fairbairn's relationship with his nanny and developing his inner world. The picture he paints, however, describes the *schizoid compromise* that Guntrip developed,[10] where the person is torn between the *desire* to make contact with his objects in the world, but is thrown back in fear upon living primarily in internal fantasy. Indeed, Sutherland describes Fairbairn's personal creation as a boy his own version of what today is a popular schizoid preoccupation, the computer game, *SimCity.* This modern computer simulation of building a city from the ground up reflects the creative power of introjection over one's objects when they are handled with the use of fantasy within one's internal world. Sutherland makes this same point as he continues. "The positive aspects of his family experience, as well as establishing a rich inner world, enabled the boy to enjoy the company of others and especially those of a similar mold. He often referred in later life to the great joy of spending holidays in Yorkshire and in London where he always felt warmly welcomed by his uncles, aunts and cousins."[11] This compensation for lack of emotional closeness with his own parents again portrays this dialectic between the oral hunger for contact that had its consummation in friends and relatives, and that of the "bad objects" of parental harshness and distancing that Fairbairn "swallowed" which manifested in various forms of psychic indigestion.

Sutherland describes a form of symbiotic tie between Fairbairn and his "omnipresent" mother as an effect of her being "ever watchful lest inappropriate influences or activities should be adopted," the net result producing "a rather unassertive young man with a strong lifelong attachment to her. . . . Her Victorian taboo on sex was so strong that sexual curiosity became an anxiously preoccupying concern for the boy."[12]

In a similar fashion, a particular neurotic symptom of his father was a "taboo" that was to find its impact on the young Ronald. His father had the "inability to urinate in the presence of others, so that, even at home, there had to be no one near the toilet door when he went to uri-

---

[9] Ibid., 3.

[10] Guntrip, *Schizoid Phenomena, Object Relations and the Self* (New York: International Universities Press, 1968) chapter 11.

[11] Sutherland, *Fairbairn's Journey,* 3.

[12] Ibid., 3.

nate. Ronald was thus made regularly aware of his father's mysterious affliction."[13] Sutherland traces this as an introjection or internalization that Ronald made of his father, a fascinating dynamic that illustrates an aspect of the schizoid process. The theme reflects Ronald's preoccupation with his own masculinity, played out in a number of different venues. The first was that of his pursuit of a commission in the Army in 1915 during the First World War, only to be medically rejected because he had a *varicocele*. This is a *testicular varicose vein*, which he had removed finally to gain his commission as an officer. The genital symptomotology relating to literal phallic potency is striking. His military career brought him to the medical unit for "Nerve-Shocked Officers" in Edinburgh where he worked under Dr. W. H. R. Rivers of Cambridge, a pioneer of medical psychology. "The manifestations of conversion hysteria that he saw on this visit greatly impressed him," developing his interest in what was called at the time the "new psychology," the psychoanalytic interest in the unconscious.[14] At the end of the war in 1919 he "embarked on a condensed four-year training in medicine with a view to becoming a psychotherapist."[15] Sutherland notes that his military experience, which included participating in the liberation of Palestine from the Turks under Allenby, along with his achievement of the MD and then being trained as a psychoanalyst, bolstered his masculine identity and sense of prowess. The subject matter of psychoanalysis afforded him the opportunity to study in detail the array of sexual taboos which were his heritage from his parents.

Sutherland notes that Fairbairn's marriage also became the occasion where his sexuality was received and confirmed and thereby enhances the sense of masculinity with which he struggled. Wedding Mary More Gordon from a landed Scottish family in 1926, she was fond of the social scene, and they enjoyed a social life together for a number of years. But as Fairbairn became more successful and therefore busy with his psychoanalytic practice, and as he was writing a number of clinical papers, his wife became resentful at his increasing withdrawal from their joint social activities. Sutherland described the scene:

> When his wife became destructive to his work she clearly threatened to castrate his psychological masculinity. There seemed to ensue a regression to a defensive identification with his father, who could assert himself against being controlled by his wife.

[13] Ibid., 4.
[14] Ibid., 8.
[15] Ibid., 9.

Unfortunately, his father's masculinity, as mentioned earlier, was deeply and mysteriously linked to his phobia of urinating in the presence of others, and Fairbairn began to manifest this symptom during 1934. It then became entrenched early in 1935 after a traumatic experience. There had been an unusually aggressive outburst from his wife, which was followed later that night by his having an acute renal colic with haematuria.[16]

It appears that Fairbairn was unable to be *pissed off* with his wife, echoing his relationship with his parents. Sutherland's analysis of the symptom articulates the object relations of the externally affable schizoid who harbors smoldering rage.

Clinical experience would at once suggest that the symptom had arisen from a sharp splitting off in his self of a deep sadistic rage against his internal bad mother. Formed out of early experience and subsequently overlain by good relationships, this primitive structuring was now activated by its resuscitation in the external world both from his wife's close fit with the past and the loss of the good figure of his father. Not associated with strong conscious affectionate bonds, his father had nevertheless been a caring figure to him, one who later took pleasure in his achievements.[17]

Fairbairn's papers manifest professionally the themes that reverberated within himself personally: "Features in the analysis of a patient with a physical genital abnormality," written in 1931, and "The repression and return of bad objects," *British Journal of Medical Psychology*, 1943, (both published in *Psychoanalytic Studies of the Personality*, 1952), are examples. Yet in terms of sources of influence on the psychoanalytic thinking of Fairbairn, Sutherland champions the paper read to the London Psychoanalytic Society by Melanie Klein in 1934 as perhaps the most influential: "A contribution to the psychogenesis of manic-depressive states." He argues that history would show that this was a "momentous occasion for the future of psychoanalysis" in general, and of Fairbairn's in particular.[18] Her innovative view of the development of the personality "made great use of Freud's death instinct as the biological energic source" of the infant's oral aggression, yet Sutherland argues that the origin of violent aggression was ultimately "inessential to her developmental scheme."[19] This

[16] Ibid., 36.

[17] Ibid.

[18] Ibid., 37.

[19] Ibid.

flexibility in thinking, stated directly here by Sutherland himself, reflected the mentality of the *Independent tradition* that received insights from Klein and applied and developed them in their own way. That "a world of internal objects was fashioned from *experience*, with each of these structures embodying the intense quality of the primitive affects which had cohered in their formation," reflects this *Independent* reinterpretation of Klein by Sutherland[20] (emphasis added). Klein's instinctual, phylogenetic model of internal objects seems very different than this experiential tack. "*Frustration* could be felt as a violent attack from an object, and, with repetition, the latter was made into a persecutor because it was merged with all the rage originally evoked by it" (emphasis added).[21] The *frustration* of *experience* is a central tenet to the environmental-developmental emphasis of the *Independents,* in contrast to the Kleinian determinism. It is both Sutherland's "statement of faith" in regards to this, his own tradition, and also the framework for understanding the development of Fairbairn's thinking. Fairbairn's personal history of object relations "structured the self" that was characterized by submerged and symptomatic rage. In short, the theories of object relations are generated by the *experience* of object relations. Phyllis Grosskurth in her marvelous biography of Melanie Klein presents much of the same thesis. Clinical papers written by psychoanalysts ultimately reflect their own lives.

As noted above, the titles of Fairbairn's papers reflect such personal concerns, even though the clinical material in them was *not* directly self-analysis as they were about patients seen in his clinical practice. Indeed, his very first clinical paper reflects this trend in being a kind of parapraxis, (slip of tongue, or in this case, the pen), for his personal interests and beliefs that have been all but ignored by the psychoanalytic community, or of which they are ignorant. In 1927 Fairbairn wrote, "Notes on the religious phantasies of a female patient."[22] Fairbairn's own theological interest and beliefs are something that, according to Sutherland, he never abandoned, and, as is the thesis of this writer, reflect a dynamic understanding of human beings that he developed through the medium of the psychology of object relations. So when we come to Fairbairn's protégé, Harry Guntrip, we will see how Guntrip continues this tradition of "doing theology" in the existential clinical setting of psychoanalytic work with his patients.

[20] Ibid.

[21] Ibid.

[22] Ronald Fairbairn, *Psychoanalytic Studies of the Personality* (London: Routledge, Kegan Paul, 1952).

Not widely known is that Fairbairn's first choice of career was the clergy. Growing up he attended church every Sunday with his parents for both morning and evening services. "The Presbyterian services, however, gradually came to seem harsh and drab for him compared with the Episcopalian ones which he often attended on holiday with relatives and family friends, who included some Anglican clergy."[23] Sutherland notes his "marked altruistic and religious feelings" found expression "in much 'practical Christianity'" through his membership in various clubs and organizations that served deprived sections of the community. His faith was within the context of his general conservative outlook, and expressed within the established structure of society. Devoted to the monarchy, idealizing the traditional social order and values, Fairbairn embodied a benevolent, concerned elitism that sought to effect social change through *evolutionary*, (that is, slow), processes. Sutherland interprets this as an inevitable outcome "for one so enmeshed with his powerful conservative mother and his successful father."[24]

His early interest in moral and psychological issues progressed to the point where philosophy became his area of study at Edinburgh University in 1907, which reflected a grounding in classical studies. He graduated with honors in philosophy four years later. During these University years he decided to become a clergyman. An entry taken from his personal diary around his twenty-first birthday captures "his conception of the religious life and his decision to adopt it."[25] He had attended a Bible conference a few days earlier, and included in his diary the social activities that reflected his both "serious and frivolous" membership in being "one of the boys." Sutherland is here tracing his theme of Fairbairn's concerns about his "lack of masculine assertiveness," which is a thread he follows through Fairbairn's statement of faith in his diary entry in 1910.

> August 11th, which is notable as the 21st birthday of that humble servant of King George V, Ronald Dodds Fairbairn. Not only a humble servant of King George, I hope, however, but also of Jesus Christ; for, at time such as this, it is well to be serious for a moment, and to pause at this great turning point of life to take a breath of heavenly air, before plunging into the work and stress of manhood. It is hard to combine in the right mixture the jollity and the seriousness which are both essential for a presentable life. It is of ultimate importance to be solid at the bottom, but continuous

---

[23] Sutherland, *Fairbairn's Journey*, 5.

[24] Ibid.

[25] Ibid.

solidity acquires a 't" and becomes 'stolidity." Now, of all things, stolidity is the most depressing, and, therefore, to be consummately avoided. This is where so many Christians *cut themselves off from life.* They are serious, and rightly so, but never jolly. There is a call to look on the happy side of life and things, no less divine than that which bids us remember that life is a Great Reality. . . . Is the religion of the average Church today of a nature to capture and mold the full-blown life of the healthy-minded young man or woman? Or does it only provide for one type of mind? Is it only suited for half of the individual's life? True Christianity ought to satisfy every legitimate instinct and aspiration. It ought to be a working and workable philosophy of life for man and boy, matron and maiden; it ought to be adaptable to the condition of the schoolroom and football field, of office and golf-course, of factory and home. God give me the strength to do my share, however little, to effect that unspeakably desirable consummation. I have decided to devote my life to the cause of religion; but may it be a manly, healthy, whole-hearted strong religion, appealing to enthusiasm of youth, as well as to the quiescence of old age—in other words may it be a Christlike religion (emphasis added).[26]

Fairbairn, at the age of 21, speaks to the issue of the *schizoid phenomena* in both his personal and Presbyterian background as he critiques the theological version of the schizoid's *cutting off from life.* It is a "full blooded Christianity" that he expounds, reflecting a theology that integrates the bodily, instinctual, and sexual, and that has its autobiographical application as a rallying cry for his own pursuit of a bodily sense of aliveness and integration into life. This foreshadows, I think, a harmony with the philosophy and mindset of that other famous British Independent, Donald Winnicott. Winnicott embodied in his daily existence this "full blooded" living, what Fairbairn developed theoretically in his psychoanalytic writing, yet was always in a kind of pursuit of personally, struggling with his schizoid self. Christopher Bollas delineated the philosophical differences between this British Independent stance and those of Freud and Klein in terms of the character of the psychological *object.* Freud's *object* was of the Cartesian-rationalistic variety. Klein's was the phenomenological type of intrapsychic internal phantasy. Bollas calls Winnicott's object *corporeal,* that is, of the flesh and blood of the *actual mother's body* which is *actually there,* or *actually absent.*[27] This *incarnational* theology is a thread that

---

[26] Ibid., 6–7.

[27] Christopher Bollas, *Winnicott Lectures* (cassette recording) (Tustin, CA: Newport Psychoanalytic Institute, 1982).

runs through both the environmental object interest of the *Independent* psychoanalysts in general, and in Fairbairn's psychoanalytic writings in particular.

Sutherland entitles the period of 1939 as Fairbairn's *Prelude to Creative Articulation*. This was in the context of the professional attacks against psychoanalysis and himself by the psychological establishment in Scotland in the persons of Drever and Henderson, as well as the ongoing tension between his wife and himself. His writings about *aggression* at this time were far from being an academic exercise. On the one hand, "Klein had crystallized for Fairbairn the importance of internal objects from birth; but by focusing on orality and oral sadism as the salient instinctual influences in the experience of the object, she gave the impression of neglecting the influence of the actual behavior of the object as the first determinant of the experience with it—and, above all, of the behaviour at a personal level."[28] Fairbairn in response drew attention to the impact of family relationships in the earliest stages of growth during his clinical writing in this period. He was both "captivated at first by the dramatic nature of the infant's inner world as she [Klein] portrayed it," and he also added "his concern for the fundamental role of the whole or personal object," citing the "craving to be loved" with its inevitable frustration by the actual, flesh and blood caretaker as the complementary object relation to the intrapsychic one. Ten years earlier in 1929 in his address to the Edinburgh medical students he had critiqued Freud's use of the term "sexual" as extending too wide, and proposed "sensuous" as the more appropriate descriptor for the full range of the appetitive feelings. The seeds of his revision of Freudian metapsychology were beginning to germinate here in 1939.[29]

Early in February 1939 he took to the offensive after years of criticism, both at home and at the University. He presented his paper, "Psychology as a proscribed and prescribed subject" to the St. Andrews University Philosophical Society, a counterattack directed at Drever's paper presented there the year before where Drever stated "that psychoanalysis could not be recognized because it was not a scientific discipline," putting it in the same category as alchemy and astrology.[30] Fairbairn countered in stating that the academic psychologists were really the unscientific ones, ignoring the "most significant psychological phenomena in man such as the unconscious, sex, love, conscience, sin and guilt along with the entire range

---

[28] Sutherland, *Fairbairn's Journey*, 58.

[29] Ibid., 59.

[30] Ibid., 61.

of the manifestations of hate and aggression: war, persecution, revolution and fanaticism."[31] All of these dynamics were in the air as World War II was to *break out* in September of that year. Europe was *pregnant* with such internal objects. Fairbairn associated such academics with the history of religious leaders who decry the dangers of such self-knowledge, "destroy the heretics" who challenge the status quo, and are themselves actually in fear of what psychoanalysis uncovers in man. He cited the university (which includes Drever, et al.), as protecting the common culture of repression. "The traditional role of a university is to safeguard the culture of its society and it was thus inevitably in conflict with another of its functions, namely to advance knowledge by free scientific inquiry, for the latter inevitably 'has had a disintegrating effect upon the prevalent culture.'"[32] Sutherland himself expands on this notion of "prevalent culture" where "'the traditional culture' to be preserved by the academics was essentially the scientific materialism which had dominated science progressively since the middle of the nineteenth century."[33]

After his presentation of the paper, Fairbairn found himself a following as, in the face of some lobbying against him by Drever, he was elected the President of the Scottish branch of the British Psychological Society. Within a week, he was in London being granted full membership of the British Psycho-Analytical Society. He now "belonged" in the psychoanalytic movement, seemingly being rewarded for "defending the faith." Ironically, he would turn this same critical thinking on the grip that scientific materialism *also* had on psychoanalysis, with its reification of concepts and resistance to "unorthodox" thinking. Sutherland sees merging with the conscious considerations of this paper, "the echoes of the boy protesting against the parents who prohibited the pursuit of his natural curiosity."[34] Sutherland through his language implies this as the occasion of Fairbairn's moving beyond Klein's model as well, moving from a *depressive position* to the *assertive position*, a developmental stage that she does not address, per se.

Fairbairn was "increasingly stimulated" by his schizoid patients during this year, characterized by their demanding dependence. The sadistic urination phantasies prominent in one of his patients would have reverberated with his own urinary symptom. Sutherland analyzed "the promi-

[31] Ibid.

[32] Ibid.

[33] Ibid., 62.

[34] Ibid.

nent features of his inner world that led him to turn the traditional pre-occupation away from impulses to personal relations."[35] He drew from Fairbairn's self-analytic notes written between October and November of 1939 during the time of uncertainty of where the war would lead. The central object under analysis *was* his urinary symptom. He recalled a dramatic incident which he recollected as one of his "traumatic incidents that left a permanent effect."[36]

> Incident on Highland Railway in old days. No corridor; train very late; stopping at every station. Father's bladder very full. Ladies in carriage—all ladies except father and me. Father conferred in whispers with Mother. Mother whispered to her friend and the other woman. Then Father urinated at his end of the compartment, while Mother and perhaps her friend, held up newspapers as screen. I was on the same side of newspaper screen as Father. It was [an] appalling experience. Father seemed in great pain and had the greatest difficulty in passing water. It took a tremendous time for him to pass it; and it only came in driblets. He "sweated blood." It was like seeing Christ on the Cross. I was closely identified with Father in the experience. I was on his side of the newspaper screen, and I wanted to urinate very badly too. I watched the scene aghast. I was terribly sorry for Father. It seemed awful to be unable to urinate when you wanted to so badly, and to be confronted with [the] danger of [one's] bladder bursting (a danger which Father had often dwelt upon me). It seemed bad enough for him to be placed in a situation in which he could not go to [the] lavatory when he required to; but it seemed even worse that the presence of women imposed a barrier upon his urinating in the carriage. I believe that first of all he tired to urinate out of the carriage window or through the slightly open door; but he failed and had to urinate on the carriage floor, which eventually was swimming in urine. I remember the sound of the urine trickling down on the floor. I wanted very badly to urinate too; and I think that, after Father had succeeded in urinating, I urinated through the door, which was held slightly open by Father. . . . The train swung about terribly and I was afraid of the door shutting and trapping my penis—which it nearly did. I think I had a bit of difficulty in urinating myself. I felt pretty anxious and worked up after watching my Father's performance. . . . Being unable to urinate when the bladder is full seems to be almost the most intolerable situation conceivable. I fancy that, when Father had that awful experience in the train, I must have held

[35] Ibid., 64.

[36] Ibid., 70.

myself responsible for his suffering—quite irrationally. Guilt over secret hostility towards him probably made me assume responsibility. I think I must have derived a secret satisfaction from his suffering, although I was [The notes break off here.][37]

Sutherland offers his analytic summary. He notes the experience for Fairbairn as highly traumatic in feeling, "powerfully present yet not really assimilated." The trains had no toilets in light of their frequent stops in stations, so that Sutherland suggests that his father "may have withheld his urine unconsciously to release it in the presence of the women." This reflects the emphasis on repressed hostility. "Ronald was put alongside his father behind the newspaper screen and he too then shared the need to urinate. His castration fears quickly followed."[38] He notes Fairbairn's identification with his father and his accompanying sadistic pleasure as an expression of his "secret hostility" toward him. Sutherland at first cites and later develops the crucifixion theme as related to retaliatory punishment, presumably for the secret hostility.

He develops this and the others themes from Fairbairn's self-analysis as a perspective on Fairbairn's early choice of the clergy for a profession. On the one hand, his mother's hostility toward sexuality combined with her narcissistic holding him as "special" as the "object of her ambition" created a "puzzling and painful contradiction" that "had built deeply serious splitting into his self."[39] His single-minded professional intellect was side by side with the symptom that insulated his intellectual work from his "secret hostility." On the other, he both identified with and resented the impotence of his father in reference his mother's controlling. His "persecutory bad mother as an unduly dominating internal object" would be a prototype for what he would later call the *antilibidinal Ego*. Sutherland reflects upon his own experience of Presbyterian ministers as frequently having ambitious mothers and a father who defers to her dominance in the family. "The resultant deep hatred of the mother for moulding their [the minister's] self is extremely difficult to release because of its intensity along with idealization of the mother. A splitting off of all aggression takes place which makes for resistance to recognizing and coping with it in themselves and others."[40] The highly ambivalent feeling toward the mother that results, Sutherland proposes, would dispose these boys toward the "Christian

[37] Ibid., 71–72.

[38] Ibid., 72.

[39] Ibid., 82, 87.

[40] Ibid., 88.

myths" with an identification with Christ "who abjures hate and gains the love of God, who is internalized as the unconditionally loving Father."[41] Sutherland thereby sees the Son of God as a model for an autonomous male sub-self whose capacities are supported by the dominant mother's desire for her son to be "special." In short, Sutherland offers an interesting object relational analysis of Fairbairn's theological interests as reverberating with, and reflecting the introjection of his parental figures.

Fairbairn's undergraduate philosophy curriculum along with his post-graduate Hellenistic studies was in opposition to his father's Calvinistic conservatism, both theological and financial, and in concert with his mother's ambition for him to achieve great things. The experiences and deprivations of the "bad mother," or *antilibidinal object,* were successfully split off as threats to her other inner presence as the one who supported their shared ideal self as "the man who was going to understand the mysteries of human nature, who would marry and have a family, and who would fulfill the Christian ideal of loving others by helping them to free themselves from inner sufferings by understanding their nature and origin. The support from his inner relationship with God had, however, an aura of secrecy about it. He turned away from the ministry, in which it had to be declared more openly."[42]

I propose that Fairbairn's theology and personal relationship with God was ultimately something that was beyond Sutherland's psychoanalysis of his family's object relations as *only* the psychological structure of such things. Let us now turn to a description of his metapsychological thinking where I will *exegete* his implicit theology, which was a core introject for Harry Guntrip.

A Revised Psychopathology of the Psychoses and Psychoneuroses

Fairbairn's developmental scheme is based upon the tradition of Karl Abraham carried through Melanie Klein that emphasizes the "mouth ego" of the infant, the "chief organ of desire, the chief instrument of activity, the chief medium of satisfaction and frustration, the chief channel of love and hate, and most important of all, the first means of intimate social contact,"[43] (see figure 1). Fairbairn ties together "splitting of the ego and

---

[41] Ibid.

[42] Ibid., 90.

[43] Fairbairn, *Psychoanalytic Studies of the Personality,* 10.

a libidinal attitude of oral incorporation," where states of "fullness and emptiness" organize the infant's experience. "The anxiety which he experiences over emptying the breast thus gives rise to *anxiety over destroying his libidinal object;* and the fact that his mother customarily leaves him after suckling must have the effect of contributing to this impression."[44] Fairbairn's classic statement about the schizoid state is the fear of destroying one's love object through hunger and "loving it too much" or intensely, that is, gobbling it up.

The Primacy of the Schizoid Concept

Fairbairn sees paranoid, hysteric, phobic, and obsessional features as "techniques" that defend against an underlying schizoid state, which he cites as "the most deep-seated of all psychopathological states,"[45] (see figures 1 and 2). Fairbairn notes that while "psychoneurotic defences are employed by the frankly schizoid patient in a vain attempt to defend his personality, they give no indication of the extent to which an underlying schizoid trend may be masked by the success of such defences."[46] The central features of the schizoid condition include the milder "social inhibitions and inability to concentrate" to the more severe examples of "depersonalization and derealization" as well as dissociative phenomena. The developmental feature that is central to Fairbairn's formulation is that "the fundamental schizoid phenomenon is the presence of splits in the ego;" a phenomena so basic that "everyone without exception is schizoid at the deeper levels."[47] The normal developmental use of such splitting is in the service of basic differentiation: between desirable and undesirable experience, and between inner and outer reality. The adaptive or pathological version of splitting, which is central to Klein and Guntrip as well as Fairbairn, is that of internalizing the "bad object" of psychically distressing experience in order to control it in phantasy as an affective, self-regulatory mechanism. These "bad object" experiences are "split off from" ego control, (referred to by Fairbairn as the *central ego*), and repressed into the unconscious as unassimilated experience.

---

[44] Ibid., 12.
[45] Ibid., 3.
[46] Ibid., 3.
[47] Ibid., 8.

A Revised Psychopathology of the Psychoses and Psychoneuroses

W. R. D. Fairbairn

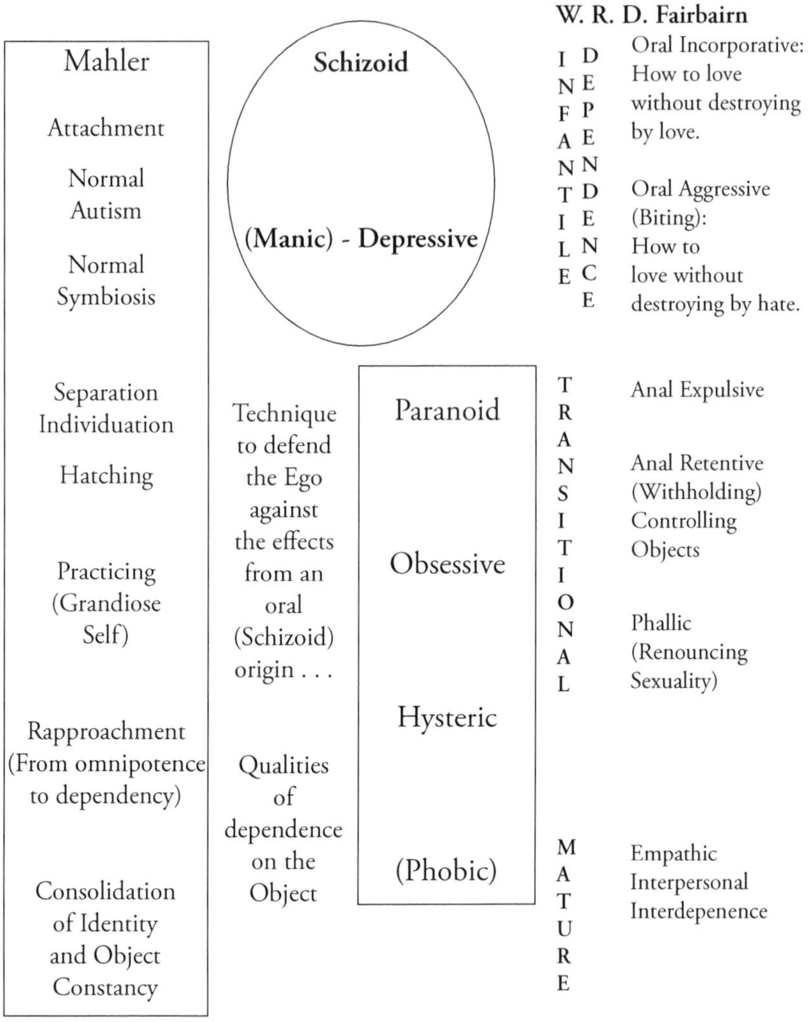

Mahler	Schizoid	INFANTILE	DEPENDENCE	Oral Incorporative: How to love without destroying by love.
Attachment				
Normal Autism				Oral Aggressive (Biting): How to love without destroying by hate.
Normal Symbiosis	(Manic) - Depressive			

(Schizoid / (Manic) - Depressive shown within oval)

Separation Individuation	Technique to defend the Ego against the effects from an oral (Schizoid) origin . . .	Paranoid	Anal Expulsive
Hatching			Anal Retentive (Withholding) Controlling Objects
Practicing (Grandiose Self)		Obsessive	
			Phallic (Renouncing Sexuality)
Rapproachment (From omnipotence to dependency)	Qualities of dependence on the Object	Hysteric	
Consolidation of Identity and Object Constancy		(Phobic)	Empathic Interpersonal Interdepenence

(Right vertical column: TRANSITIONAL ... MATURE)

Fairbairn's Basic Assumptions:

(1) Humans as Object Seeking: Attachment is the most central and basic developmental task.
(2) Schizoid: "Splitting" of the Ego into multiple egos.

Each ego (*Central, Libidinal, Antilibidinal*) is "schizoid" (split off) in this sense.

(Right vertical: DEPENDENCE)

FIGURE 1

Techniques to Defend the Ego from
Effects that are Schizoid in Origin

R E T E N T I V E	*Phobic*
	
	Escape/Submit
	  Masochistic
	  Passive
	  Externalization of both the
	  Accepted & Rejected Objects
	    [Satir Distracter]
	    Moving Toward/Moving Away
	    Approach/Avoid
		Obsessive
		
		Control/ Be Controlled
		  Sadistic (Aggressive)
		  Active
		  Internalization of both the
		  Accepted & Rejected Objects
		    [Satir Computer]
		    Moving Away
		    Retain/Expel
			R E T E N T I V E

P
H
A
L
L
I
C

←COMPLEMENTARY→
"Flipping"

A
N
A
L

E X P U L S I V E	Hysteric
	Self-Depreciating
	Overcompensation for
	  underlying rejection
	Dissociative: from organ/function
	  in self
	Externalization of the accepted
	Moving Toward
	[Satir Placater]
	Internalization of the rejected object
		Paranoid
		Extravagant Grandiosity
		
		Projection of the Bad Self
		
		Externalization of the Rejected
		Moving Against
		[Satir Blamer]
		Internalization of the accepted
		Grandiose
			E X P U L S I V E

FIGURE 2

Endopsychic Structure Considered in Terms of Object Relationships

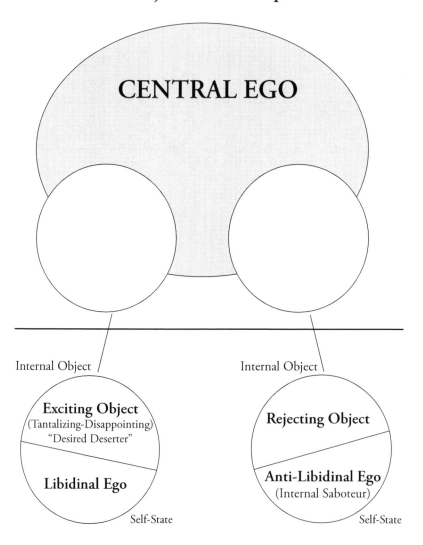

SPLIT-OFF & REPRESSED

FIGURE 3

Endopsychic Structure Considered in Terms of Object-Relationships

Fairbairn's notions of the splitting of the ego in the service of internalizing distressing experience gave rise to his reformulation of Freud's classic structural theory where *id, ego and superego* are replaced by *libidinal ego, central ego, and antilibidinal ego*, although with a very different emphasis and frame of reference (see figure 3). He sees "the realm of internalized good objects" as that of the superego, while he sees "the realm of internalized bad objects" as the foundation of psychopathology. These internalized bad objects come in two basic forms:

The *libidinal* psychic structure is the attachment-seeking part of the self that is so central to Fairbairn's reformulation of Freudian structural theory. On the surface its name appears to reflect "good object" experiences, yet Fairbairn is describing the experience of *desiring* a secure, affective attachment to the parental figure, only to be disappointed by the premature withdrawal of the *libidinal object's* availability. This led Fairbairn to characterize this *tantalizing* parental object as the *desired deserter* (See figure 3).

Fairbairn describes the *antilibidinal ego* as the psychic structure that protects the self from what becomes an anticipated abandonment and disappointment by the parental figure whose contact is desired by the *libidinal ego*. Fairbairn's original term for the *antilibidinal ego, the internal saboteur,* describes the familiar clinical phenomena of a patient who uses self-hate in the service of undermining the development of intimacy in relationships due to this inherent vulnerability of abandonment. Schematically, the *antilibidinal ego* carries out internal attacks on the patient's own *libidinal ego* for daring to desire attachment or intimacy, seeing it as a foolish and dangerous pursuit (Figure 3).

> The uncompromisingly aggressive attitude of the internal saboteur towards the libidinal ego is based on the latter's cathexis of the exciting object and its own cathexis of the rejecting object; and it is thus a reflection of the original ambivalence of the individual towards his libidinal objects. According to my view, ambivalence is not itself a primal state, but one which arises as a reaction to deprivation and frustration. Thus I do not consider that in the absence of frustration the infant would direct aggression spontaneously toward the libidinal object. Accordingly, whilst I regard aggression as a primary dynamic factor in that it does not appear capable of being resolved into libido, I also regard it as ultimately

subordinate to libido and essentially representing a reaction on the part of the infant to deprivation and frustration in his libidinal relationships.[48]

The Moral Defense

Fairbairn presented some of his central psychoanalytic concepts through the use of theological motifs. One of his more famous ones he called "the moral defense." This is where the patient takes the "badness" of the object into himself, resulting in the chronic pursuit of making oneself good. The defense is often manifest in such pursuits as reading countless self-help books, practicing fundamentalist piety, (religious or otherwise), and constantly berating oneself internally. As Fairbairn describes it:

> It becomes obvious, therefore, that the child would rather be bad himself than have bad objects (parents); and accordingly we have some justification in surmising that one of his motives in becoming bad is to make his parents "good." In becoming bad he is really taking upon himself the burden of badness which appears to reside in his parents. By this means he seeks to purge them of their badness; and in proportion as he succeeds in doing so, he is awarded by that sense of security which an environment of good parents so characteristically confers. To say that the child takes upon herself the burden of badness which appears to reside in her parents is, of course, the same thing as to say that she internalizes bad parents. The sense of our security resulting in this process of internalization is, however, liable to be seriously compromised by the resulting presence within her of internalized bad parents. Outer security is best purchased at the price of inner insecurity; and her ego is henceforth left at the mercy of the band of internal fifth columnists or persecutors, against which defenses have to be, first hastily erected, and later, laboriously consolidated.[49]

This is a survival technique, where it is better to "bad" than "weak." This is why Fairbairn calls it the "moral defense." The child makes the situation conditional: "If only I am good, then I won't be punished for being bad anymore." The child then tries to find ways to please the parent, to be "good," as an answer to the experience of pain. This is the religion: finding ways to placate and appease their angry creator, father or mother. Morality in this sense is a defensive response to the reality of the creator who flies

---

[48] Ibid., 171–72.

[49] Ibid., 66.

into rages, inflicts fear and pain, often accompanied by criticisms of the child as lazy, worthless, ungrateful, and the like.

Fairbairn makes a sophisticated, psychoanalytic critique of the *total depravity* theology of the Augustinian/Calvinist tradition that defined his Presbyterian background. The picture is that of the psychological manifestation of this theological tradition within the object relationship between the hostile and condemning *antilibidinal object* that represents the internalized parental figure, and the attachment-seeking *libidinal ego* of the child: "You are right, father, I am just a worm. Evil. Depraved. Unworthy. Please, forgive me." The child returns to this confessional week-in and week-out. The child feels safer to be the one who does not measure up; the one who "if I can just find a way to be good in your eyes, then, perhaps, you will not rage at me." Otherwise the child is faced with the terror of not being able to do anything about the situation. "Dad or Mom is going to be a rage-aholic, or an alcoholic no matter what I do?" That is just too devastating. Better to get religion.

Mature Dependence

Another of Fairbairn's theological concepts is that of formulating a developmental line of thinking that retains *dependency* as constant throughout. In contrast to the movement toward *autonomy* (Erik Erikson), *separation-individuation* (Margaret Mahler), and other forms of *independency* represented by the Freudian traditions, Fairbairn cites the goal of development as the attainment of *mature dependency*, essentially manifest in forms of adult *interdependency* (See figure 1). This echoes, I believe, the influence of his theological background where "dependence upon God" need not be taken as *infantile*, but reflects a theo-psychology that sees relationship as central to human existence and lifelong in duration.

Psychoanalyst as Exorcist

The most striking of Fairbairn's theological motifs is that of his clinical description of "the release of bad objects" that have been repressed. He cites that the deepest source of resistance in psychoanalysis is the "fear of the release of bad objects from the unconscious; for, when such bad objects are released, the world around the patient becomes peopled with devils which are too terrifying for him to face."[50] One of Fairbairn's central clinical goals is the very release of such bad objects which requires the provision of an

---

[50] Ibid., 69.

analytic relationship in which the analyst is a "sufficiently good object" in order to support such a regressive transference. Fairbairn here critiques the Kleinian contention that psychopathology lies in the realm of the super-ego, (even the harsh, critical one). He is differentiating the nature of the *antilibidinal object* as "attacking the good" from the classic concept of the super-ego as attacking the ego in the moralistic service of the "good." He contrasts the moralistic function of super-ego where "a True Mass is being celebrated in the chancel (of the church)," with the *internal saboteur or antilibidinal ego* whose "pact" with the *antilibidinal object* is to provide the schizoid function of defending against the vulnerability of attachment. This "pact with Satan" is "a Black Mass being celebrated in the crypt."[51] Hence the world of the *antilibidinal self* is experienced as a hellish underworld where demonic forces must be appeased through maintaining the tie with the "bad object." This is the same type of reversal with which the *moral defense* operates: entering into a relationship with a "bad object" in order not to feel *at its mercy,* of which none is expected. The ultimate goal of psychoanalysis, according to Fairbairn, is the reintegration of these bad object experiences into consciousness and thereby into the *central ego.* As an ambivalent holding of the object as both good and bad, their release from repressive captivity is essential. Hence Fairbairn writes, "it is evident that the psychotherapist is the true successor to the exorcist, and that he is concerned, not only with 'the forgiveness of sins,' (i.e., the analytic resolution of guilt), but also with 'the casting out of devils.'"[52] Fairbairn is not only using theological terminology as metaphors for a psychological process, he is validating the theological concern of freeing persons from "internalized badness." His theological shift, however, is from the *depravity theology* that denies the "need for redemption" for such demons. The ultimate clinical metaphor of the *antilibidinal self,* as I would construe it, is the rageful "inner child," who though unattractive as the "street urchin" of *Oliver Twist* fame, is nonetheless one to be embraced and held.

Guntrip's Move from Theory to the Pursuit of "Regression to Dependence"

Guntrip would pick up these metaphors in his own writings as he carried on Fairbairn's tradition. Guntrip wrote an article which was re-titled in

---

[51] Ibid., 70.
[52] Ibid., 70.

his *Collected Papers* as "Psychotherapist as Parent and Exorcist."[53] Guntrip was so taken with Fairbairn's psychoanalytic writings that he chose him as his second psychoanalyst. Yet, while he saw Fairbairn's model as a brilliant (Protestant) Reformation of classical Freudian metapsychology, Guntrip's own protest was that Fairbairn practiced a clinical technique that was too distant and oedipally classical for his liking. Guntrip eventually set out on a third analysis with one whose writings also captured his attention, and with whom he apparently hoped for a "regression to dependence" for which this analyst was famous. Let us now turn to Donald W. Winnicott.

[53] Jeremy Hazell, ed., *Personal Relations Therapy: The Collected Papers of H.J.S. Guntrip* (Northvale, N.J.: Aronson, 1994) chapter 2.

6

The Influence of D. W. Winnicott on Harry Guntrip

Winnicott as Psychoanalytic Artist

"**S**PONTANEOUS expression of his inner being." This is the tag line that Dodi Goldman uses to capture both the heart and style of Donald W. Winnicott.[1] While Christopher Bollas has characterized Winnicott as "the court jester of the London Psycho-Analytic Society."[2] Goldman develops a portrait of Winnicott as psychoanalytic artist, whose own "scribbled signature resembled one of his squiggle games, a technique he developed to facilitate his therapeutic consultations with children."[3] He actually liked to paint, not merely as a clinical technique of working with children, but as a personal hobby. Yet the description is still more than that of vocation or avocation, but a metaphor of his personality. A colleague and a friend who translated most of his work into French entitled their essay about him "A Splash of Paint in His Style," a phrase borrowed from his own 1935 paper on "The Manic Defense." There he responded to some analysts' "objection to his unconventional use of the word, 'fantasy.' 'The invention of a new word,' Winnicott replied, 'would have been less easily justified than the treatment of an already existing word *with a splash of paint*'" (emphasis added).[4] This is a marvelous example of his impish, artistic, and intuitive genius for which he has become famous, to the point of sentimentalizing him as the "teddy bear" play therapist. Often lost is the complicated, dis-

---

[1] Dodi Goldman, *In Search of The Real: The Origins and Originality of D.W. Winnicott.* (New York: Aronson, 1993) 1.

[2] Christopher Bollas, *Winnicott Lectures* (cassette recording) (Tustin, CA: Newport Psychoanalytic Institute, 1982).

[3] Goldman, *In Search of The Real,* 1.

[4] Ibid., 2.

ciplined, and dialectical nature of his mind that gave depth to his thinking as a psychoanalyst. Less well known is his work with psychotic patients and others whose adult version of primitive mental states is addressed in the 1935 and subsequent papers. This depth and capacity for complexity appealed to the critically thinking mind of Harry Guntrip. Winnicott's maternal presence would ultimately soften Guntrip's personal rigidity and obsessional formalism, and invite him to venture forth from the prison of his own obsessionally brilliant mind, his schizoid stronghold.

Perhaps one of Guntrip's significant contributions to the psychoanalytic community was his *exegetical* study and application of Winnicott's writings, as they were characteristically unsystematized, dialectically and paradoxically confusing, resembling poetry rather than prose. Famous for his concept of *transitional phenomena,* where the child's teddy bear is representative of the mother's body, his use of theory was similarly that of a stuffed animal. He took concepts and then reinvented them in reference to his own sensibilities. "Winnicott seems to ignore serious inquiry as to whether his use of a particular concept is something he made or something he found." This mirrors the *in-betweeness* of the *transitional space* between the mother's and the baby's sense of what is real. Goldman notes that Winnicott's "insistence on being himself" disposed him to be either enormously appealing or ignored if not distrusted by those who came in contact with him. Another of his famous concepts, that of the *True Self,* in contrast and in relation to the *False Self,* would be something I think would resonate with Guntrip's schizoid version of false self relating through intellectual distancing. Guntrip would eventually state that the schizoid keeps his true self in protective cold storage, a notion as personal as it is clinical for Guntrip.

In concert with one of the basic themes of this study is that Winnicott's theory is also autobiographical in nature. "Winnicott's personal strivings were so consistently echoed in his theoretical conceptualizations that one cannot easily disentangle his creative concepts from the persona that he was. One senses a basic congruity between what he espoused—the ideas he articulated—and the way he was in the world."[5]

In that this originality of thought and person were so inseparably linked, Goldman points out a price that Winnicott paid in his unswerving pursuit of it. He notes that Winnicott was reluctant to read the works of Ferenczi "lest he discover that he had actually stolen ideas from him. (F. Robert Rodman, personal communication, February 14, 1992). The

---

[5] Ibid., 3.

pride he took in his own inventiveness and concomitant fear of any inauthentic ventriloquism were both core features of his character."[6] Goldman describes a number of features of Winnicott where he was protecting his own sense of sensitivity, including avoiding in-patient cases with the accompanying din of distress of babies and small children in a hospital ward, so as to "avoid becoming callous in order to be efficient."[7] This kind of behavior won him the description as "crypto-prima donna" by a psychoanalytic colleague, Charles Rycroft. Goldman muses that Winnicott was defending his own spontaneity from perceived encroachments, rearranging one's external environment to make it one that would hold without impinging. This is in contrast to the schizoid's solution of withdrawal from impingements and threats to create an alternative internal world; between Winnicott's *being-in-the-world* and that of both Fairbairn and Guntrip's schizoid adaptation. The narcissistic trend in his character was a central theme in his theory. "Healthy narcissism" was a developmental outcome of having had a primary experience in which "the infant is allowed to feel itself to be the creator of the world," without which, life for the child "would feel futile and unreal."[8] So what were the sources that fed who Winnicott was in the world?

A Methodist Childhood:
Winnicott's Facilitating Environment

"The struggle to feel real begins, Winnicott argues, in earliest childhood."[9] So begins Dodi Goldman's treatment of Winnicott's own childhood and home life and the impact it made on his psychoanalytic theorizing. Winnicott's hallmark publication was *Maturational Processes and the Facilitating Environment,*[10] highlighting his commitment to the priority of the nurture of the person's *true self* in order to feel real.

Born into a prosperous Methodist family in Plymouth, England, Donald was the only son and youngest child of a local merchant and politician who was often absent from the home. His father, Frederick Winnicott, twice elected mayor of Plymouth, and knighted in 1924, was described by Clare Winnicott as a tall and slim man with an "old fashioned

---

[6] Ibid., 5.

[7] Ibid., 6.

[8] Ibid.

[9] Ibid., xxiv.

[10] Donald Winnicott, *Maturational Processes and the Facilitating Environment* (New York: International Universities Press, 1965).

quiet dignity and poise about him, and a deep sense of fun."[11] Goldman makes note that although he was "a person of high intelligence and sound judgment," Clare Winnicott went on to describe him as having certain learning difficulties, "sensitive about his lack of education. . . . He always said that because of this he had not aspired to Parliament, but had kept to local politics—lively enough in those days in faraway Plymouth."[12] He then speculates on Donald's own modest style of writing: avoiding specialized technical language, distrusting intellectual formalism, and reluctance to cite authoritative texts as scholarly references. "Perhaps it also helps explain why for every one lecture that Winnicott was asked to give before professional societies he gave at least a dozen to gatherings of less elitist audiences and why it gave him particular pleasure to speak before ordinary people who were involved in the care of others (Khan, 1975)."[13]

In light of his father's conspicuous absences, Winnicott's facilitating environment consisted of a nanny, governess, mother, and two older sisters, one which Goldman suggests predisposed him toward his interest in things "maternal" in many ways. His mother, Elizabeth, was only described in "vague terms" by Clare Winnicott, as vivacious and outgoing, "able to show and express her feelings easily."[14] Donald's overall household was described as a "lively one, bustling with activity," including garden, orchard, croquet lawn, tennis court, a pond, and high trees ringing the entire estate. He is described as retreating to the branches of one particular tree for homework and reverie. Of particular interest is that he would frequent the family kitchen, a practice he is said to have continued on his adult travels "to strange places [where] he would invariably be drawn to seek out and spend time in the local kitchen."[15] His mother complained that he spent more time with the cook than with the rest of the family.

Complementing his own household was that of his uncle Richard and his family across the road. The eight cousins would together provide an abundance of playmates, things to do, and space to do it in. There was also always room to be alone, "secret hiding places in which a child's imagination could soar and to which he or she could withdraw," facilitating solitude and escape along with the social encounters.[16] The fam-

[11] Goldman, *In Search of The Real*, 34.
[12] Ibid.
[13] Ibid., 34–35.
[14] Ibid., 35.
[15] Ibid.
[16] Ibid.

ily atmosphere is described by Goldman as having a cheerful disposition, possessing an irrepressible sense of humor. He concludes that "a consistent line can be drawn from this relatively benign and nonintrusive setting to Winnicott's capacity for belief and faith in natural processes."[17] Such a home provided him with an "elemental sense of security in the world," where Clare Winnicott "used to tell him that he knew from the moment he opened his eyes on the world that he was loved, and she teased him that he suffered from 'benignity.'"[18] In short, Donald's social setting was an *environmental mother,* the community of which he was a proud and integral part. In anticipation of such a portrait of family life being *too good to be true,* Clare Winnicott noted that "the truth is that it *was* good, and try as I will I cannot present it in any other light. Essentially he was a deeply happy person whose capacity for enjoyment never failed to triumph over the setbacks and disappointments that came his way."[19] Yet it is important to consider that this idyllic picture was *not* devoid of any aggression.

The Place of Aggression in Winnicott's Childhood

Goldman describes Donald's autobiographical account of an incident where his father would taunt and irritate him with one of his sister's wax dolls. In response Donald took his own private croquet mallet and "bashed flat the nose of the wax doll."

> I was perhaps somewhat relieved when my father took a series of matches and, warming up the wax nose enough, remoulded it so that the face once more became a face. This early demonstration of the restitutive and reparative act certainly made an impression on me, and perhaps made me able to accept the fact that I myself, dear innocent child, had actually become violent directly with a doll, but indirectly with my good-tempered father who was just then entering my conscious life.[20]

Goldman reflects on Donald's "perhaps disingenuously benign" portrayal of his father here in light of the taunting that evoked his own violence, and suggests that "within the Winnicott household there was not much room for the direct expression of anger. Michael Eigen points out that any expression of anger would have seemed out of place in this

[17] Ibid., 36.
[18] Ibid.
[19] Ibid., 38.
[20] Ibid., 40.

family,"[21] and therefore such angry moments would have made a great impression on Winnicott. Goldman develops this theme more in the direction of its impact on Winnicott's "profound interest in, and propensity for, ambiguity."[22] A hallmark of Winnicott's theorizing is his emphasis on accepting, without resolving, paradoxes, as well as avoiding confrontations, which Goldman sees as a manifestation of Winnicott's way of dealing with his own aggressive impulses. Margaret Little gave an example of this in her account of her analysis with Winnicott as detailed in her *Psychotic Anxieties and Containment: A Personal Record of an Analysis with Winnicott.*[23] She described one session where she smashed a favorite oriental vase of Winnicott's in his office, only to have him say nothing about it but to replace it without comment by the next session. She reflected that she regretted his not speaking to her violence directly. Winnicott's own vision of such containment of violent aggressiveness was that of a necessary developmental stage where the child, who would fear having destroyed the adult, could realize when the smoke cleared that the parent/analyst still existed. I would speculate that what Guntrip would find attractive in this Winnicottian quality was Donald's keen awareness of such rage in Guntrip's own primitive schizoid states, yet providing a non-verbal absorption of it, bypassing the problematic schizoid tendency to intellectualize with words.

Winnicott as Darwinian Empiricist with a Romantic Heart

What might we say about Winnicott as philosopher and theologian? As noted above, he was steeped in both the British empiricist tradition that abhorred dogmatism on the one hand, as well as the Romantic tradition that echoed his intuitive sense for primary creativity. "Creative apperception must accompany passive perception. An experiencing self—a notion more akin to existentialism than empiricism—is central to Winnicott's worldview."[24] Most striking of his worldview was his dialectical bent, the "playful use of nonsense" where he would treat things both lightly and seriously at the same time. Goldman compares him to Lewis Carroll of *Alice in Wonderland* fame as the "whimsical writer" who bridges the sciences

---

[21] Ibid.

[22] Ibid.

[23] Margaret Little, *Psychotic Anxieties and Containment: A Personal Record of an Analysis with Winnicott* (Northvale, NJ: Aronson, 1990).

[24] Goldman, *In Search of The Real,* 92.

and humanities. He sees them both as "deeply concerned with the radical ambiguity between that which is absolutely subjective and that which is absolutely objective."[25] Winnicott described the two traditions and the poetic and the scientific roads to truth.

> The link between these two forms of truth is *surely in the person,* in you and me. The poet in me reaches to a whole truth in a flash, and the scientist in me gropes toward a facet of the truth; as the scientist reaches the immediate objective, a new objective presents itself. Poetic truth has certain advantages. For the individual, poetic truth offers deep satisfactions, and in the new expression of an old truth there is opportunity for new creative experience in terms of beauty. It is very difficult, however to use poetic truth. Poetic truth is a matter of feeling, and we may not all feel the same about one problem. By scientific truth, with limited objective, we hope to bring people who can use their minds and who can be influenced by intellectual considerations to agreement in certain areas of practice. In poetry, something true crystallizes out: to plan our lives we need science. But science boggles at the problem of human nature, and tends to lose sight of the whole human being.[26]

The ultimate reconciliation of paradox, (as opposed to its resolution), Guntrip himself will champion as being found *in the person.* This embracing of polarities in tension as a function of being a person was the philosophical response of John Macmurray to the same type of issue in terms of science and religion that was to have such a profound impact on Guntrip.

Winnicott fell in love with the works of Charles Darwin while a student at Cambridge, noting that he "knew Darwin was my cup of tea . . . I felt this tremendously."

> At the time I do not know why it was so important to me, but I see now that the main thing was that it showed that living things could be examined scientifically with the corollary that gaps in knowledge and understanding need not scare me. For me this idea meant a great lessening of tension and consequently a release of energy for work and play.[27]

What was it about Darwin that spoke so directly to Winnicott? Goldman asks. "Fundamentally, it was the same thing that was to later at-

---

[25] Ibid., 93.

[26] Ibid., 97 (emphasis added).

[27] Ibid., 108.

tract him to Freud: the thrill of discovering an objective way of looking at things."[28] Clare Winnicott noted his discovery of Darwin as a "revelation" that "changed his whole life." This appears to be Winnicott's "conversion experience" of his college days, which was a similar movement in a different direction than the one noted above about Fairbairn as a collegiate. Winnicott was drawn to the freedom from dogmatism in science, while Fairbairn was drawn to the freedom from repression in religion.

Winnicott reflected the philosophical movement within both science and the "New Theology" that came to characterize the Modernist movement that would affect Guntrip: rejection of the "god of the gaps."

> About scientists I would say this: that when a gap in knowledge turns up, the scientist does not flee to a supernatural explanation. This would imply panic, fear of the unknown. . . . For the scientist every gap in understanding provides an exciting challenge. Ignorance is held, and a research programme is devised. The stimulus for the work done is the existence of the gap.[29]

"Just as Darwin labored to fill the gaps in the historical evidence regarding the origin of the species, Winnicott focused on the gaps in the historical evidence regarding the earliest relationship between mother and infant."[30] Here Winnicott's empiricism was that which also allowed him to be a "romantic at heart." In contrast to the Rationalism that tended to want and to provide answers for all questions, which was reflected in various forms of orthodoxy, both theological and psychoanalytic, his capacity to "not know" freed him to pursue a psychoanalytic inquiry that was empirical, romantic, and postulated the "area of faith," all at the same time. He coined the term, the "non-interpretive function," which was the psychoanalytic technique of *keeping one's brilliant interpretations to oneself* rather than disrupt the patient's unfolding and movement toward a "regression to dependence" upon the analyst. Along these lines, Winnicott was profoundly influenced by the Romantic poet, John Keats, whose notion of "Negative Capability" was in concert with Winnicott's ideas of creative play. Keats was exploring the nature of poetic genius and imagination as "when a man is capable of being in uncertainties, Mysteries, doubts, without any irritable reaching after fact and reason; . . . with a great poet the sense of Beauty overcomes every other consideration, or rather oblit-

---

[28] Ibid., 109.

[29] Ibid., 104.

[30] Ibid., 109.

erates all consideration."[31] "Negative," in this sense, is that of "absence," or "being devoid of," and essentially embodies the kind of paradox that Winnicott found attractive, as in his "capacity to be alone in the presence of another," as well as his notion of the use of "space" as "potential" and waiting to be filled. This is the area within which creative play manifests: "the ability to be open, in the presence of mother, to whatever spontaneous gestures may arise, without the need to flee into compliance."[32]

The Area of Faith

In the same talk to the Oxford University Scientific Society where he noted his view of gaps in knowledge as the potential space that evokes inquiry, Winnicott added his paradoxical twist to the common notion of science as secular.

> The stimulus for the work done is the existence of the gap. The scientist can afford to wait and to be ignorant. This means he has some sort of faith—not faith in this or in that, but a faith, or a capacity for faith. . . .[33]

Winnicott cites the common notion of "religion" and that which replaces doubt with certainty, and describes the real scientist as the one whose capacity for faith enables one to tolerate doubt, to "shudder" at the thought of complete knowledge, where "the formulation of questions is everything; answers, when found, lead to new questions."[34] Goldman describes Winnicott as having a complex relationship to *religious faith*. On the one hand, he saw organized religion as an escape to the security of supernatural explanations. He rejected notions of miracles, an afterlife, and saw moral educators as suffocating the spirit and inhibiting creativity. "It was not religion generally that he opposed, but religion as a closed dogmatic system, thwarting individual creativity and demanding obedient worshippers."[35] He also opposed such religion within the British society of Psychoanalysis in terms of those who would worship at the altars of either Mrs. Klein or The Freuds.

To a degree, Winnicott reflected the Freudian tradition as he also saw religion as a form of projection, but not as a wish fulfillment of an ideal-

---

[31] Ibid., 103.

[32] Ibid., 104.

[33] Ibid., 105.

[34] Ibid., 114.

[35] Ibid.

ized father. In contrast, Winnicott seems to reflect the Kleinian influence of the paranoid position in seeing the projection as "rooted in the dangerous and tenuous attainment of individuality. God's name, after all, means 'I AM THAT I AM.'"

> Does not this name given to God reflect the danger that the individual feels he or she is in on reaching the state of individual being? If I am, then I have gathered together this and that and have claimed it as me, and I have repudiated everything else; in repudiating the not-me I have, so to speak, insulted the world, and I must expect to be attacked. So when people first came to the concept of individuality, they quickly put it up in the sky and gave it a voice that only Moses could hear.[36]

In the face of this traditional psychoanalytic stance, Goldman points out what he describes as Winnicott's "lingering religiosity." Clare Winnicott insisted that he was never "anti-religion," and "was only too thankful if anybody could believe in anything." In a private letter, Winnicott clarifies his difference from the traditional antagonism of mainstream psychoanalysis.

> One must be able to look at religious beliefs and their place in psychology without being considered to be antagonistic to anyone's personal religion. I found others who thought I was anti-religious in some of my writings but it has always turned out that what they were annoyed about was that I was not myself religious in their own particular way.[37]

Winnicott does not share the Freudian conviction about the incompatibility between the scientific worldview and the theological/metaphysical. He had a different view of what *illusion* itself was, in contrast to Freud's use of it as distortion or contradiction of reality for the purpose of wish fulfillment, where organized religion was an example of mass *delusion*. Just as Winnicott saw *illusion* as a normal developmental step in the formation of the capacity for creativity, so religious experience carries these same positive and creative aspects.

Winnicottian Methodism

Raised a Wesleyan Methodist, Winnicott's family went to church every Sunday morning, his father acting as church treasurer and singing in the

---

[36] Ibid., 114.
[37] Ibid., 115.

choir. The Revivalist roots of Methodism were retained in the emphasis on the individual's "personal, direct, moral contract with God." Winnicott recalls such an emphasis in regards to a particular interaction with his father.

> My father had a simple [religious] faith and once when I asked him
> a question that could have involved us in a long argument he just
> said: read the Bible and what you find there will be the true answer
> for you. So I was left, thank God, to get on with it myself.[38]

This idea was echoed in a talk Winnicott gave to the Christian Teamwork Institute of Education: "Brought up as a Wesleyan Methodist, I suppose I just grew up out of church religious practice, and I am always glad that my religious upbringing was of a kind that allowed for growing up out of."[39] Goldman notes that Winnicott grew up out of religious practice, but not as one who abandoned everything associated with a religious outlook, citing the capacity for wonder as characteristic. I would add that Winnicott was a rather *Wesleyan Methodist Psychoanalyst* in this regard. "Theirs was a nonconformist and questioning religion, rather than a strict, oppressive and doctrinaire one. It was based on the simple notion of helping people through love."[40] He carried the *Independent* spirit in his confrontations of the strict, oppressive, and doctrinaire practices of *Psychoanalytic religion* within the British Psychoanalytic Society, posing the challenge of *Revival* to the orthodox Kleinians, challenging their Calvinistic metapsychology in favor of a historical and empirical delineation of the mother infant drama. Goldman notes how Winnicott gave secular expression to some of the fundamental doctrines of Methodism.

> These include insistence that the heart of religion lies in personal
> relationship with God; simplicity of worship; the partnership of
> ordained ministers and laity in the worship and administration of
> the church; concern for the underprivileged and the betterment of
> social conditions; tolerance for differences of conviction regarding
> various theological disputes; worship that is partly liturgical, but
> partly spontaneous.[41]

Goldman notes how these "atmospheric conditions" would have fostered a sensitivity within Winnicott toward the personal and spontaneous

---

[38] Ibid., 116.
[39] Ibid., 117.
[40] Ibid.
[41] Ibid., 118.

in human nature, "a non-dogmatic attitude toward theory, and mutuality in the therapeutic alliance."[42] It could be said, therefore, that Winnicott practiced his *religion* as a psychoanalyst, a theme implicit in Winnicott that Guntrip was to make explicit in his own writings.

As Fairbairn did as well, Winnicott eventually joined the Anglican church to which his first wife belonged, somewhere around the age of 27. "This conversion was not uncommon at the time; many young aspiring people abandoned the somewhat working-class and simplistic Methodist church for the more polished and intellectually sophisticated Anglican church."[43] Another parallel to Fairbairn was that Winnicott's mother also was originally from the Anglican church, and had settled into the Methodist church when she married Sir Frederick. Even with his church attendance dropping off in his later years, Winnicott was said to have remained a "believing skeptic."[44]

John Macmurray was the Marxist who eventually gravitated toward the Quaker notion of "God as Friend." Ronald Fairbairn was the Calvinist Presbyterian who became one of the most influential "Protestants" in the "Reformation" of Freudian metapsychology. Donald Winnicott was the easy-going Wesleyan-Methodist Revivalist who sought the "spontaneous" as the psychoanalytic process and goal. Who was Harry Guntrip? What was his experience with these innovating psychoanalysts? Let us now examine his personal life history and his relationship to Fairbairn and Winnicott.

[42] Ibid.
[43] Ibid., 117.
[44] Ibid.

7

Guntrip's Relationship
with Fairbairn and Winnicott

To Depend (On One's Analyst),
Or Not to Depend: That is the Question

IN 1900 Freud published his landmark volume, *The Interpretation of Dreams,* which we might rename, "My Experience of Analysis with Sigmund," as this was material drawn from the only psychoanalysis that Freud underwent: with himself. The most consistent critique of Guntrip's reflections upon his analyses with Fairbairn and Winnicott,[1] has been of the same flavor: Guntrip exerted so much control over his analyses that one reviewer has quipped that ". . . he was never baptised in analysis. He analyzed rather than was analyzed."[2] Guntrip took copious notes during his own analyses and worked very hard to understand his own material, and yet was seen as one who "never seemed to abandon himself to the experience."[3] The core of the criticisms of his reflections on his own treatment is that his own "infantile omnipotence" and "primary narcissism" were never truly analyzed and worked through, citing his resistance and rejection of the attempts made by both Fairbairn and Winnicott to do so. Ronald Markillie, who "knew him well" in the context of their working together at the Department of Psychiatry in Leeds from 1947 until Guntrip's death in 1975, expresses both his admiration and his misgivings about him. He characterized Guntrip's practice with patients as a "ministry," keeping his fees low, especially to ministers, "and he was a man of simple tastes who

---

[1] Guntrip, "My Experience of Analysis with Fairbairn and Winnicott," *International Review of Psychoanalysis* 2 (1975) 145–56.

[2] Ronald Markillie, "Some Personal Reflections and Impressions of Harry Guntrip," *International Journal of Psychoanalysis* 77 (1996) 767.

[3] Ibid.

never wished to make a lot of money."[4] When they met, Guntrip was still the minister at the Congregationalist Salem Chapel in Leeds, "but was seeing patients also in an old shop in Holbeck, just like a working class GP."[5] Markillie offers an interesting observation on Guntrip's relationship with his mother who was ultimately the central figure in his analyses, noting that

> she had a reputation for being a difficult woman. . . . They would hear the old lady talking to herself in her room [she lived with Guntrip and his wife Bert at the time] and found many of the things she said very revealing about the struggle she had, and the determination she needed to succeed in her business and to rear Harry. My impression is that he was more understanding of her then than appeared later in what he said and wrote.[6]

"What he said and wrote" of her was crystallized in a dream about her and her brother, Percy, which Guntrip presented as the capstone of all of his years of analysis.

> *I saw my mother*, black, immobilized, staring fixedly into space, totally *ignoring me as* I stood at one side staring at her and feeling myself frozen into immobility: the first time I had ever seen her in a dream like that. Before she had always been attacking me. My first thought was: 'I've lost Winnicott and am left alone with mother, sunk in depression, ignoring me. That's how I felt when Percy died." I thought I must have taken the loss of Winnicott as a repetition of the Percy trauma. Only recently have I become quite clear that it was not that at all. I did not dream of mother like that when my college friend died or my ministerial colleague left. Then I felt ill, as after Percy's death. This time was quite different. That dream started a compelling dream-sequence which went on night after night, taking me back in chronological order through every house I had lived in.[7]

Guntrip goes on to describe what he saw as the final resolution for why he ostensibly sought psychoanalysis: to break his amnesia surrounding his experience of the death of his younger brother, Percy, when Guntrip was three and a half years old himself. These dreams came upon him the very

---

[4] Ibid., 764.

[5] Ibid.

[6] Ibid.

[7] Jeremy Hazell, ed., *Personal Relations Therapy: The Collected Papers of H. J. S. Guntrip* (Northvale, NJ: Aronson, 1994) 365.

night when Guntrip was told of Winnicott's death. The ensuing dreams culminated with a striking image:

> I was standing with another man, the double of myself, both reaching out to get hold of a dead object. Suddenly the other man collapsed in a heap. Immediately the dream changed to a lighted room, where I saw Percy again. I knew it was him, sitting on the lap of a woman who had no face, arms or breasts. She was merely a lap to sit on, not a person. He looked deeply depressed, with the corners of his mouth turned down, and I was trying to make him smile.[8]

Guntrip's analysis was a shift in seeing his presenting problem of "amnesia" for the loss of his brother to an image of what others referred to as his "psychotically depressed mother,"[9] who was unable to be psychologically available to foster an emotional attachment to Guntrip. He immediately tipped his hat to his two psychoanalytic mentors in touting "what better dream evidence could one have of Winnicott's view that 'There is no such thing as a baby': i.e. there must be a 'mother and baby' and what better evidence for Fairbairn's view that the basic psychic reality is the 'personal object relation'?"[10] Here Guntrip shows his *romantic* colors in all of their splendor, with central emphasis on the mother-infant dyad and how his distant mother's "total failure to relate to"[11] himself and Percy essentially starved his brother to death, and sent himself on a life-long quest for such an attachment, characterized by both driveness, and for years, the somatic symptomotology of constipation and sinusitis.

Markillie picks up his account of his experience of Guntrip with an extended description of Guntrip's rather obsessional and self-absorbed qualities that could make him rather off-putting. "He wanted to talk about his patients and wanted my analytic help, though not really to change his way of conceptualizing things, but then showed little interest in my issues so that discussions did not develop. . . . He had an urge to treat."[12] Markillie described his wife, Bert, as a very kind person and "one of the most self-effacing women I have known." She was Harry's ardent supporter, to a fault in Markillie's estimation, noting his "family felt that he was devoted to her yet used her quite inconsiderately in the pursuit of his

---

[8] Ibid.

[9] Markillie, "Some Personal Reflections," 764.

[10] Hazell, ed., *Personal Relations Therapy*, 366.

[11] Ibid.

[12] Markillie, "Some Personal Reflections," 764.

mission, which became all consuming. It seemed to conflict with his criticism of his mother's actions."[13] This was in regard to Guntrip's mother's own driveness that she applied as her own adaptation to her personal distress. After a very stormy period between Guntrip and his mother in his early childhood following Percy's death, she opened a business of her own. This was during Guntrip's latency years and precipitated a kind of peaceful coexistence where they essentially lived in their respective private worlds of "industry." Markillie essentially describes a strong identification of Harry with his mother, where the "business" to which he applied himself was the constant use of his intellect to make his adaptation and way in the world. Markillie applauded the impact of his writings as Guntrip developed "an international reputation" that surpassed the medical staff with whom he worked, yet was always uncomfortable with the rigidity of his views on the one hand, and his unorthodox clinical boundaries on the other, giving out his address and phone number to patients on his holidays.

> His experience of transference and his use of it were different than mine. I always thought that this led him to ally himself with his patients against their bad objects. One consequence is that the bad objects can then become external prize specimens and are not perceived as part of oneself. Such an alliance ultimately diminishes rather than potentates the patient's own ego capability, and militates against reparation.[14]

Markillie here makes a kind of *classical*, and perhaps, Kleinian critique of Guntrip's *romantic* use of empathy to align with patients along the line of feeling failed by parents. This, again, is the central theme of those who have critiqued Guntrip's *My analysis with Ronald and Donald* paper.

The Controversies Surrounding Guntrip's Personal Analyses

Along with Pontalis,[15] and most recently Padel's very classical reinterpretation of Guntrip's anal sado-masochism that went unanalyzed,[16] is the

---

[13]   Ibid.

[14]   Ibid., 765.

[15]   J. B. Pontalis, et al. "A propos du teste de Guntrip," *Nouvelle Revue Psychoanalyse* 16 (1977) 29–37.

[16]   John Padel, "The Case of Harry Guntrip," *International Journal of Psychoanalysis* 77 (1996) 755.

critique by Glatzer and Evans,[17] who argue for the position that Guntrip's taking control of the therapy situation was gratified ultimately by both Fairbairn and Winnicott, who "apparently colluded with him by accepting his terms rather than analyzing them," leaving covered his "hostile unconscious omnipotence."[18] Markillie considers it "hardly without significance" that Evans "was also a Congregational minister before becoming an analyst."[19] What Markillie fails to clarify (I assume that he is unaware of the possibilities) is: What Congregationalist cloth is Evans cut from? His and Glatzer's critique of Guntrip, along with Fairbairn and Winnicott, reflect an avowedly *classical* stance and set of presuppositions. As Evans is an American, it could be that he comes from the good Calvinist stock of the Puritan Congregationalists, rather than the modernist strain. Either way, as Michael Eigen details in his own critique of their critique, they ultimately reflect the pessimism of the *Calvinist-classico-Kleino-Freudian* tradition that is tempted to see "most people as trash."[20]

Eigen clarifies both Fairbairn's and Winnicott's position as not being the purist *romanticism* that is characteristically reductionistic in terms of human aggression. He describes a "transference-countertransference bind" where Winnicott played the "good mother" to the point where he told Guntrip that he enjoyed him as a patient, yet "somewhat tongue in cheek he added that Guntrip might be too good," referring to his elaborate note taking and remembering more about sessions that Winnicott himself. Eigen describes an object relational reversing of roles between them, where "if Winnicott played good mother to Guntrip, so also did Guntrip play good mother to Winnicott," with Winnicott also playing the baby role and receiving "good narcissistic mirroring from the 'gleam' in Guntrip's maternal eye." Eigen cites the importance of this in terms of identifying this as a "counter-transference reaction requiring containing and reprocessing" by Winnicott which would reflect Guntrip's lifelong history of "compulsive[ly] playing 'good mother,'" first as minister and then as therapist. He sees Winnicott as responding to this through his "pe-

[17] H. T. Glatzer and W. N. Evans, "Guntrip's Analysis with Fairbairn and Winnicott," *International Journal of Psychoanalytic Psychotherapy* 6 (1977) 81–98.

[18] Michael Eigen, "Guntrip's Analysis with Winnicott: A Critique of Glatzer and Evans," *Contemporary Psychoanalysis* 17 (1981) 105.

[19] Markillie, "Some Personal Reflections," 766.

[20] H. Meng and E. L. Freud, eds., *Psychoanalysis and Faith: The Letters of Sigmund Freud and Oskar Pfister.* (New York: Basic Books, 1963) 61.

riodic attempts to evoke in Guntrip an awareness of baby rage," repeatedly wondering where Guntrip's "baby sadism and ruthlessness were."[21]

Winnicott considered exclusion of normal aggression in humans as a form of "sentimentality," and would thereby clearly distinguish himself from Strenger's "ideal type" of *romantic* that he finds in Kohutian Self-Psychology. (Note that Kohut was not a *Kohutian*, as he himself spoke out against such sentimental notions of empathy, citing the Nazi's use of sirens on their dive-bombers in World War II as the empathic understanding of what evokes terror in humans.) Guntrip himself criticized "Winnicott as not Winnicottian enough" in terms of loyalty to the "object relations viewpoint." Eigen on the one hand does validate the *concern* of Glatzer and Evans (and the rest of the *classical* crowd), in identifying Guntrip's "trying to mould his actual emotional reactions in light of an idealized theoretical possibility:" rage would be unnecessary if mothering were perfect.[22] Glatzer and Evans cite Guntrip's defensive use of object relations theory as a "mask for 'primary narcissism,'" which Eigen sees as overly reductionistic on their part. He points out that their seeing Guntrip as blaming his mother without empathy for her actually misses Guntrip's actual statement to the contrary. Harry noted that his memory of her "lingers as a mood of sadness for my mother who so damaged in childhood that she could neither be, nor enable me to be, our 'true selves.'"[23] Eigen saw that "deep mourning work was going on," which was genuine therapeutic advance, without denying the area of grandiosity. So, what are we to make of this critiquing and counter-critiquing?

Eigen ultimately reflects Strenger's sentiment in finding a balance between two views of Guntrip, and clearly places Glatzer and Evans in the Calvinist camp in regards to their view of nature and of the human self. They quote not only Freud, Jacobson, and Mahler of the *classical* tradition, but Ferenczi as well in putting forth their argument that "the birth of the subject's knowledge of the external world is coincident with his hatred of it. 'Hate as a relation to objects is older than love.' (Freud 1915, quoted by Glatzer and Evans 1977)."[24] They deny that there can be any such thing as "primary love." Eigen critiques their own presumptiveness that they "pres-

---

[21] Eigen, "Guntrip's Analysis with Winnicott," 106.

[22] Ibid., 106–7.

[23] Guntrip, "My experience of analysis with Fairbairn and Winnicott" *International Review of Psychoanalysis* 2 (1975) 145–56.

[24] Eigen, "Guntrip's Analysis with Winnicott," 108.

ent their position as if it had been validated."[25] He challenges their premise on empirical grounds that the notion that early object perception is hate motivated is not substantiated, and instead argues for a parallel development of pleasure and reality principles, citing the "intrinsic order which characterizes primary process thinking."[26]

This is in contrast to Guntrip's view of hate as reactive to the failings of primary objects. "The implication of this view is that if love were perfect there would be no hate. It is a profoundly Christian psychology. Love is deeper than hate and without some experience of love as a point of reference hate would not make sense." I would add here that this is *romantic* Christian psychology, rather than the *classical* variety. Guntrip himself had made the move across the entire theological spectrum.

Guntrip's Personal History: Rebel in Search of a Cause

Jeremy Hazell in his *H.J.S. Guntrip: A Psychoanalytical Biography,* offers much more historical detail about Guntrip's family history than is represented in most of these discussions of Guntrip's analyses with Fairbairn and Winnicott. For instance, Harry's theological pilgrimage was one that emulated his father, Henry. The elder Guntrip was a "rebel" in his own right, whose path in terms of "mother" and "mother church" was to foreshadow the one trodden by Harry. Henry's own father, "'a saintly man of great gentleness, unselfconscious charm and attractiveness' died early, leaving Henry in the care of his authoritarian mother."[27] Henry was not able to emancipate himself until his engagement to Harriet Jessop at the age of thirty-three.

In the meantime, during his twenties, he "'rebelled' politically by forsaking the Tories for the Liberals, and religiously by leaving High Anglicanism for Wesleyan Methodism. There he once again instigated a breakaway movement of Evangelical Fundamentalist Preachers, known as the 'Ranters', whom he led with considerable success for seventeen years, before establishing an active Church on a permanent site in East Dulwich" in London.[28] The *Ranters* were a mission society, echoed in one of Harry Guntrip's dreams while in analysis with Fairbairn which took place in "the mission hall" with his father. They provided the venue for Henry's "im-

---

[25] Ibid.

[26] Ibid.

[27] Jeremy Hazell, *H.J.S. Guntrip: A Psychoanalytic Biography* (London: Free Association Books, 1996) 1.

[28] Ibid.

pressive" public speaking skills, which complemented his love of music and poetry. Indeed, his son Harry would eventually do a fair amount of "ranting" himself in his own rebellion against the "mother church" of Freudian metapsychology and the Ego Psychology of Hartmann. Both father and son developed into keen cricketeers, where sports would be a common outlet for them in their common experience of authoritarian mothers. Ironically, Henry met Harriet when she and her mother went to hear "The Ranters," where Harriet and her brother Sam "became active workers at Herne Hill Mission Hall, the 'tin tabernacle' that was the forerunner of the East Dulwich church."[29]

Antilibidinal Introjects: Violence in the Family History

Harriet herself was emerging from the "parentified child" role that she played in her own family, the third of twelve, who by her twenties "was worn out with the care of her younger siblings."[30] This role continued with the death of her father who bequeathed to her his "Dyers and Cleaners" business with the admonition to take care of her own "feather-brained and irresponsible mother, with the ominous words, 'Look after your mother. She's only a child.'"[31] Her father's public stature was that of a powerful businessman, yet inside the home he exemplified "a basically depressed personality in a bullying attitude to his sons whom he regularly thrashed. On one occasion, when Harriet, whom he never beat, intervened, she sustained a badly bruised arm, and her father was so aghast that he never beat his children again."[32] When one of these brothers, (an elder one), challenged her right to the inheritance of the family business and "took it over by force," Harriet was forced to start one of her own business and so began a feud with this brother that was fueled for the rest of her life. Hazell describes her meeting Henry already armed with "an extremely embittered and domineering personality," which Hazell connected with Henry's attachment to his "own maternal figure against whose values he rebelled."

> It is not difficult to see how Henry, faced with the probable death of his mother, was drawn towards this strong-willed energetic figure when she came to his 'tin tabernacle'; nor is it hard to suppose that Harriet, her father's favorite, saw in this fine looking, eloquent and sensitive leader, the warmer and more impressive side of her

29 Ibid.
30 Ibid., 2.
31 Ibid.
32 Ibid.

recently deceased father. Neither of them could have realised that too many years as an overburdened little mother; had rendered Harriet emotionally unable either to want or to cope with a child of her own.[33]

When they married in 1899, Harriet gave up her business, settled her mother in a small flat, and brought a brother and two sisters to live with them, still under her care. After Sam and Minnie married and moved away, the chronic invalid sister, Mary, stayed with them the rest of her life. Mary idolized Harriet, helping with the housework despite her frailty. Her bond with Mary was stronger than Harriet knew, and "she reacted drastically many years later when Mary died."[34] When Harry was born in 1901, the marriage was already deteriorating, and Harriet's disdain for the care of children was readily apparent. She breast-fed Harry in the hope of preventing further pregnancy; her breast milk apparently inadequate as Harry developed rickets, "and was a 'crying baby' in general." Hazell notes that she was "unremittingly hostile" to Henry's interests, and within a short time he "had stopped playing cricket and ceased reading poetry."[35]

Henry eventually gave up preaching for a job in the city which was jeopardized when he refused to sign a petition in support of the Boer War at the turn of the century. Harriet became alarmed and "set up a draper's shop which became the overriding focus of the family."[36] In response, Henry is said to have "lost his youthful dynamism, becoming a warm and ineffectual father who largely gave up on a life of his own."[37] The picture of Harriet as mother was that of overbearing and essentially narcissistic, giving Harry "intermittent and insensitive care" during his early years. She would take him to the shop with her when he was unhappy, but then would use him "to model girls' clothes until customers protested that this would not do."[38] Hughes has pondered if the overall effect of his mother's using Harry as an extension of herself, to this extreme of dressing him as a girl, burdened Harry to struggle with an overpowering identification with his mother as his bad object self that he resisted through both analyses.[39]

---

[33] Ibid.

[34] Ibid.

[35] Ibid., 3.

[36] Lavinia Gomez, *An Introduction to Object Relations* (New York: New York University Press 1997) 130–31.

[37] Ibid., 131.

[38] Ibid.

[39] Ibid.

The central focus of Harry's self-analysis for most of his years with both Fairbairn and Winnicott was his relation to his brother Percy, born on July 6, 1903. Harry's relationship to Percy was described as a "marked devotion," with Harriet complaining of Harry letting Percy "get the better of him 'in every way.'"

> This "devotion" is all the more remarkable for the fact that Harriet often compared Harry unfavorably with his brother, especially in-sofar as he did not actively oppose him. She did not like what she called his "Peace at any price" attitude, and curiously described it as "one of the evilest things" about Harry—an example of a curiously dual attitude she took to "goodness" both in Harry and in his father, admiring it in principle and scorning it in practice, especially when it appeared to be "unmanly."[40]

At the age of sixteen months Percy lay dead on his mother's lap, the scene of which became Harry's breakthrough dream image in his self-analysis. Harriet herself recounted the scene in one of her letters of 1944.

> When I was performing the last sad duty, somehow you (Harry) got away from Mary and came into the room. I said "Go to Aunty" but for once you would not obey me, but came right up to me, catching hold of the baby. You said firmly "What's the matter with Babs?" Not knowing what to say, I said, "He's gone to sleep." You caught hold of him and said: "Wake him up. I don't want him to sleep." I then said, "Well darling, he's gone to live with Jesus." You then gave a loud cry, "Don't let him go, Mummie. You'll never get him back." I put my free arm around you and we cried together.[41]

Ten days later Harry was so ill that the family doctor was called and, according to Harriet's account, diagnosed Harry as "fretting for the baby." Harriet's accounts of this period vary from fetching Harry's cousin, Annie, "as company for Harry," as her 1944 letter presented it, to that of taking him to Aunt Dolly and Uncle George whose small children were to take Harry's mind off of Percy, the version from the 1920s. Harry took the latter version as the true one. Indeed, "both Fairbairn and Winnicott were of the opinion that he would have died, had Harriet not sent him away from herself in that situation."[42] Henry's accusation was that the cause of Percy's death was Harriet's denial of breast-feeding him, to which she countered with a variety of explanations. One, noted as "quite wild" by Hazell, was

---

[40] Hazell, *H. J. S. Guntrip,* 4.

[41] Ibid., 5.

[42] Ibid., 6.

that the maid had tipped him out of his chair, falling on his head, incurring "abscesses in the brain." Others were of the bland variety: "I expect you know that he died in full health, fell dead in my arms."[43] Harry himself would identify with his father's sentiment: a mother unable to offer nurturance. All in all, a rather narcissistic picture of Harriet emerges.

Back to Hysteria: A Lifetime of Somatic Complaints

Another legacy of Harry's relationship with his mother was that of his somatic complaints. In the eighteen month period following Harry's return from his aunt and uncle, Harriet's business lost money in spite of very long hours, and sexual-relations disappeared between his parents as "Harriet was determined to prevent further conception."[44] The only remnant of Henry's former activity was chairing a committee at the local Congregational Church, coming from his day job to acting as book-keeper for the failing business of his wife in the evening. Within this atmosphere and until his fifth birthday, Harry developed a collection of maladies, including stomach aches, fevers, heat spots, loss of appetite, and constipation. As "no physical cause" could be found by the doctor, Harriet would leave the shop to Mary and "make Harry a 'tent-bed' on the kitchen sofa so as to shield his eyes against the light, to which he had become oversensitive. She would then feed him bread and milk and next day he would be quite recovered."[45] These apparent *hysterical* gestures by Harry toward his mother seem clearly to have created the classic detour from emotional nurturance to the compensated version received through the care of physical symptomotology. Her treatment for constipation, on the other hand, inserting glycerine suppositories into his rectum, had the adverse effect of leaving Harry feeling humiliated, "presumably because of an absence of sensitivity on Harriet's part superimposed on an already highly disturbed little boy."[46] Hazell makes note of how his symptomotology was tied to his relationship with his mother as he had no problems during the same period at the small private "Dame School," just opposite his mother's shop.

Most striking of Harry's symptoms in terms of Harriet's response was irritation under his foreskin that he experienced at the age of five. After attempts to clean him, standing him in the kitchen sink,

---

[43] Ibid.
[44] Ibid., 7.
[45] Ibid.
[46] Ibid., 7–8.

she suddenly had him circumcised, without explanation, on the table in the very parlour where he had seen Percy lying dead on her lap. When the doctor removed his stitches a few days later, he found Harry most unnaturally passive and submissive, and from that time on all the physical disturbances of the previous eighteen months disappeared. Doubtless further traumatised by this drastic and insensitive treatment, Harry withdrew from Harriet and began a slow process of growing away from her—a process aided by his move to a larger private school run by Mrs. East, an efficient bustling woman, where he played vigorous "Red Indian" games "scalping enemies by the score," thus unconsciously turning the tables in some sense upon those who had "scalped" him.[47]

Guntrip's Antilibidinal Maternal Introject

The legacy of Harriet's own father's violence eventually manifest when Harry was six, occasioned by both Harriet's failing business and her sister Mary's almost deadly bout with rheumatic fever. Harriet's temper deteriorated along with her business and her sister's health, beating Harry "cruelly on several occasions." The worst was occasioned by "a customer's malicious gossip regarding a head injury" Harry had sustained while romping about the house playing "tig" with a neighbor girl. He was caught by surprise when mother stormed in from the shop in "a towering rage," accusing him of telling lies about how he injured his head, and "began to beat him repeatedly and uncontrollably, until he was reduced to sobbing helpless terror, clinging to her skirt to support himself. When the shop bell rang he was dragged, still clinging to his mother into the shop, sobbing helplessly, and when the customer expressed concern, Harriet said, 'He's a bad boy. He's been telling lies.'"[48] Guntrip would later refer to the incident in a letter to Fairbairn in 1955, citing this as the "penis game," which raised the issue of the sexual element in the game which may have been what set Harriet off, although the mystery was never solved. Guntrip saw this as the central element of the "thrashing offence," as it "bore witness to his existence as 'an ordinary boy . . .of flesh and blood', whom his mother could not tolerate; though she despised the other-worldly self demanded of him."[49]

---

[47] Ibid., 8.

[48] Ibid., 9.

[49] Ibid.

Theological Organization of Violence

Harry's theology of the period came to reflect this theme as Harriet would read to him on Sunday nights while Henry and Mary were at church from "The Bible in Fortnightly Parts." His favorite story of Nimrod carried this theme of violence that preoccupied him. Nimrod was the mighty hunter with spear poised in confrontation of a roaring lion clinging to the front of his chariot. Guntrip would later reflect: "was he Nimrod defying his roaring, attacking mother, or was he the hungry lion clinging on the front to his mother with her cane raised, ready to strike?—a question which was to be taken up in both his analyses."[50]

The influence of Guntrip's father can be seen in what Hazell described as Harry's period of "growing away" from his family at the age of seven. The first move was to a new school, a mile away from his mother's dress shop. Most significant was the period of time that his father Henry would walk with him to school every morning. Harry "greatly valued his walks with his impressive looking father. In June 1951, in analysis with Fairbairn, Guntrip recalled that it was after this period of walking up Dog Kennel Hill to school that he began to develop 'obsessional characteristics' in an attempt to 'organize himself inwardly' and thus grow away from Harriet."[51] At this early age Harry continued his *schizoid* development which created an internal world as a barrier to the problematic interpersonal dynamics with his mother. The second event was the arrival of the East Dulwich Salvation Army who held "Open Air Meetings" just outside of his mother's shop itself, which became "a warm, cheerful family throughout the remainder of his childhood and adolescence."[52] A third significant event of this period was his mother's relocation of her shop to a more prosperous location as well, where as Hazell puts it, "the new business thrived, and Harriet's temper as well."[53]

During his adolescent years, Harry, with his best friend at the time, Alf, who Hazell described as one of many "Percy substitutes," joined the Salvation Army Scout troop where he practiced a number of interests, including cricket, carpentry, music as a "solo drummer," where sporting in general eclipsed intellectual interests. He followed Alf out of school and into civil service training at the age of fifteen, all the while emulating the religious zealousness of his new adjutant of his Salvation Army Corps,

[50] Ibid., 9–10.
[51] Ibid., 11.
[52] Ibid.
[53] Ibid.

throwing himself into "witnessing and evangelism." He even would wear his Salvation Army jersey under his jacket while at work at the Treasury, his Civil service position, to the snickering of those around him. After only nine months at the Treasury, (which apparently served as a draft deferment), at the end of the Great War in 1918, Harry accepted a temporary appointment as Sub-Lieutenant of Corps in the Old Kent Road slum area. At this time he "declined" his mother's invitation to join her in the business, reflecting on this with Fairbairn as inheriting his mother's determination to survive. Even within the atmosphere of religious zealotry, he maintained his critical faculties, critiquing "the perception that many people managed to convince themselves that they had experienced 'conversion' and 'the Second Blessing of Entire Sanctification,'" which essentially is a theological position of grandiosity and perfectionism.[54] The "appalling poverty and housing conditions" helped lead his interest to studying the *Social Psychology* (1908) of Professor William McDougal, which Hazell cites as almost certainly the book "which first awakened him intellectually to the significance of psychological understanding for himself and others."[55] Guntrip was later to reflect upon this period as the tension between his desire to pursue and perfect a *schizoid* withdrawal into "other-worldly religious experience," while at the same time happily engaged in the busy activities of ministry to the down and out. In the same obsessional fervor that he applied to the diaries of his many years of dreaming and his own analyses, he adopted twenty-four "Rules for Life and Work" which he reflected on regularly in the keeping of a "Devotional Diary." In 1945 he would reflect on these experiences in this way:

> My need of communion suggests that I had missed the basis of that experience in the kin of mother-love that is warm, understanding, yet helps the child to freedom. I must have grown to feel that love could only be bought with the price of submission, and I turned all that into the religious channel. I was seeking in religion something that I had missed in human experience.[56]

By 1920 with his commission as Captain of a Corps at Bideford in Devon, Harry was a smashing success in running the activities of his group, building it up to three hundred from its dwindling origins. This was the beginning of the end with the Salvation Army as his intellectual pursuits drew him to study the modern scholarship that questioned the

---

[54] Ibid., 13.

[55] Ibid., 13–14.

[56] Ibid., 15.

verbal authority of the Bible. The Army itself at the time grew more authoritarian and "intolerant of any policy disagreements," and "Harry had
seen enough to realize that he could not reconcile his personal values with
the authoritarian structure of the Salvation Army at that time."[57] In his
decision to resign he was supported by many fellow officers, as well as his
father, "for it was exactly the kind of 'matter of principle' on which he too
would have made a stand." He was his father's son; *Independent* to the core,
(and now, "from the Corps").[58]

From Fundamentalism to Philosophy and Theology

Harry entered New College and University College of London University
to study Divinity at the former, and philosophy and psychology at the
latter. In Congregationalism's New College Harry received his "progres-
sive" theological training. At University College he studied philosophy
under Professor John Macmurray, and psychoanalysis under J.G. Flugel.
This was also the occasion of meeting his future wife, Bertha, at the family Congregational church, ironically introduced by his mother herself.
Bertha had been one of Harriet's "favourite lieutenants in the church Girl
Guide troop for some years,"[59] although Harriet would come to oppose
their union in her characteristic style of attempting to control Harry. In
this atmosphere Harry succumbed to what would become a recurring state
for the rest of his life: "drastic loss of energy, with a tight sensation in the
head and eye-strain."[60] This echoed the "tent-bed" illness of his childhood,
yet also, as Hazell notes, "represented a 'schizoid withdrawal' from the
emotional demands of the developing relationship with Bertha."[61] So in
some harmony with Markillie's observation of Guntrip championing the
external bad object, Hazell notes its internalization and replication with
Bertha.

   These somatic conditions would cycle, typically evoked by the loss of
his current "Percy substitute," as when his close college friend and future
famous Congregational preacher, Leslie Tizard, left for Oxford. So debili-
tated would he become with his "exhaustion illness" that he would "return
home to mother afterwards with his collapse into apparent dying that had
followed Percy's death. The subsequent return to college with his "other

[57] Ibid., 16.
[58] Ibid., 17.
[59] Ibid., 18.
[60] Ibid., 19.
[61] Ibid.

brothers" would essentially revive him.[62] Hazell here traces the replications that Guntrip would later reconstruct as tied to Percy's death and his amnesia around it.

Death as the Missed Opportunity for Maternal Contact

Soon after Harry's graduation with honors, taking "the Class Psychology Prize" from University College, and his Bachelor of Divinity from New College, his father manifest the jaundice of liver cancer. The medical specialist

> told them that there was nothing to be done and that he expected Henry to live for about a week. At that moment Harriet lost control and began to cry, and Harry moved to comfort her. Before he could do so, however, the specialist said, "Sit down. Your mother will control herself." Overawed by the gravity of the situation, Harry obeyed. But he was later greatly to regret having lost this opportunity of crossing the emotional barrier between himself and his mother—the one occasion when a deeper personal relationship might have grown between them. Harriet never revealed her need again, even on the day Henry died, exactly a week later.[63]

With the striking imagery of one death, (Percy's), that symbolized the chasm between him and his mother, whether actively hostile and violent or that of living in parallel universes, the loss of this critical opportunity to make emotional contact with her at the second most significant death in his family life is striking. We perhaps see the roots of Harry's rage and ranting at the stoic and mechanistic "medical specialist" reflected in his polemical attacks on the Freud-Hartmann tradition. His longing for such contact was one already theorized in his training with Professor Macmurray just these previous few years. It was a theory that would be organized and articulated through his years of analysis and collaboration with Fairbairn. Yet, according to one witness, it would be one that would not be *incarnated* in his own experience until his analysis with Winnicott. That witness is his biographer and protégé, Jeremy Hazell.

Winnicott as Opportunity for Maternal Contact

When Hazell entered into analysis with Guntrip in 1964, Harry was still plagued by his periodic exhaustion illnesses, even after "just over 1,000

---

[62] Ibid., 20–21.
[63] Ibid., 22.

hours of analysis with Fairbairn."[64] During this early stage of his therapy with Guntrip Harry's "general restlessness was something of a problem" to Hazell, where he "fidgeted and interrupted constantly, whenever I said anything, and noisily cleared his throat throughout the sessions. It was difficult at times to reconcile so gifted a writer, whose writings exuded a depth of compassionate understanding, with the noisy and often intrusive personal reality."[65] What captured Hazell's loyalty to enduring such a process was Guntrip's disciplined mind "so as to understand others" which was characterized by a formidable intellectual energy. It seemed clear to Hazell that it "was due partly to these troublesome symptoms that Guntrip developed such penetrating insights into the 'schizoid' problem."[66] In anticipation of yet another death, that of Fairbairn himself as foreshadowed by his failing health, Guntrip "phased out his analysis" with him, "re-instated repression, and brilliantly conceptualized his own problem in the form of an extension to Fairbairn's theory of endo-psychic structure, to include a 'regressed libidinal ego' (Guntrip 1968)."[67] This original contribution was in harmony with Winnicott's own notion of "true self in cold storage," and Guntrip began a second analysis with Winnicott. At the rate of two sessions a month, 150 over six years, Winnicott reconceptualized Guntrip's problem from that of amnesia about Percy's death to his mother's initial inability to emotionally attach to him. Winnicott from the first session on addressed this in the transference with himself.

> Winnicott said, "I've nothing particular to say yet, but if I don't say something you may begin to feel I'm not here." At the second session he said, "You know about me but I'm not a person to you yet. You may go away feeling alone and that I'm not real. You must have had an earlier illness before Percy was born and felt mother left you to look after yourself. You accepted Percy as your infant self that needed looking after. When he died you had nothing and collapsed."[68]

Another theme of the analysis was Winnicott's interpretation of Guntrip's pervasive manic defense. "You have to work hard to keep yourself in existence. You're afraid to stop acting, talking or keeping awake. You

---

[64] Jeremy Hazell, "Reflections on My Experience of Psychoanalysis with Guntrip," *Contemporary Psychoanalysis* 27 (1991) 148.

[65] Ibid., 149.

[66] Ibid., 148.

[67] Ibid., 150.

[68] Ibid., 151–52.

feel you might die in a gap like Percy because if you stop acting, mother can't do anything. She couldn't save you or Percy. You're bound to fear that I can't keep you alive, so you link up monthly sessions for me by your records. No gaps."[69] Hazell describes this process as developing a sense of basic ego relatedness. In essence, Guntrip was to observe Winnicott as ultimately entering into this sphere where, "thanks to his profound insight I was not now alone with a non-relating mother."[70]

Hazell began analysis with Guntrip in 1964; two years after Guntrip began seeing Winnicott on his twice per month frequency. At this time, Guntrip still reflected the many years of Fairbairn's more classical *style* of analysis, as well as Guntrip's own *schizoid* style of self-analysis. Hazell's impression of Guntrip was "that he gave very little indication of that capacity for maternal care" that he came to experience with Guntrip *after* the effects of his analysis with Winnicott began to take hold. Hazell described Guntrip's ability in the early stage to ally with Hazell in his internal struggles with the "bad objects" that dominated his internal world. He saw that Guntrip's own problems "put him into an excellent position to come right into my 'object relations' situation, . . . but it was not until, under Winnicott's influence, this 'strong father figure' developed the capacity for maternal warmth that I felt radically eased of my internal burden."[71]

Hazell's early years with Guntrip witnessed his very obsessional style, to the point of sending Hazell a "printed plan of the house, the path to the waiting-room and the exact position in which I should park my car, together with instructions to enter the waiting-room by a side door and wait for him collect me." Hazell recounts Guntrip taking "copious notes of almost everything I said—aloof and writing rapidly during the entire session, a practice he continued for about a year."[72] Guntrip kept to a strict forty-five minute hour, never going over, yet being "more firm about my leaving punctually than over his punctual arrival."[73] Hazell at a certain point confronted Guntrip on being shorted on his own time on an occasion when Guntrip was late. After this presentation of rigidity and control, Hazell was "amazed to hear him apologise."[74] Guntrip then even rearranged his morning schedule at the University to improve his own

---

[69] Ibid., 151.

[70] Ibid., 152.

[71] Ibid., 153.

[72] Ibid., 154.

[73] Ibid., 153.

[74] Ibid.

time-keeping. Hazell never encountered another patient within the five years that he saw Guntrip, never saw his wife, and only on one occasion did he bend his "frame" to come out to the parking area to greet Hazell's wife and children who had come to meet Hazell. Even then, Hazell felt that Guntrip "did not want to, and the meeting was brief."[75]

Hazell described the mixed effect of Guntrip's "restless formality." On the one hand, Guntrip's own very *classical* style (to the point of caricature with his obsessional note-taking), provided the *classical* psychoanalytic father figure: "someone with a strong, confident sense of purpose, whom I could hardly manipulate," yet as Hazell "came and went (on time)" he could "remember very little to hang onto."[76] Hazell reflects that Guntrip "was only just coming to experience the feeling of being relaxed and 'real' as a person with Winnicott, after years of extremely marked formality with Fairbairn."[77] Therein developed a shift in Guntrip's style and way of being with Hazell, one that retained his rather "daunting framework," yet began to be permeated by Guntrip's "caring understanding and interest in" Hazell. Ironically in the move from the chair to the couch, Guntrip made his own move from the obsessional "doing" of note-taking and the like, to that of "simply 'being' with" Hazell. Guntrip "would say, 'Just rest, and let nature work,' moving his chair alongside me. . . . Gradually, he would let himself go into a dream with me, making slight movements of his clothing which I found so reassuring, and we would rest together—surely a result of his experience with Winnicott."[78]

In light of Guntrip's own relaxing and settling in, his descent from his own psychoanalytic *schizoid citadel*, keeping Hazell's "needs for regression a matter for respect," Hazell reports that he has "not the slightest doubt that it was under the influence of this quality of relationship that my basic nature grew strong enough to achieve some adequacy of mature interdependence. These were the curative aspects, of that I have no doubt."[79] Yet this was not at the expense of the "painstaking working through dreams and phantasies," piecing together early struggles to form the picture of how he was "trapped and isolated in [his] personal relations predicament."[80] It appears that Hazell found in Guntrip a *trailblazer* of the

[75] Ibid., 154.

[76] Ibid., 155.

[77] Ibid.

[78] Ibid., 156.

[79] Ibid.

[80] Ibid., 156–57.

schizoid and *isolated* and one who therefore could help him with his own *schizoid phenomena*. Yet the implementation of the "personal" and perhaps the "maternal" sense of "being with" a patient that Guntrip had already championed with Fairbairn in their respective writings was not *incarnated* into his *flesh and blood* presence until he had had such an experience with Winnicott himself.

In summary, Hazell characterized Guntrip as having a "sense of balance" between supporting "the need for controlled regression in search of recognition" without it becoming either sentimental or a popular bypassing of the conscious process with hypnosis, drugs, cathartic groups or "touch therapy." He noted Guntrip's concept of the "continuum of disturbed experience" as one where he "partnered" Hazell through a range of levels and mental states, "'neurotic' and 'psychotic,' 'True' and 'False.'"[81]

> He was never only an analyst and I was not only a patient. There was, instead, a growing feeling of mutual personal significance in which no state was unimportant. His perception of the human individual's right to be loved "for his own sake as a person in his own right" (Fairbairn, 1952) meant that I gained from my relationship with him a greatly enhanced sense of my own value as an adult. My job was important, my relations with my wife and with other adults whom I met professionally, my ambitions—he took me seriously as a whole person, my adult purposes and capacities receiving as much respect as my needs as a regressed ego.[82]

After the end of their analytic sessions, Hazell noted an even furthering of the "gradual erosion of Guntrip's habitual formality" as reflected in letters they exchanged. Guntrip went from "Dear Hazell" for two years to where he both changed his salutation addressing him with "his Christian name," (Jeremy), and advised Hazell to "Dispense with 'Dr.' in writing" and came to sign himself, "Yours aye, Harry."[83] The intellectual champion of the *personal* had finally become *somewhat personable*.

---

[81] Ibid., 159.

[82] Ibid., 159.

[83] Ibid., 161.

PART THREE

Guntrip's Theology as Internal Object to His Psychoanalytic Psychology

GUNTRIP'S experience of analysis with Winnicott evidenced a movement from the citadel of his self-contained schizoid and obsessionally driven existence toward a lessening of symptoms. On the one hand his magnum opus, *Schizoid Phenomena, Object Relations and the Self* (1968), champions the experience of embracing one's own *weakness* as the key that unlocks the prison tower of schizoid living. I contend that this object relational concept is the external form of his implicit theology, which I will demonstrate in chapter eight.

On the other hand, I will also address what I see as the *tragedy* of the ironic breakthrough of maternal dream material from his analysis with Winnicott: the death of his *environmental mother analyst* as the occasion for such an accomplishment. In chapter nine I will argue for an object relational critique of Guntrip's unintegrated hostility: the lack of his capacity to "be weak *in the presence of* Winnicott," with the resultant loss of *antilibidinal* integration in himself.

8

Guntrip's Psychoanalytic Theology

From Morality to "Grace Made Perfect in Weakness"

From Morality to Relationship

Jacques Ellul in his *Subversion of Christianity*[1] echoes a theme of Macmurray in differentiating *Christianity* from *Christendom,* where the latter is a corruption of the former. Ellul argues that the essence of Christianity is relational while in its historical development of institutionalization it has been reduced to a system of *morality,* a self and societal regulatory process characterized by rules of conduct. Macmurray described this process as the "inner springs of human life" being taken under the control of the institution of medieval Christianity. The theologian, Dietrich Bonhoeffer, offered a similar position in his theological exegesis of the Genesis story of the Fall. The partaking of the "forbidden fruit" which represented the "fall from grace" was from the "tree of the knowledge of good and evil." Knowing "good and evil," which is *morality itself,* represented the substitution of autonomous self-direction in place of a relationship with God; hence the fall from external object relations, or what Guntrip prefers to call "personal relations," into one's internal schizoid world, the self-contained "I" of Cartesian rationalism.[2] Harry Guntrip in his classic text, *Schizoid Phenomena, Object Relations and the Self,*[3] presents this identical contrast between morality and relationship. On the one hand he refers to the *moral standpoint* of classic Freudian metapsychology with its emphasis on the *ego* "civilizing" the sexual and aggressive impulses

---

[1] Jacques Ellul, *The Subversion of Christianity,* trans. Geoffrey W. Bromiley (Grand Rapids: Eerdmans, 1986).

[2] Dietrich Bonhoeffer, *Creation and Fall,* trans. John C. Fletcher (New York: Harper & Row, 1954).

[3] Guntrip, *Schizoid Phenomena, Object Relations and the Self* (New York: International Universities Press, 1968).

of the *id*. On the other, he contrasts this with the personal object relations which underlie such concerns and form the core of the *person*.

Guntrip, the veteran of the Salvation Army with its military style of discipline and "by the book" code of morality, has emerged as the *Oliver Stone of psychoanalysis*, that military veteran who came to critique the military-political establishment through the genre of his motion pictures, "Platoon," and "The Fourth of July." While it is easy to cite Guntrip's critique of *"the moral standpoint"* of classical psychoanalysis as merely a transferencial response to his own personal history, he argues his position very clearly and thoroughly in both of his major works, *Personality Structure and Human Interaction*, 1961, his historical and comparative study of the development of psychoanalytic theory, as well as his magnum opus: *Schizoid Phenomena, Object Relations and the Self*, 1968. In short, Guntrip cites the dominant thinking of the psychoanalytic tradition (up until his time) as "the moral standpoint" that emphasizes "the need for the control of anti-social impulses and for the production of properly socialized characters." In the larger societal arena this was pursued through "training and discipline, education and religion, authoritative guidance and direction by 'reason' and the value of the spiritual life." He clearly cites the *classical vision* of western culture, and applies his critique to the classical-Freudian tradition of psychoanalysis proper. Guntrip refers to Freud's seminal work in the 1880s where the clinical problems that Freud dealt with reflected both moral issues and illness. A vague confusion arose in how to draw the dividing line between the two, captured "bluntly if crudely in the question, 'Are neurotics really ill or only selfish?'"[4]

> After starting with the study of hysteria, psychoanalysis in its first creative period analysed thoroughly the moral and pseudo-moral (or pathologically moral) level of human experience, the area of the control of impulses of sex and aggression working antisocially, generating guilt, and leading to obsessional neurosis and depression.[5]

Alluding to the structural model with its dual concern of an *ego* managing the impulsive *id*, as well as the interest in the *superego* with its manifestations of guilt, Guntrip captions this ego psychological model as the "moral approach." Rather than a critique of this psychoanalysis of the neurotic level of depressive issues with its focus on aggression and guilt, Guntrip tips his hat to Freud's success in this area as opening "the way

[4] Ibid., 6.

[5] Ibid., 9.

to a deeper and more primitive level of our psychic life, denoted by the term 'the schizoid problem.'"[6] He essentially describes his allegiance to Fairbairn's paradigm shift in psychoanalytic metapsychology from, on the one hand, an instinctual, tension regulating model whose aim is organismic homeostasis, to that of an object relational one whose aim is attachment to the object. On the other hand, Guntrip here reflects Fairbairn's roots in English Kleinian thought as he proposes a developmental scheme, as did Klein, that saw the most fundamental period as pre-oedipal, pre-neurotic, and centered on the infant's earliest relationship with his/her mother. This Guntrip referred to as "a fundamentally different point of view from that of the moral approach;" in other words, a paradigm shift. In a nutshell, Guntrip argues for analysis of what in classical psychoanalysis and ego psychology was seen as "unanalyzable," in concert with, again, the Kleinian preponderance for psychoanalysis of "primitive mental states." Such analysis of the "unanalyzable" only found acceptance in the United States under the influence of Margaret Mahler's work and notables such as Peter Giovachinni, Otto Kernberg, and William W. Meissner in the 1970s, formulated around the psychoanalysis of the Borderline Personality.[7] Guntrip made his pitch for the analysis of "the underlying, unconscious strata" that predates depressive-aggressive concerns as "the pre-moral level of infantile *fear, ego-weakness, and flight from life.*"[8] In essence, Guntrip in following, articulating, and expanding upon Fairbairn's revision of Freudian structural theory, championed what I would describe as an *attachment theory,*[9] although his and Fairbairn's terminology throughout reflected attachment's pathological breakdown in *schizoid phenomena.*

An Ego Psychology Formed by Object Relations

In this Introduction to *Schizoid Phenomena, Object Relations and the Self,* Guntrip lays down his basic philosophical presuppositions about the nature of human beings. In contrast to the "atomistic scientific theory" that takes an outside observer role and performs a reductionistic and stoic *analysis* of the "organism," for Guntrip, "all this seemed to me to miss the final key to human problems by not beginning with *the primary fact about human be-*

---

[6] Ibid.

[7] Peter Giovanchi, ed., *Tactics and Techniques in Psychoanalytic Therapy III: The Implications of Winncott's Contributions* (Northvale, NJ: Aronson, 1990) xv–xxiii.

[8] Ibid., 10, (emphasis added).

[9] Popularized in John Bowlby's work, notably, *Attachment and Loss,* 2d ed. (New York: Basic Books, 1982).

ings, namely their experience of themselves as that significant and meaningful 'whole' which we call a 'person.'"[10] In this one statement, perhaps, he brings together the cumulative influence of John Macmurray, Ronald Fairbairn, and Donald Winnicott. In an interesting use of terminology, he titles this approach "to man as a 'whole person'" as "ego-psychology," essentially a revision of the classic structural model of Fairbairn to his object relational structural model, yet one that is very different from the Freud-Hartmann "ego-psychology." Guntrip, however, in spite of his rhetoric, still shares the basic "ego-psychology" interest in how the *ego* is structured and to what level it is developed in the patient. This becomes the basis for his way of differentiating *mental illness* from *immorality*. "Mental Illness springs specifically from the ravages of early fear and basic weakness of the ego, with consequent inability to cope with life in any other than a dangerous state of anxiety." In contrast, immorality is manifest in a "reasonably stable individual" who is manifesting "bad values and standards of behavior" and "is not necessarily undermined by deep-seated fears." Guntrip then identifies the work of both Fairbairn and Winnicott as "interacting together" and as the "main stimulus" to his thinking, culminating in his exposition of *schizoid phenomena* as the heart of the problem:

> the failure of strong ego-formation in earliest infancy, the persistence of a fear-ridden and withdrawn (or regressed) infantile self in the depths of the unconscious, and even the fact of unrealized potentialities of the personality that have never been evoked. *The rebirth and regrowth of the lost living heart of the personality is the ultimate problem psychotherapy seeks to solve.*[11]

What is this indebtedness to Fairbairn to which Guntrip refers? In essence, the formulation of the "schizoid position" as the earliest developmental stage was central to Fairbairn's reformulation of the Freudian "oral stage," with a different emphasis than that of Melanie Klein's own reformulation in her *Paranoid Position*. Yet so influential was Fairbairn's contribution that even Klein eventually amended her formulation to be the *Paranoid-Schizoid Position*. Both Fairbairn and Guntrip share the milieu of the British Object Relations founded by Klein with its existential emphasis on the basic anxiety of being, variously referred to by Guntrip as "irresistible fears" and "simply elementary fear." The contrast of these two traditions *within* British Object Relations is between the aggressive-destructive-envious manifestations of the "death instinct" on the Kleinian

---

[10] Guntrip, *Schizoid Phenomena*, 10.

[11] Ibid., 11–12, (emphasis in the original).

side, reflected in her interest in the persecutory anxiety of the *Paranoid* projective processes and defenses. On the *Independent* side, the interest is in attachment-seeking and its interruption, characterized by *Schizoid* processes and defense, where the anxiety was a "fear carrying with it the feeling of weakness and inability to cope with life; fear possessing the psyche to such an extent that 'ego-experience' cannot get started."[12] For Klein, *schizoid* was more of the splitting of the ego for the purpose of aggressive, paranoid projections outward. For Fairbairn and Guntrip, *schizoid* was the splitting of the ego for protective withdrawal inward.

Guntrip's opening chapter echoed Fairbairn in his definition and description of "the schizoid problem," and was indeed a revision of Guntrip's earlier paper, "A study of Fairbairn's Theory of Schizoid Reactions" in the *British Journal of Medical Psychology* in 1952.[13] He captions his description of the *Schizoid Personality* or *Condition* as *The Picture of the Shut-in Individual.* The heart of his description is that of the mental state of a patient who "becomes inaccessible emotionally, when the patient seems to be bodily present but mentally absent. One patient said, 'I don't seem to come here', as if she came in body but did not bring herself with her."[14] He describes the various aspects of the phenomena of *depersonalization,* "feeling cut off, shut off, out of touch, feeling apart or strange, of things being out of focus or unreal, . . . things seeming futile and meaningless."[15] Guntrip notes that many patients will describe this state of mind as "depression," yet this does not reflect classical depression's more extraverted and object relational turning of anger inward in the service of keeping it from breaking out into overt anger. The schizoid person, on the other hand, takes an introverted path, having renounced objects themselves, "even though he still needs them."[16] Guntrip reflects Fairbairn's developmental hierarchy in citing the *schizoid* phase (or *position* in Kleinian terms) as *oral* and therefore "below," or preceding the *depressive* and *anal* phase (or *position).*

Guntrip's exposition of *The Schizoid Personality* can perhaps best be seen as his own articulation of Fairbairn's object-relations theory. He cites his common source with Fairbairn whose own theory "arose out of his

---

[12] Ibid., 13.

[13] Guntrip, "A Study of Fairbairn's Theory of Schizoid Reactions," *British Journal of Medical Psychology* 25 (1952) 86–103.

[14] Guntrip, *Schizoid Phenomena,* 17.

[15] Ibid., 17–18.

[16] Ibid., 18.

study of schizoid problems."[17] Guntrip throughout this work continually cites clinical examples from his own practice to illustrate the phenomena of schizoid cutting-off, detachment, and withdrawal, all in the service of protection from disappointment and attack at the hands of the love object, both external and internal.

> Patient: "I feel hopeless, resigned, no way out, stuck. I'm wondering how I can manage somehow just to get around and put up with it."
>
> Analyst: "Your solution is to damp everything down, don't feel anything, give up all real relationship to people on the emotional level, and just 'do things' in a mechanical way, be a robot."
>
> Her reaction clearly brought out the schizoid trait: "Yes, I felt I didn't care, didn't register anything. Then I felt alarmed, felt this was dangerous. If I hadn't made myself do something I'd have just sat, not bothered, not interested."
>
> Analyst: "That's your reaction in analysis to me: don't be influenced, don't be moved, don't be lured into reacting to me."
>
> Her reply was: "If I were moved at all, I'd feel very annoyed with you. I hate and detest you for making me feel like this. The more I'm inclined to be drawn towards you, the more I feel a fool, undermined."[18]

Following Fairbairn, the ultimate or core source of the danger is *not* the aggression whose attack is destructive and *immoral*, rather it is the love hunger itself, the *object seeking* desire which threatens to *gobble up* the love object. His patient illustrated this point for Guntrip when she said, "I'd rather hate you than love you," with the former being less dangerous than the latter. "The mere fact of the analyst's presence as another human being with whom she needed to be emotionally real, that is, express what she was actually feeling, created an emotional crisis in her with which she could only deal by *abolishing the relationship*. So her major defense against her anxieties was to keep herself emotionally out of reach, inaccessible, and keep everyone at arm's length."[19] The clinical presentation of detachment and boredom, which are permutations of depersonalization, is the central issue to be understood, according to Guntrip.

Guntrip clearly spells out his core philosophical-psychological belief: *"The significance of human living lies in object-relationships, and only in such*

[17] Ibid., 19.
[18] Ibid., 18–19.
[19] Ibid., 19.

terms can our life be said to have a meaning, for without object relations the ego itself cannot develop."[20] Object relationships are not optional but a "basic need," because we "are constitutionally incapable of living as isolated units." The influence of both Macmurray and Fairbairn clearly can be seen here. The sum effect of the breakdown of relationship with external objects is to retreat to *Living in an Internal World.*[21] "The more people cut themselves off from human relations in the outer world, the more they are driven back on emotionally charged fantasized object-relations in their inner mental world, till the psychotic lives only in his inner world. But it is still a world of object relations."[22]

The Metapsychology of Internalized Objects

As illustrated above, it is the patient's *Antilibidinal Ego* who calls the patient "a fool" for daring to want to be in relationship, attacking the patient's *Libidinal Ego* for even contemplating such a temptation. The *Antilibidinal Ego* acts as the patient's *Internal Saboteur* to undermine such movement toward contact, all in the service of protecting oneself from the danger of the pain in relating to another human being.[23] Again, this model of Fairbairn and Guntrip reflects Erik Erikson's concept of *basic mistrust,*[24] where the lack of "good enough" attachments to their own childhood caretakers facilitated the schizoid flight into their own respective inner worlds. It is a developmental model that stresses pathology; an attachment theory whose terminology of *schizoid* echoes the attachment failures in the lives of its two principal architects.

Guntrip follows both the Kleinian and Fairbairnian use of "introjection" (or mental internalization) of the object as a way of controlling and managing the frustrating and distressing experiences with the external object. As he articulates his own version of "this metapsychology," he actually lands somewhere between the two of them. For Klein, internal objects are of both the good and bad varieties. Guntrip notes Klein's difference with Fairbairn, in citing him as regarding the "good object" as not needing to be internalized since the internalization of the "bad object" is a defensive operation. Hence, the *Libidinal Ego* itself does not relate to an internalized "good object" in that sense, but its correlate is the *tantalizing, Libidinal*

---

[20] Ibid., 19–20, (emphasis in the original).

[21] Ibid., 19.

[22] Ibid., 20.

[23] Ibid., 71–72.

[24] Erik Erikson, *Childhood and Society* (New York: Norton, 1993).

Object that promises fulfillment but does not deliver. Guntrip describes Fairbairn's notion of internalization of the "good" as taking the form of "memory," rather than as an "internal object" proper. Here Guntrip seems to follow Wilford Bion rather than Fairbairn.[25]

Guntrip is a true *Romantic* in the *Independent spirit* as he confirms his failure-of-the-environment emphasis in the formation of the bad object experience.

> When someone we need and love ceases to love us, or behaves in a way that we interpret it as cessation of love, or disappears, dies, i.e. deserts us, that person becomes, in an emotional, libidinal sense, a bad object. . . . All that is experienced as frustration of the most important of all needs, as rejection and desertion, or else as perse-cution and attack. Then the lost object, now become a bad object, is mentally internalized in a much more vital and fundamental sense than memory. In the language of Bion, bad experiences can-not be *digested* and absorbed; they are retained as foreign objects which the psyche seeks to project.[26]

Guntrip here references both sides of the oral stage according to British object relations: "rejection and desertion": the *schizoid position* as articulated by Fairbairn; and "persecution and attack": the *paranoid posi-tion* championed by Melanie Klein. As noted previously, she amended her rendering of this stage to include Fairbairn's notion, then calling it the *paranoid-schizoid position.* Guntrip cites Klein as Fairbairn's source of this reworking of the Freudian scheme, where the classical psychoneuroses, paranoia, obsessions, hysteria and phobias, are merely defenses "against internal bad-object situations which would otherwise set up depressive or schizoid states."[27] Treatment, therefore, is moving behind the symptom producing defenses which are born of the *anal* and *phallic* stages, to be-come conscious of these bad-object situations that stem from the earliest, or *oral* stage.

The two fundamental reactions to these internal bad-object relation-ships, again parallel Klein's two developmental positions: the primary *paranoid-schizoid position* of earliest infancy followed by the *depressive posi-tion.* For Fairbairn, (and hence Guntrip), the *schizoid* and *depressive* states

---

[25] Guntrip, *Schizoid Phenomena*, 21.

[26] Ibid., 22.

[27] Ibid., 23.

are "the two basic or ultimate dangers to be escaped from."[28] Guntrip then describes them in his characteristic simple and articulate fashion.

> When you want love from a person who will not give it and be-
> comes a bad object to you, you can react in either or both of two
> ways. You may become angry and enraged at the frustration and
> want to make an aggressive attack on the bad object to force it to
> become good and stop frustrating you—like a small child who flies
> into a temper tantrum and hammers on her with his fists. This is
> the problem of *hate, or love made angry.* It is an attack on a hostile,
> rejecting, actively refusing bad object. It leads to *depression* for it
> rouses the fear that one's hate will destroy the very person one
> needs and loves, a fear that grows into guilt.[29]

Guntrip in summary fashion describes the locus of the *classic vision* in psychoanalysis, with its interest in sublimating and socializing the can-tankerous *id*. Yet even in describing these *aggressive-depressive-guilt induc-ing* dynamics, he has as its core the experience of *lost love,* or, *love made angry.* Developmentally he alludes to the "temper tantrum" of the classic Mahlerian *separation-individuation* dynamics of toddlerhood,[30] essentially an *anal* expulsive and retentive dynamic in the classic Freud-Abraham tra-dition. He, in accord with Klein, (with her own roots in her analysis and training with Abraham), seeks the *oral* as the "earlier and more basic reac-tion." He continues:

> When you cannot get what you want from the person you need,
> instead of getting angry you may simply go on getting more and
> more hungry, and full of a sense of painful craving, and a longing
> to get total and complete possession of your love-object so that you
> cannot be left to starve. Fairbairn arrived at the view that *love made
> hungry* is the *schizoid* problem and it rouses the terrible fear that
> one's love has become so devouring and incorporative that love
> itself has become destructive. Depression is the fear of loving lest
> one's hate should destroy. Schizoid aloofness is the fear of loving
> lest love or need of love should destroy, which is far worse.[31]

---

[28] Ibid., 23.

[29] Ibid., 24.

[30] Margaret Mahler, *The Psychological Birth of the Infant: Symbiosis and Individuation* (New York: Basic Books, 1975).

[31] Guntrip, *Schizoid Phenomena,* 24.

The Schizoid Dilemma and The Schizoid Compromise: Guntrip's Core Polarity

The sum effect of these earliest schizoid phenomena is the *schizoid dilemma:* a basic "approach-avoidance" situation best illustrated in the schizoid's reactions to food and eating, (a derivative of the paradigm of the infant's relationship to the mother's breast). "His reactions to people and food are basically the same. These may be described as a *need* to possess and incorporate, checkmated by a *fear* to take, accept, and devour."[32] Guntrip's description is interestingly similar to that of bulimic patients. *"There is a constant oscillation between hungry eating and refusal to eat, longing for people and rejecting them."*[33] This oscillation becomes a characteristic of the transference situation where "the analyst excites by his presence, but does not libidinally satisfy, and so constantly arouses a hungry craving."[34] The frustrating aspect of the non-gratification of the psychoanalytic situation itself "is certain to bring out schizoid reactions." This was well attested by Jeremy Hazell's own experience in his analysis with Guntrip's formal and non-gratifying analytic style, as noted above.

> The patient longs for the analyst's love, may recognize intellec-tually that a steady, consistent, genuine concern for the patient's well-being is a true form of love, yet, because it is not love in a full libidinal sense (Fairbairn reminds us that it is *agape*, not *eros*), the patient does not 'feel' it as love. He feels rather that the analyst is cold, indifferent, bored, not interested, not listening, busy with something else while the patient talks, rejecting. . . . The patient will then begin to feel he is bad for the analyst, . . . in general feels he is draining and exhausting, i.e. devouring, the analyst.[35]

The Theology of Love

Guntrip here demonstrates his first piece of what I will call *theology as an internal object.* As he illustrates the *schizoid dilemma* of approach-avoid, he cites a theological construct in defining the *love* of the analytic situa-tion. *Agape* is the standard New Testament Greek term for an intentional form of love that gives to the need of the other without necessitating a

---

[32] Ibid., 30.
[33] Ibid., 31.
[34] Ibid., 33.
[35] Ibid.

mutual response on the same level.[36] Guntrip (with Fairbairn) contrasts the analyst's *agape* with *eros,* not only of the standard sexual arousal toward the other, but also with the Freudian tradition itself, with its classic drive polarities of *eros* and *thanatos,* or the "death instinct." What is interesting is Hazell's description above of the staunchly *agape,* formal analytic style of Guntrip through most of his relationship with Hazell. Yet his style, under the influence of Winnicott, softened and *moved somewhat* in the direction of Winnicott himself: a warm and almost whimsical love perhaps best described by the Greek word, *phileo.*[37] This is the Greek word from which the name of the city, Philadelphia, is derived: "The city of brotherly love." *Phileo* is the form of love that is characterized by warmth and affection, essentially the "affective bond" that eventually grew to be *somewhat* overt between Guntrip and Hazell. It is part and parcel of the Winnicottian *romantic* style.

Destructiveness in Relation to Love

Of paradoxical interest is how Guntrip contrasts the complementary dynamic of "destructiveness" between Fairbairn's view and that of Winnicott. "Fairbairn regards the destructive element in infantile "love" or "need of the object" as a direct reaction to rejection. Winnicott regards a destructive element in infantile "need" as normal and natural."[38] Guntrip sides with the Fairbairn emphasis, critiquing Winnicott's description of

> "destructive primitive love" as simply "hate," but though it is experienced by the mother as wearing, exhausting, and ruthless, we can hardly say that the infant is intentionally "ruthless." He is rather energetic, vigorous, alive, one might almost say enthusiastic, and he presumably experiences a sense of "shock" when he finds mother cannot indefinitely cope with his needs. He may then grow at first angry and demanding, then frightened and withdrawing. Finally, if no satisfactory solution of the problem is found, if the mother becomes hostile, intolerant, and rejective, then the combination of natural vigour, natural anger, and natural fear develops into the pathological form of "need" or "love" which is correctly called "hate".[39]

[36] Walter Bauer et al., *A Greek-English Lexicon of the New Testament and Other Early Christian Literature,* 3d ed., revised by Frederick W. Danker (Chicago: University of Chicago, 2000) 5.

[37] Ibid., 866.

[38] Guntrip, *Schizoid Phenomena,* 32.

[39] Ibid.

Guntrip, given his personal history as detailed by Hazell, seems to be clearly speaking from personal experience in regards to his relationship with his own mother. He continues this passage with a detailed discussion arguing for a "more careful definition and accepted use" of both of the terms "love" and "hate," rather than how they "have been used in loose ways for so long."[40] He clearly reflects his concern for preciseness in contrast to Winnicott's characteristic "loose" and poetic use of language. Guntrip is a good schizoid, after all. Even beyond that, Guntrip essentially has difficulty in having *normative hate,* reserving the term for a rather well developed breakdown with one's mother. Guntrip leans rather strongly in the *romantic* direction, in contrast to Winnicott who preferred to hold such polarities in dynamic and paradoxical tension, as will be further developed in chapter nine.

Types of Schizoid Dilemmas

Guntrip describes his own version of dynamic tension through a number of catch-phrases. The first he called *"The 'In and Out' Programme."*

> *The chronic dilemma in which the schizoid individual is placed, namely that he can neither be in a relationship with another person nor out of it, without in various ways risking the loss of both his object and himself,* is due to the fact that he has not yet outgrown the particular kind of dependence on love-objects that is characteristic of infancy. This has two different but clearly related aspects: identification and a wish to incorporate. Identification is passive, incorporation is active. Identification can feel like being swallowed up in another person, incorporation is the wish to swallow the object into oneself. Identification suggests regression to a womb state, and incorporative urges belong to the post-natal, oral infant at the breast.[41]

Guntrip echoes what Fairbairn had called *the moral defense,*[42] where the child cannot tolerate particular bad object experiences of the caretaker, and rather than feel out of control, internalizes the bad in herself as the *Antilibidinal Ego* in oneself. The internal logic of the process is the sense that it is better to be *bad* oneself than have the external caretaker (object) be the one who is *bad,* and therefore live with a sense of having

[40] Ibid.

[41] Ibid., 36.

[42] Ronald Fairbairn, *Psychoanalytic Studies of the Personality* (London: Routledge, Kegan Paul, 1952).

no control and therefore feeling doomed. If I make myself the *bad* one in the relationship, then I have the hope that someday I will figure out how to become *good*. The *moral* aspect is the prospect of figuring out how to be *good*, which is essentially finding a way to please the caretaker so as to restore some sense of connection and thereby security. Small children in abusive environments typically do not "run away from home" and employ Fairbairn's *moral defense* strategy as a way of maintaining a connection with the object, or parent. In the child abuse literature, Roland Summit has described a similar process in what he termed "The Accommodation Syndrome,"[43] where the child reports and then recants the complaint of abuse, an "accommodation" to keep the family together. Hence, according to Guntrip, the child must "incorporate" or "swallow" the bad object (trauma) experience, never being free to "get over it" or "move beyond" bad experiences with the caretaker, always with "one foot in and one foot out" of relationships when this becomes the dominant pattern or dynamic. Ironically, Guntrip here supports Markillie and others' contention that Guntrip never really came to terms with his internalization of his own narcissistic and violent mother, rather than merely suffered the deficit of her unavailability. Given Hazell's account of Mrs. Guntrip's savage beatings of Harry, his internalization of such violence would not be a far flung notion. In his own words, *"Return to the womb is a flight from life,"*[44] and Harry's womb was his obsessional, "schizoid citadel."[45]

Guntrip's other polarity of dynamic tension is what he called *The Schizoid Compromise*. The "compromise" between the oscillation of the "alternating in and out policy" that makes life so difficult, (as is characteristic of the Borderline Personality's lability as described in the tradition of Margaret Mahler),[46] is the *"compromise in a half-way-house position, neither in nor out."*[47] This dynamic can take many forms. One is a split between the mental and the bodily self, where if "he is 'in' with the mind he must be 'out' with the body, and *vice versa*. He cannot commit the whole of himself to one person."[48] Another is a version of "attention deficit," as with the "bibliophilic Don Juan" who collects books but never reads them. "This

[43] Roland Summitt, *The Accomodation Syndrome* (Los Angeles: University of California, 1980).

[44] Guntrip, *Schizoid Phenomena*, 53.

[45] Ibid., 22.

[46] W. W. Meissner, *The Borderline Spectrum* (Northvale, NJ: Aronson, 1984).

[47] Guntrip, *Schizoid Phenomena*, 61.

[48] Ibid., 60.

schizoid fear of full self-committal accounts for much inability to concentrate attention in study."[49] Guntrip describes various versions of what I think is best illustrated by James Thurber's classic character, *Walter Mitty*, the mousy man who externally defers to his domineering wife, and in any spare moment is some World War I flying ace or some other hero who has adventure after adventure in the private world of his fantasies. Another variation would be that which I call the *gregarious introvert*, whose "outer self, like a skilled actor, can act even an emotional part mechanically while thinking of other things."[50] Guntrip, again, argues for the schizoid state as the foundational one that underlies all others.

> It is far more common to find people exhibiting mild traits of introversion, and poor affective contact with their outer world, than exhibiting signs of true depression, and as Fairbairn pointed out (1952) most people, when they say they are depressed, really mean that they are apathetic and feel life to be futile—the schizoid state.[51]

Greek Dualism:
The Schizoid Philosophy of Western Culture

Guntrip continues his exposition of the schizoid polarity in view of its "struggle to preserve an ego," in bringing in his next piece of his theological philosophy. He is offering more clinical examples of patient's self-descriptions such as wearing unneeded glasses in order to "feel safer behind that screen," or "the feeling of a plateglass wall between the patient and the world."[52] He then gives an example of what I call Guntrip's *theological internal object.*

> Another patient says: "I feel I'm safe inside my body looking out at the world through my eyes." One is reminded of the Greek idea of the body as the prison of the soul, one of many marks of a schizoid mentality in the Greek intellectualist view of life. Winnicott's account of the split between the psyche and the soma throws much light on this. The healthy personality does not feel to be in two

---

[49] Ibid., 61.

[50] Ibid., 63.

[51] Ibid., 62.

[52] Ibid., 63.

parts, one hiding from the world within the other, but whole, all of a piece, and active as unity.[53]

He begins a thread that will run through the rest of the book, addressing the Greek philosophical dualism that is characteristic of Western culture in general, and of Western Christianity in particular. At the same time he is developing the theme of his own innovation to the Fairbarinian scheme: a second split in Fairbairn's *Libidinal Ego* that becomes the *Withdrawn Ego*, a contribution acknowledged by Fairbairn himself.

> *The part of the self that struggles to keep touch with life feels intense fear of the deeper and more secret, withdrawn self, which appears to be endowed with a great capacity to attract and draw down more and more of the rest of the personality into itself. Hence, extensive defences are operated against it.* (emphasis in original). If those defences fail, the ego of everyday consciousness experiences a progressively terrifying loss of interest, *energy, zest, verging toward exhaustion,* (emphasis added), apathy, derealization of the environment, and depersonalization of the conscious ego.[54]

Recalling Hazell's account of one of Harry's savage beatings at the hands of his mother, where he was left sobbing, clinging to her skirt, one can conceive of Guntrip's own withdrawal into a secret self, and his own "extensive" defenses characterized by his "exhaustion illness" that plagued him on and off during his entire lifetime, and which was significantly evoked in direct relation to events surrounding his mother. The autobiographical piece here seems rather transparent. Guntrip employed a number of ways "in which life in the outer world can be kept going in spite of a considerable measure of withdrawal of the vital feeling-self."[55] He lists three ways, which again, I see as autobiographical in nature.

> The schizoid intellectual lives on the basis of "thinking", the obsessional moralist on the basis of "duty" and the "organizational-man" on the basis of carrying on automatically a fixed routine. If the emotionally withdrawn person can by such means ward off a great deal of the impact of real life, and prevent its pressures from playing on the secret inner fear-ridden feeling-life, then a relatively stabilized schizoid character may result, a human being who functions as an efficient robot within a restricted and safe conception of how life is to be lived. Life is the pursuit of truth, not love, the

---

[53] Ibid.
[54] Ibid., 64.
[55] Ibid.

thinking out of an ideology; and ideas become more important than people.[56]

Guntrip, I propose, is describing his "secret inner fear ridden feeling life" that is the derivative of life with a hostile, violent, and explosive mother. Hazell gave his personal experience of Guntrip's *dutiful* adherence to *classical* psychoanalytic technique (as opposed to his own theory); his overall obsessional lifestyle characterized by his obsessive note-taking; the *organizational-man* of the Salvation Army, but again, better seen in his *fixed routine*; and perhaps most strikingly, his *intellectualized* containment of his *fear-ridden* life in his writing about the centrality of relationships and attachments that he so poorly practiced.

Guntrip continues his veiled autobiographical exposition into the area of the *theological character structure* of the schizoid individual.

> He tends to hold the Greek rather than the Christian view of life, and the scientific rather than the religious view. In religion theology is exalted above love of one's neighbour. . . . Highly abstract philosophy seems unwittingly designed to prove Descartes' dictum, "Cogito, ergo sum", "I think, therefore I am", the perfect formula for the schizoid intellectual's struggle to possess an ego. A natural human being would be more likely to start from "I feel, therefore I am."[57]

Macmurray's contrast of science and religion comes through clearly, along with the intellectualization of Cartesian enlightenment philosophy. The paradox of Guntrip's "intellectual struggle" was that it was not his philosophy that was "highly abstract," and he obviously critiques the Greek dualism as a worldview, both psychologically and theologically. His particular schizoid struggle was that he *intellectualized about feeling* and its vicissitudes in writing his object relations psychology. Markillie is a good example, along with Hazell, of those who knew Guntrip personally and experienced Harry's self-absorption. The contrast between the personable tone of his writing, and the report of his interpersonal awkwardness and emotional distancing by those who knew him, is striking.

---

[56] Ibid.

[57] Ibid., 64–65.

Guntrip's Central Theological Concept: Weakness That Calls for Dependence

In a latter chapter on "Psychodynamic Theory" Guntrip picks up the thread of his *internal theological object*. He begins with referencing his mentor, Macmurray, as the philosopher who "has given the *coup de grace* to instinct theory," and then parades by Klein, Fairbairn, Winnicott, Bowlby, and Bion as those in support in seeing instinctual manifestations such as aggression and the classical conflicts (aggressive, Oedipal, etc.) as derivatives of the "self-exhausting struggle of *an already divided self* to maintain psychic defences against ego-collapse."[58] He then makes his next theological installment.

> Freud actually took over the traditionalist and popular psychology of Plato and St. Paul as his starting point (cf. Chapter V, p. 132). Plato's charioteer of reason and St. Paul's "law of the mind" became the controlling ego with its scientific reason. Just as Plato's "reason" made an ally of the lion (aggression), turning it against the beast (instincts) to enforce control, so Freud envisaged the ego working with the sadistic superego to turn aggression inwards against the id, and showed how pathological guilt produced depression. . . . But Freud did not answer, indeed failed to ask, the crucial question: since man is without doubt social by nature, how does it come about that he feels such antisocial impulses so often? Why do men have antisocial impulses? Freud, like all his predecessors, simply assumed that they were innate, that in man's nature there was an unresolvable contradiction of good and evil. This is the traditional view of man in our own and other cultures.[59]

Guntrip applies a very *classical vision* critique of the theory of the source of antisocial impulses as "innate" in seeing this as "our greatest rationalization and self-deception. We have preferred to boost our egos by the belief that even if we are bad, we are at any rate strong in the possession of 'mighty instincts.'" He sees antisocial drives as *distortions* of our more basic drive to attachment and social connection; a defense against experiencing our own "weak, fear ridden infantile ego that we never completely outgrow," and as the "root cause of neurosis."[60] Here Guntrip makes his application of Fairbairn's notion of the *moral defense* again, and in doing so, makes his most fundamental psychological *and theological* statement.

---

[58] Ibid., 124.

[59] Ibid., 124–25.

[60] Ibid., 125.

Antisocial drives are a defense against basic dependency, a kind of *reaction formation* against a core sense of *weakness*. He goes so far as to say that this is "the real basis of psychodynamic theory, for human beings would rather see themselves as bad than weak."[61] Guntrip illustrates this further in the cultural bias, (including that of psychoanalysis, by the way), of valuing obsessiveness over hysteria. This is a direct parallel to valuing the *classic vision* of psychoanalysis over the *romantic* one. "Obsessionals get more respect than hysterics. Obsessionals are thought to be mastering bad impulses, while hysterics are held to be only trying to find someone to cling to in their weakness. . . . But it is hysteria that takes us closer to the fundamental problem."[62] *Ego weakness,* thereby, becomes the centerpiece of Guntrip's psychoanalytic psychology and his theological philosophy.

Guntrip's theological thread resurfaces in his next chapter, V, "The Clinical Diagnostic Framework," originally published as the article, "The Manic-Depressive Problem in the Light of the Schizoid Process."[63] Referring to Freud's use of "the traditional theory of human nature" of "conflicts arising from the need to control bad impulses rooted in 'the flesh,'" Guntrip here alludes to the theology of "St. Paul" that he referenced earlier. He draws a historical line for Freud's approach starting all the way back at Charcot in the 1890s, simply characterized as "natural instincts versus social controls." An important juncture came in 1920 where an "increasing range of facts" pressed Freud to consider other points of view. Guntrip does not identify what these "facts" would be, but in light of Gay's picture of historical influences on Freud, this would at least be the profound effect of the carnage of the First World War, with the concomitant losses to Freud of his own children, including his daughter Sophie to influenza. The traditional view was "the pre-scientific philosophical and religious psychology of Greece and Palestine, and [this] had always been the universal common-sense view, as indeed it is today. The ancient Persian Zoroastrians thought of a warfare between matter as evil and mind as good."[64] Guntrip then gives a reprise of his earlier reference to the Platonic simile of men looking like human beings on the outside, but concealing three creatures inside: a many headed monster with various dispositions; the spirited lion, and the rational human being. Plato's admonition was

---

[61] Ibid., 125–26.

[62] Ibid., 126.

[63] Guntrip, "The Manic-Depressive Problem in the Light of the Schizoid Process," *International Journal of Psycho-Analyis* 43 (1962) 98–112.

[64] Guntrip, *Schizoid Phenomena,* 132.

to make man supreme, and with the help of the lion, to control the many headed beast. This decade of the 1920s was the development of Freud's tripartite structural model: *monster, man,* and *lion,* which is embodied in his *id, ego* and *superego.* Guntrip will then go on to cite the long standing tradition of Pauline theology as being read as Platonic.

> St. Paul's doctrine of unceasing warfare between the flesh and the spirit, the law of the members and the law of the mind, the Platonic simile, and the traditional trichotomy of body, mind, and spirit, all represent the same diagnosis of the human predicament. As a first hypothetical basis for his investigations Freud adopted this "theory" and gave it scientific dress.[65]

Guntrip's basic critique, again, is to locate this as representing concerns surrounding the *depressive position,* and not the core of neurosis. "*Mankind's universal preference [is] for feeling bad but strong rather than feeling weak and afraid. The 'depressive' diagnosis fixes our attention on our badness, the 'schizoid' diagnosis fixes it on our weakness.*"[66] He sees the Freudian tradition as both Platonic and Pauline.

> I do not think there is any real difference in principle here between Plato, St. Paul, and Freud. For all three, human nature is the scene of an unending internal strife and there is no real possibility of "cure", only of "compromise and relative stability" so long as man remains "in the flesh". The views of all three involve the underlying dualistic philosophy of body and mind, id and ego, as original, separate, and opposed entities.[67]

Following Macmurray, Guntrip notes how "official Christianity took the side of repression" in the task of managing the internal strife. Here Guntrip introduces his first biblical polarity as he refers to "the Gospels, the *later St. Paul,* (emphasis added), and the Johannine tradition" as having "wiser insights."[68] Guntrip credits Freud with taking the side of "easing repression and showing more toleration of instincts while strengthening the ego," yet then gives extensive examples from Freud's stoic and pessimistic *classical vision* of the "masses [who] are lazy and unintelligent: they have no love for instinctual renunciation."[69] He then illustrates how Freud himself

---

[65] Ibid.
[66] Ibid., 134.
[67] Ibid., 135.
[68] Ibid.
[69] Ibid., 136.

employs the reaction formation of substituting the *strength of badness* for the *basic ego weakness.*

> Nevertheless, though it seems to be proved beyond all doubt that we are very bad, since who dare gainsay such a trio as Plato, St. Paul, and Freud, we may console ourselves that we are not weak. We have a *mighty sexual instinct* (Freud, 1908) and *a powerful and destructive aggressive instinct* (Freud, 1927), . . . at least we can glorify aggression as heroism, and live like Sir Tristram and Sir Palomydes and others of King Arthur's knights who idealized the role of picking quarrels with all and sundry to prove what "mighty men of valour" they were.[70]

Guntrip then offers a clinical illustration to point to the weakness that underlies aggressive strength. A woman who felt "regarded by her family as inferior" and "was the perpetual butt of criticism of a very unstable mother" would often withdraw to the corner of the room in her family and came to be known as the "quiet one." In her late teens she had "a serious mental breakdown" which alarmed her parents. "Her father became sympathetic and devoted to her, her mother said she was mad. She would say: 'No, I'm not mad, I'm bad', because her most obvious symptom was her compulsion to curse God, her parents, her sisters and 'bad words and bad thoughts' . . . would be running in her head." Later, as Guntrip's adult patient, she recalled how she insisted on telling her parents these thoughts and that she knew that she was shocking them. "She felt proud of herself for being so daring, though she felt she could not stop it. The reason was clear when she said: 'I feel strong, powerful, when I was cursing and swearing. If I wasn't being bad, I could only shrink away into a corner and feel I was nobody.'"[71]

The Apostle Paul:
"Hebrew of Hebrews," or Hellenized Neo-Platonist?

So if the ultimately inadequate Platonic-Pauline viewpoint was the source of Freud's own metapsychologizing in terms of this Western cultural heritage, what did Guntrip mean by the *wiser insights* of the *later Paul?* First of all, we need to *exegete* the "St. Paul" to which Guntrip took exception. Alexander LeBreque has chronicled the traditional view of the Apostle Paul, author of most of the "letters" that make up the New Testament of

---

[70] Ibid., 137.
[71] Ibid., 137–38.

the Bible, as the *Diaspora* Jew of the first century AD (or CE, *the Common Era*, as is the nomenclature in scholarly theological circles). This Paul was influenced by the Greek or *Hellenic* culture of his native Tarsus of Cilicia in Asia Minor, so as to be considered a *neo-platonist.* This is Guntrip's viewpoint, one that is reflected in many if not most of the western theological circles of the modern era. The *Diaspora* Jews are those who centuries earlier were *dispersed* to live outside of Israel and Palestine by various historical events. The empire of Alexander the Great was to bring the *Hellenic* or Greek culture and philosophical systems to influence the vast area that Alexander conquered, including that of Paul of Tarsus, the St. Paul of Christian history. *Neo-platonism* is the philosophical system of dualism described by Guntrip that promotes the various dualisms and polarities of the mind and body that is split along the lines of the "evil or irrelevant" material body, and the "good" "spirit" or "mind" of the human being. This philosophy is well represented in the long history of monasticism and asceticism in Christian church history, which is typically attributed to the profound influence of the Platonic and other Greek philosophies. In this light, Pauline theology is read to reflect this dualism, where the terminology of "in the flesh," as referred to by Guntrip, is a pejorative devaluation, if not an all out rejection, of bodily existence, yearning for release from the Platonic "prison of the body." Indeed, Pauline theology is peppered with metaphors that lend themselves to this interpretation, such as "the body of sin and death," and "this earthly tent in which we live." (Romans, Chapter 7, in the New Testament of the Bible).

Yet the other tradition about Pauline theology is that Paul was in a literal sense a "Hebrew of Hebrews," meaning that he reflected that ancient near eastern philosophy and worldview: one characteristically that was holistic in outlook. One might characterize the western Greek worldview as *left brain*, traditionally reductionistic in the Aristotelian sense, categorical, and intellectual, lending itself to dualisms and trichotomies. The east is to the *right*, a spatial-visual apprehension of reality where even the languages are typically written right to left, opposite to the western traditions. In *starting on the right,* the Hebrew language and culture represented anthropology and psychology metaphorically, with bodily metaphors reflecting psychological states. In the west, one thinks with the head. For the Hebrew, the *heart* is the seat of the intellect, and decision making itself is more of an intuitive process than the logical, deductive emphasis of the Greek, Aristotelian, western mind. Even the concept of *soul*, which is the tripartite *mind, will and emotions* in the west, is translated as *life* in a much more whole-person sense for the Middle Eastern Hebrew.[72] The Hebrew language itself is characterized by *parallelism*, where words and concepts are used, in a sense, interchangeably, reflecting the *analogical* representational system of the right hemisphere of the brain, where also the unconscious process of dream states has been postulated to live.[73] I think that it is no accident that psychoanalysis itself was invented by one who grew up within this whole tradition, and had probably studied Hebrew himself, according to Meissner's account of Freud's childhood. The capacity to be a psychoanalyst ultimately requires one to listen to the patient's unconscious with one's own, which is argued by Alan Schore[74] to be significantly represented in the right hemisphere of the brain where one finds "psychoanalysis's right mind."[75]

So, had Paul of Tarsus become *Hellenized* and thereby reflected the dualism rejected by Guntrip? Alexander LeBreque argues for Paul's intact Hebrew worldview, and cites Augustine, the famous fourth century theologian who is unarguably the most influential voice in the western Christian tradition, as the *neo-platonist* who is responsible for our mind-body dualism. In fact, LeBreque characterizes him as not even a *neo-platonist* Christian, but a Christian *neo-platonist,* an emphasis that reflects the same thinking of Ellul, Macmurray, and Guntrip himself, that the western tradition has compromised the original (object) relational heart of the movement.[76] A study of the word that Guntrip often referenced, "in the flesh," also looks very different when seen from the right side of the brain rather than the left. The Greek word in question, (the language in which Paul wrote his New Testament letters), *sarx,*[77] or "flesh," rather than being seen in the Platonic dualism of the meaningless if not evil body, can be seen in the Hebrew sense of "muscle" where the notion is to operate solely from one's own strength. Viewed in this way, Paul is aligning himself both with Fairbairn's language of growing into "mature dependence" rather than an impoverished independence, as well as Guntrip's frequent

---

[72] Hans Walter Wolff, *Anthropology of the Old Testament,* trans. Margaret Kohl (Philadelphia: Fortress, 1974) 17.

[73] Allan N. Schore, *Affect Regulation and the Origin of the Self: The Neurobiology of Emotional Development* (New York: Erlbaum, 1994).

[74] Schore, *Affect Regulation and the Repair of the Self* (New York: Norton, 2003) 207–14.

[75] Ibid., 208.

[76] Alexander LeBreque, "The Cross in Perspective," *Evangelica* 7 (1987) 4.

[77] Walter Bauer et al., *A Greek-English Lexicon of the New Testament and Other Early Christian Literature,* 3d ed., revised by Frederick W. Danker (Chicago: University of Chicago, 2000).

refrain of the impossibility of living as an isolated individual, out of one's own "strength," which is the schizoid situation itself. Indeed, this is a central tenet of Pauline theology as represented in Paul's classic metaphor of the Christian church as the "body" of Christ, where "the eye cannot say to the hand, I have no need of you." The interdependency described by both Fairbairn and Guntrip as one of the hallmarks of healthy object relationships is the central theme throughout the Pauline corpus. I would offer, therefore, that Guntrip need not *split* Paul into one with a pathological model on the one hand, and a "latter one" with "wiser insights" on the other, resulting in a theological polarity.

The *wiser* Paul that Guntrip alluded to was the one who actually penned Guntrip's central metapsychological construction: the *weak ego* as the core self to be embraced and integrated by each person. This is drawn from Paul's account of his own physical ailment that he "prayed three times" to be removed, but was still left with his "thorn in the flesh."

> Three times I pleaded with the Lord to take it away from me. But he said to me, "My grace is made perfect in weakness." Therefore I will boast all the more gladly about my weaknesses, so that Christ's power may rest on me. That is why, for Christ's sake, I delight in weaknesses, in insults, in hardships, in persecutions, in difficulties. For when I am weak, then I am strong (2 Corinthians 12:8–10 in the New Testament).

This is paradoxical thinking of which Winnicott would be proud, where the last line is similar to the statement that Winnicott made about himself: "I want to be alive when I die."[78] One can add to the interpretation of this statement by Paul the notion that when he refers to Christ, he is not limiting himself to a personal devotional prayer life, but refers to the interpersonal and object relational church community, captured in the Pauline metaphor: the *body of Christ*. The masochistic tone of *delighting* in "weaknesses and insults" would certainly make Paul look like the self-deprecating dualist that most think him to be. Yet if giving up a defensively oriented sense of *strength* allows one to enter into what Guntrip will develop as the central therapeutic road for the schizoid state, *regression to dependence*, Guntrip himself could see these words of Paul as embracing one's weak ego and vulnerability, rather than as an expression of asceticism.

---

[78] Dodi Goldman, *In Search of The Real: The Origins and Originality of D. W. Winnicott.* (New York: Aronson, 1993).

Four chapters of Guntrip's *Schizoid Phenomena* book (chapters 6–9) carry the heading of "The Nature of Basic Ego Weakness." Over and over he describes the strong resistance to "admitting and facing 'basic ego weakness rooted in fear' that all human beings show both in social life and as patients, which is reflected in the slowness with which psychiatric and psychoanalytic research has come to face this problem. It may be that we ourselves would rather not be forced to see it too clearly lest we should find a text-book in our own hearts."[79] Praying to have "thorns in the flesh" removed lest we experience such weakness is not given up easily.

What are we to say, then, of Guntrip's grand scheme in light of his apparent disappointment of not having attained such an experience in his psychoanalytic experience with Fairbairn? Hazell pointed to the observable influence of Winnicott on Guntrip's interpersonal functioning, yet to a limited degree. What are we to make of Guntrip's assertion that the ultimate effect of his time with Winnicott was his breakthrough series of dreams about his mother? Had he reached a "regression to dependence" with Winnicott and thereby achieved the liberation and embrace of his own *weak ego*? Theologically, had he therefore achieved a personal liberation from living in the isolation of his depending upon "knowing good and evil" with his intellect, and not knowing others in a personal way? I will now take up these questions along with the task of proposing a Winnicottian paradoxical model of integration for psychoanalysis and theology.

---

[79] Guntrip, *Schizoid Phenomena*, 178.

9

Paradox

The Integration of Polarities

Freud has constructed a quasi-neurophysiological explanatory system which never departed in its foundations from the pre-conceptions of the "Project for a Scientific Psychology." Melanie Klein constructed a quasi-theological system in which internal objects have the significance of deity. Bion has constructed a quasi-philosophical system where thought sits amazed in Plato's cave, straining itself to apprehend the noumena of the world.

—Donald Meltzer (1978)

IN this study I have traced the development of a number of polarities within the history of the psychoanalytic tradition. This includes the larger psychoanalytic movement itself, the British *Independent* tradition, the metapsychology of object relations theory, as well as the personal lives of the principal contributors to the development of the thought of Harry Guntrip. In this final chapter I shall: (1) summarize the essential influences of Guntrip's personal mentors; (2) describe Winnicott's paradoxical paradigm that serves as a model for the integration of psychology and theology; and (3) examine Guntrip's analysis with Winnicott in terms of the degree to which he achieved a therapeutic integration within himself. I will analyze the degree to which he accomplished the clinical goal of his own theory: entering into a regression to dependence upon the analyst in order to embrace and integrate one's own *weak ego*.

Guntrip's Internalizations and Identifications with Macmurray, Fairbairn, and Winnicott

John Macmurray: Theoretical Influences

Philosopher John Macmurray was the most foundational figure for Guntrip in emphasizing the *personal* as his philosophical presupposition in developing psychoanalytic metapsychology. Macmurray essentially constructed an object relations theory within moral philosophy. This training prepared Guntrip to adopt Fairbairn as the psychoanalytic theorist who most appealed to him. Guntrip eventually even used this catch-phrase of the *personal* to critique Fairbairn's continuation of the use of the classic psychoanalytic nomenclature of *object,* preferring *personal relations* over the term *object relations.*

Macmurray critiqued the western philosophical tradition essentially as a *schizoid landscape,* where the concept of *reason* had been reduced to *a state of mind which is cold, detached and unemotional,* as well as individualistic or *ego-centric.* Macmurray's alternative was the concept of "emotional reason," which is the "capacity to behave in terms of the nature of the object, that is to say, objectively."[1] He describes the central problem of those living out western culture as the tendency toward ego-centrism, which prefers the illusion of self-sufficiency over the painful awareness of one's need for connectedness to the outside world. "Against the assumption that the Self is an isolated individual, I have set the view that the Self is a *person,* and that personal existence is *constituted* by the relation of persons."[2] This theoretical and philosophical model spoke directly to Guntrip as I believe that it reverberated within his own schizoid existence of emotional detachment and interpersonal isolation.

John Macmurray: Object Relational Impact

Macmurray was Guntrip's professor while an undergraduate at London University. This came at a time of Guntrip's transition from the fundamentalism of his Salvation Army days, punctuated by his resignation from this career track in protest of the "mismanagement of persons" by the Salvation Army leadership. This protest was supported and celebrated by his mentor in this area, his father Henry, who wholeheartedly encouraged his "taking a stand." Macmurray can be seen as akin to Guntrip's paternal introject, a

[1] John Macmurray, *Reason and Emotion* (London: Faber & Faber, 1935) 16, 19.

[2] Macmurray, *The Self as Agent* (New York: Harper & Brothers, 1953) 12.

libidinal object who offers the hope and promise of emotional connection, yet one, which for Guntrip, had not progressed beyond the level of a *taste,* which although compelling, was not sufficient enough to be satiating. His father Henry modeled brazen critiques of the status quo in church matters as Macmurray did in philosophy. Yet Harry's depressed and withdrawn *libidinal ego* can be seen in relation to the insufficiency of his *libidinal object* attachment, manifest in his father's ultimate withdrawal and deferral to the *antilibidinal object* of the Guntrip family system, Harry's mother, Harriet.

Ronald Fairbairn: Theoretical Impact

I propose that Fairbairn's key concept was to define libidinal drive in the service of seeking attachment to the object, a fundamental shift from the classical notion of drives seeking tension reduction. For Guntrip this would clearly echo Macmurray's emphasis on a relationally defined self rather than of the adaptation of the individual organism. On the grand theoretical scale, Guntrip would then construct his Hegelian dialectical model of Fairbairn's Object Relations theory as the theoretical synthesis between Freudian drive theory and American interpersonal-behavioral psychology, linking the inside with the outside of the person. On the micro theoretical scale he would take up Fairbairn's concept of *schizoid* as the most foundational psychological issue to be addressed, the pathological version of the capacity for attachment. To this paradigm Guntrip would add his own contribution of the concept of the *weak* or *regressed ego*. This is formed by a secondary split within the *libidinal ego* that is completely withdrawn from contact with the object world. This *weak ego* is akin to Winnicott's *unknowable self,* yet is presented as *reachable* according to Guntrip.

Ronald Fairbairn: Object Relations Impact

Guntrip chronicled the ongoing *split in his affections* for Fairbairn: agreeing with and elaborating on Fairbairn's theoretical developments, yet taking him to task for offering oedipal interpretations and conducting his analysis in a stiff and formal style. Guntrip commented on the split that he experienced in the difference between Fairbairn offering such interpretations sitting behind his desk, and the more personal interaction on walks together *after the session.* Hazell points clearly to the parallel and projective process that Guntrip employed as seen in Guntrip's own formal and rigid psychoanalytic style. I would describe this as an identification between the two where both Fairbairn and Guntrip employed a schizoid adaptation to their personal worlds. In this area Guntrip saw and experienced with Fairbairn what he could not see and hated in himself.

Donald Winnicott: Theoretical Impact

I would argue that *regression to dependence* is the most central Winnicottian concept to influence Guntrip. Guntrip's emphasis on schizoid phenomena as foundational and *beneath* the *depressive* dynamics that he associates with classical psychoanalysis points to the need for a deep regressive experience in order to ultimately resolve the *schizoid dilemma*. This dilemma is the person's approach-avoidance stalemate in regards to the duality of the desire for, and the fear of, experiencing an intimate attachment to another. The recovery of the *regressed ego* is Guntrip's response to Winnicott's notion that there exists in every person a core True Self that is unreachable and unknowable. Guntrip uses the *regression to dependence* concept is in the service of this *mission impossible:* recovery and integration of the repressed and withdrawn *weak ego*. Guntrip essentially argues that this "lost sheep" of the ego can "be found," as it *does belong* within the life of an interpersonal relationship.

Donald Winnicott: Object Relations Impact

Guntrip gave Winnicott much higher marks in his analysis with him than he did Fairbairn, yet at times, he still critiqued Winnicott as not being "object relational enough." Guntrip ultimately cast Winnicott as a paradoxical introject, a maternal object whose effect was in essence manifest upon the loss of the external maternal object in Winnicott's actual death, the catalyst that set into motion the series of dreams that Guntrip cites as the breakthrough in his analysis with Winnicott.

Guntrip as a Polarity in Search of a Paradox

I would offer at this point that Winnicott's paradoxical bent is a dynamic thread that runs through Guntrip's work as he was significantly influenced by Winnicott theoretically in conjunction with his personal experience with him. Yet Guntrip, both psychologically and theologically, seems to lean more strongly toward the *romantic* side of the coin, as noted above in his rather wholesale rejection of instinctual, or perhaps better put, temperamental sources of psychic conflict. As Markillie described him, Guntrip never met a bad object that he did not like-to-hate as an *antilibidinal object,* yet I think Guntrip fell short in identifying the *antilibidinal ego* of his own identifications with his mother, although not to the degree of neglect attributed by his detractors.

Guntrip's Integration of Religion and Psychoanalysis

Theologically, Guntrip has essentially adopted the human interpersonal relationship, in the tradition of Macmurray, as the place where religion is best understood.

> I take *"religion"* not as theological doctrine, nor as an intellectual activity, or an organization; . . . I take it as *an overall way of experiencing life, of integration or self-realization through communion with all that is around us, and finally our way of relating to the universe, the total reality, which has, after all, evolved us with the intelligence and motivation to explore this problem: all that is meant by "experience of God."*[3]

Guntrip's *personal relations factor*, rather than being limited to *infantile dependence* in the classic stage-dependent model, Guntrip sees as *the essential permanent factor in our existence at every stage of life, and is itself undergoing a process of maturing that is central to all our development as persons.*[4] A sense of "dependence upon God" is implicitly manifest in human object relationships *not only* as infantile dependence, but also as a lifelong *mature dependence*, echoing Fairbairn.

Illusion and Its Future:
Winnicott's "Area of Faith" as Transitional Object

Meissner traces this dynamic as it is played out in the traditional polarity of *psychoanalysis versus religion* in his treatment of Winnicott's notion of transitional phenomena and the transitional object. After reintroducing Freud's *classic* repudiation of illusion, and along with it, religion, Meissner presents an extended study on *Religion as Transitional*. Indeed, he describes a shift of attitude within psychoanalysis that not only has found a place for illusion but has defined it as a powerful and necessary force in human psychic development and in the continuing nourishment and health of the human spirit as well.[5]

---

[3] Jeremy Hazell, ed., *Personal Relations Therapy: The Collected Papers of H.J.S. Guntrip* (Northvale, NJ: Aronson, 1994) 275.

[4] Ibid., 274.

[5] W. W. Meissner, *Psychoanalysis and Religious Experience* (New Haven: Yale University Press, 1984) 164.

Meissner describes Winnicott's notion of the child's early use of transitional objects, beginning with the fist, fingers or thumb to stimulate the mouth and to bring satisfaction. In just a few months, the infant begins to play with some special object to which it becomes attached, even addicted, in a peculiarly intense manner.[6] This phenomenon is thought by Winnicott to spring from the earliest mother-infant interaction which reflects his notion of *undifferentiated unity* between them. This *dual participation* is where the good enough mother provides a sense of *going on being*, preserving the infant's sense of continuity in his existence. Such a mother's empathic ability to meet the baby's emerging need and to harmonize with his biological rhythms becomes crucial for achieving this function.[7] The mother's capacity for holding in this way promotes a sense of basic trust that is so lacking in Guntrip's *schizoid state.* The various aspects of the transitional process, beginning with the use of the hand for self-pacification, are seen as the first step in separation from this maternal matrix. Borrowing from the Kleinian tradition, Winnicott identifies the infant's hand as the substitute for the mother's breast in particular, and transitional objects for the mother's body in general. A variety of transitional objects are chosen, from the blanket made famous by Linus from the cartoon strip, Peanuts, to the proverbial teddy bear. The object provides a soothing purpose that builds a defense against anxiety connected with the loss of the mothering figure. The adopted object becomes of crucial importance and must be available at all times.[8]

The *intermediate area* that Winnicott calls "experiencing" is the bridge between the intrapsychic world of phantasy of the Kleinian tradition and the interpersonal and external world that must be "adapted to" as portrayed by Ego Psychology. Winnicott himself describes it as an area that is not challenged, because no claim is made on its behalf except that it shall exist as a resting-place for the individual engaged in the perpetual human task of keeping inner and outer reality separate, yet interrelated.[9] This is a break with the Freudian and Kleinian *classical* tradition that most definitely *challenges* such *illusions* as infantile, defensive, and ultimately pathological. Winnicott goes on to argue for the capacity of illusion as necessary for normal human psychological development and functioning.

---

[6] Ibid., 165.

[7] Ibid.

[8] Ibid.

[9] Ibid., 166.

It is usual to refer to reality testing, and to make a clear distinction between apperception and perception. I am staking a claim for an intermediate state between a baby's ability and his growing ability to recognize and accept reality. I am therefore studying the substance of *illusion*, that which is allowed to the infant, and which in adult life is inherent in art and religion, and yet becomes the hallmark of madness when an adult puts too powerful a claim on the credulity of others, forcing them to acknowledge a sharing of illusion that is not their own. We can share a respect for *illusory experience*, and if we wish we may collect together and form a group on the basis of the similarity of our illusory experience. This is a natural root of grouping among human beings.[10]

Winnicott is citing the normative nature of illusion in the human enterprise, an *allusion* to the fact that each group within the British Psychoanalytic Society each had their own respective "primary illusion" of omnipotence in regard to their particular view of things. The child's (and psychoanalyst's) illusion of magical control over satisfying objects is necessary not only for the capacity to do more than *test* reality in the stoic sense, but to learn to *love* reality. This is the basis of which Goldman spoke in reference to Winnicott's emphasis on "feeling real," rather than just performing mechanical ego functioning.

Disillusionment is the natural development within the infant when the "primarily preoccupied mother," whose swift responses to the infant help foster the capacity for illusory omnipotence, begins to slow over time. This provides the "optimal frustration" that is the counterbalance to the illusory control through fantasy, making the object real in a concrete sense.

An essential part of Winnicott's view is that the dialectic and tension between illusion and disillusionment plays itself out through the whole of human experience and human life. The task of coming to know and accept reality is never fully completed. No human being is ever free from the tension of relating inner to outer reality. Further, relief from this unending tension is gained only in the intermediate area of illusory experience, which even in the life of the adult remains unchallenged, as in the arts and religion, for example.[11]

Meissner then develops Winnicott's own notion of religion as transitional phenomena.

---

10 Ibid., 166–67.
11 Ibid., 168.

The faith experience has a number of attributes that characterize it as a form of transitional experience. The believer does not regard his faith as a matter of wishful hallucination or of purely subjective implications. Rather, his faith speaks to him of the nature of the world in which he lives, of the meaning and purpose of his existence there, and, in most religious traditions, of the relationship of that world and himself to a divine being who creates, loves, guides, and judges. At the same time that faith asserts, however, it cannot demonstrate the independent reality of the spiritual world and to which it lays claim. Consequently, the experience of faith is not totally subjective, nor is it totally objective. Rather, it represents a realm in which the subjective and the objective interpenetrate.[12]

God as Transitional Object

The concept of the figure, or representation of God, as a transitional object is developed in the work of Rizzuto (1979) based upon the clinical study of her patients. Her conclusion is that the child creates God as a special kind of object representation in the intermediate psychic space, neither a hallucination, nor beyond the reach of subjectivity, but, in Winnicott's terms, "outside, inside," and "at the border."[13] God, as a special order of transitional object, does not gradually decathect and become forgotten or relegated to psychic limbo, but is even intensified by the oedipal experience. Essentially, Meissner describes the God representation as going from the status of *transitional object* to that of *transitional phenomena*, where it reflects the ongoing process of exchange that develops in relation to the individuals evolving self-representation (p. 180).

I would interpret Meissner's thesis here as reflecting the developmental dynamics of the facilitation of one's *self-representation* through the interaction with the caretaker, with God being a special case of caretaking. The question in regards to Guntrip is determining the location of the presence of God which he argues is within the *personal relations factor.* It is said of his mentor, Macmurray, that after rejecting his own childhood fundamentalism and then adopting Marxism for many years, that he eventually looked to the Quaker concept of God as *Friend* as the one which captured his own theological perspective.[14] Guntrip, in the process, seemingly has abandoned theological doctrine as an approach to organizing his own the-

---

[12] Ibid., 178.

[13] Ibid., 179.

[14] Ray S. Anderson, *Historical Transcendence and the Reality of God: A Christological Critique* (Grand Rapids: Eerdmans, 1975) 205.

ology, and my own thesis is that he has instead expressed it as the *internal theological object* within his object relations theorizing.

Kierkegaardian Paradox as the Key to Integration

Rather than rely upon Strenger's proposal that the dialectical spectrum from *romantic* to *classical* viewpoints is one upon which an analyst moves back and forth, I would propose that *paradox* in the Kierkegaardian spirit of Winnicott himself is a more helpful integrative position. The Hegelian dialectic (employed by Guntrip) between *thesis* and *antithesis* that reduces itself into a *synthesis,* ultimately falls prey to intellectual abstraction, and hence retreats from the experience of *being there* in a fully integrated sense of being a person-in-relationship. The Kierkegaardian notion of paradox is that of entering into a situation *without knowing what will happen and without being able even to predict the outcome.* This is the classic "leap of faith" coined by Kierkegaard, a very Winnicottian notion. This, I will argue, is the missing piece from Guntrip's analytic experience where he ultimately was never able to give up the control of "knowing," and thereby enter into a regression to dependence *on* Winnicott at this paradoxical level.

Guntrip's concept of the *weak ego* is the one who needs *holding* rather than knowing, and who must take this *leap of faith* in order to be "baptized in analysis," Markillie's metaphor for "dependent immersion" into the experience.

The Development of Guntrip's Capacity for Weakness in Winnicott's Faith Paradigm

As described in chapter 8, Guntrip identifies the capacity to embrace one's own weakness as the necessary condition to experience the "grace" of dependency within a growth facilitating object relationship. Following Winnicott, the "dual unity" of this relationship facilitates the development of one's illusory (omni)potency that is the basis for the development of the capacity for basic trust in the world of others, as well as in oneself. When experienced with the "good enough" caretaker, the ensuing stage of "disillusionment" that accompanies such a relationship develops an ego boundary that allows the person to differentiate his "inside" from his "outside." The net result is the development of the ongoing *capacity for illusion,* or imagination, and therefore a relationally generated *faith* that moves (if not leaps) into the "unknown." This mature openness to new experience is the quality that the schizoid person needs so desperately. The "God" who facilitates such discovery of feeling "really" alive is manifest in this caretaker relationship.

Winnicott was confronted with Guntrip's own *schizoid problem* of living within his internal, intellectually omnipotent, illusory world as a defense against interpersonal intimacy. The final focus of this study is to examine the degree to which Guntrip himself achieved a resolution of his own schizoid defensive structure. To what extent was Guntrip able to experience his own "grace made perfect in weakness" through the theo-psychoanalytic experience with Winnicott?

How Complete a Result Does Psycho-analytic Therapy Achieve?

Guntrip entitled his account of his analyses with both Fairbairn and Winnicott with this question. He identified his time in analysis with Winnicott as the catalyst that facilitated the evocation of his dream series. Here he identified his mother as "faceless and without arms," the picture of a failure of attachment in the most fundamental sense. This breakdown around the developmental stage of Fairbairn's "love made hungry" is the psychic experience of one's very hunger for connection as destructive to the other and thereby dangerous for one's own survival. If I "devour" my love object, then I am utterly alone. I am left with a sense of being defective at my core, where my essential self is unlovable. The symptomatic portrayal of this can be seen throughout Guntrip's entire life. His "exhaustion illness" is reenacted over and over again as representative of the psychic collapse of his core self.

Evocation of Dreams of the Unattachable Mother: Triumph or Tragedy?

The central issue that pertains to this particular influence of Winnicott on Guntrip was that it was precipitated by news of Winnicott's actual death, the loss of the one to whom Guntrip attributed a true psychoanalytic maternal holding of himself. The crucial question is whether, on the one hand, his loss of Winnicott's living presence was a necessary condition of the evocation of his repressed self in relationship with a mother who could not emotionally hold him and in whose face he could not see his own reflection. On the other, was this evidence of the intractability of his schizoid defensive structure to the point that he could not allow such a *return of the repressed* while *in a relationship of dependence upon Winnicott in the flesh?*

I propose that the *triumph* of Guntrip's breakthrough of dreams was paradoxical in nature, and a tragic paradox at that. Guntrip told of how Winnicott in his own way had made contact with the proverbial "baby" part of his unconscious, due to *"Winnicott's profound intuitive insights into the very infancy period I so needed to get down to"*[15] (emphasis in the original). He described the impasse that he reached in his analysis with Fairbairn as the "dilemma of not being able either to end analysis or go on with it, once my analyst (Fairbairn) became Percy in the transference. Ending would be equivalent to Percy dying and I would have no one to help me with the aftermath. If I did not end it, I would be using my analyst to prevent the eruption of the trauma and so get no help with it, and risk his dying on me."[16] Guntrip credits Winnicott with altering "the whole nature of the problem by enabling me to reach right back to *an ultimate good mother, and to find her recreated in him in the transference.* I discovered later that he had put me in a position to face what was a double trauma of both Percy's death and mother's failing me"[17] (emphasis in the original).

Guntrip essentially describes Winnicott *not* as the good object *replacement* for his unattachable mother, but as the connection with an initial period where his mother's "natural maternalism" made a rudimentary attachment to him "before her personality problems robbed [him] of that 'good mother.'"[18] Without such an attachment, both Fairbairn and Winnicott doubted that Guntrip would have actually survived at all. This is what I have called the "paradoxical introject" that Winnicott became for Guntrip, one that "put [him] in the position to face" the loss not only of his brother Percy, but of a mother who could hold him.

The tragedy, I propose, is that the paradoxical twist around his "finding" this armless and faceless mother is that it was evoked by the loss of Winnicott. "If you want to find your life, then you must lose it" is the paradoxical parable of the Christian tradition. From an object relations standpoint, if Guntrip's tie to Winnicott was through his *non-regressed libidinal ego*, then to facilitate the recovery of his *regressed libidinal ego* which was completely cut off in concert with the "armless and faceless mother," this libidinal tie must die. This is an object relational representation of the clas-

---

[15] Hazell, ed., *Personal Relations Therapy*, 361.

[16] Ibid.

[17] Ibid.

[18] Ibid.

sic "death and resurrection" theme of the Christian theological tradition of Jesus "descending into Hell to minister to imprisoned spirits." The tragic outcome, however, was the enactment of what Guntrip had feared about ending with Fairbairn, that he would "have no one to help [him] with the aftermath." I see this as the triumph of the schizoid defense.

The Schizoid Compromise: Guntrip "Half-in" with Winnicott, Yet Still "Half-out"

In concert with the various critiques of Guntrip's account of his analyses with both Fairbairn and Winnicott, it appears that Guntrip successfully defended *against* experiencing what he had argued *for* throughout his writings: a truly dependent relationship upon another human being. Only with a dead Winnicott could he have his breakthrough about his "faceless mother without arms" who was unable to emotionally hold him. Guntrip appears to have triumphed in the schizoid defense of keeping emotional distance from the experience of *human weakness within a human relationship,* which was his theoretical clinical goal. Whether seen as the uninterpreted negative transference, as do Glazner and Evans, or as the narcissistic self-preoccupation of the schizoid, as described by Markillie, Guntrip tragically never reached the clinical experience of *weakness* for which he argued so strongly. I would conceptualize this as the *schizoid avoidance of the paradox of weakness*: entering into an existential experience without knowing its outcome; the Kierkegaardian "leap of faith."

The net effect of Guntrip's experience of analysis is that he retained "knowing" as belonging to himself, reserving the interpretation of his "breakthrough" dreams to himself, as if he dare not dream this while still in a living relationship with Winnicott. Perhaps it was only with a "dead" mother that this piece of dreamwork could emerge. Apparently the only other opportunity that Guntrip had for making a desirable emotional connection with his mother was on the occasion of his father's death.

> The medical specialist told them that there was nothing to be done and that he expected Henry to live for about a week. At that moment Harriet lost control and began to cry, and Harry moved to comfort her. Before he could do so, however, the specialist said, "Sit down. Your mother will control herself." Overawed by the gravity of the situation, Harry obeyed. But he was later greatly to regret having lost this opportunity of crossing the emotional barrier between himself and his mother—the one occasion when a deeper personal relationship might have grown between them.

Harriet never revealed her need again, even on the day Henry died, exactly a week later.[19]

Harry's *antilibidinal ego* also never allowed revealing *his need* again, tragically illustrated in the "medical specialist" *antilibidinal object* who had no place for such affectations of *weakness*. This "specialist" guarded against the danger of inevitable rejection in the form of the *libidinal object's* tantalizing offer of closeness that is expected to vanish into thin air. He was never able to "cross the emotional barrier" between himself and his psychoanalytic mother as well, as if his *antilibidinal self* told him to "sit down" each time before he would "lie down" on the analyst's couch.

This is where I would propose that Guntrip too strongly defended against the *classical* tradition of psychoanalysis: to be able to regress and depend upon the analyst who *can* know something that the analysand does not, and *depends* upon the analyst to provide for the patient/child. This would not necessarily have to be in the form of a verbal interpretation on the part of the analyst, as in what might be called *classical* technique, but nevertheless would be a process of becoming aware *within* the experience of the dependent relationship. The dead Winnicott could not be *existentially* present as the *holding mother* who would provide an object relational situation within which Guntrip could experience and explore what *romantically* would be seen as his attachment deficit *with* his own mother. This would fit within the *romantic* view of such a situation without the need even to postulate uninterpreted hostility on Guntrip's part. I would argue that Guntrip was unable to avail himself of even such paradoxical knowing, one that reflects the Hebrew sense of *yada,* the intimacy of "being inside of another person." This is the right-brain, sexual knowing where "Adam knew Eve and she conceived." *Essentially Guntrip's psychoanalytic mother died in childbirth and he remained an orphan.*

Michael Polanyi, best known for his work on the paradigm shifts in the history of the philosophy of science, has presented this same notion that we ultimately *know* more than we can explain (1958). This knowing, therefore, is the Kierkegaardian existential knowing without prior cognitive insight; an insight which, if at all, can be gained upon reflection *after* having entered into the event. Psychoanalytically speaking, this would refer to an approach of allowing the transference with the patient to evolve and grow without premature cognitization of it.

---

[19] Jeremy Hazell, *H.J.S. Guntrip: A Psychoanalytic Biography* (London: Free Association Books, 1996) 22.

The other dimension of the *classical view* that I would argue is defended against is Guntrip's unintegrated maternal introject, his physically violent and abusive mother. As represented above in Fairbairn's own biography, the capacity to be *pissed off* was the unintegrated personal hostility that lived within Fairbairn's own hysterical symptom. Guntrip's entire life history is characterized by his own hysterical adaptation in his exhaustion illness which was evoked directly in response to events regarding his mother. Harry's response to the repeated reminders of her lack of capacity emotionally to hold him was this chronic manifestation of his ego collapse. He never progressed to the point of appreciably focusing any of his hostility toward her in *direct protest within* his relationship with her.

Instead, Guntrip focused the lion's share of his own hostility in theoretical dueling with both Heinz Hartmann and Hans Eysenck. I would suggest that they are representatives of the "medical specialist" whose mechanistic approach reflects his internal *antilibidinal object* that tells him to "sit down" and restrain his desire to embrace his mother. Guntrip made the *classical* Freudian tradition his *antilibidinal object* of concern, yet he does not identify his own *antilibidinal ego* that would be in ongoing relationship with it. Guntrip's *classical* critics, Glazner et al., have a point to be made, yet not in the simple instinctual notion of unintegrated or unmodulated aggression, but in the object relational scheme of hostility in the service of protection against the expected abandonment in an intimate, and therefore vulnerable relationship. This is the sentry function of the *antilibidinal ego*, the *internal saboteur*, who guards against such abandonment by the *libidinal object*.

A way to conceptualize this intellectualized version of aggression as reflected in Guntrip's theoretical wrangling is that it lives within Fairbairn's *central ego:* intellectual arguments and abstract concepts. (See Figure 4). I would suggest that this is where Guntrip organized and contained his own aggression: within schizoid intellectual abstraction. Again, in contrast to the classic critique by Glatzer, et al., Guntrip's lack of integration of this aggression, I would argue, is a later developmental failure of the capacity to protest. As Guntrip's sense of core self was already compromised, his inability to develop an integrated capacity to protest within the interpersonal relationship, anger with his mother (as well as his father) was split off and displaced into his intellectualizations. The message to be found in his hysterical symptom of exhaustion, in contrast to Fairbairn's inability to be *pissed off,* was the more foundational collapse of his ego itself. This is in direct line with Guntrip's own metapsychological formulation that the schizoid condition is prior to, and foundational for, the *depressive* concerns of aggression and its vicissitudes.

Guntrip's intellectualized protests within the area of psychological theory *never availed themselves* to the evocation of *an emotionally charged* negative transference experience with Winnicott. Guntrip never regressed *to the degree* that his corresponding sense of loss that lay *beneath* such an *emotional* protest would have allowed him to depend upon Winnicott to hold his collapsed, fragile and *weak ego*. This is the tragedy not only of Guntrip's analysis, but of his very life. It is tragically the evidence of the great strength of the schizoid defensive structure.

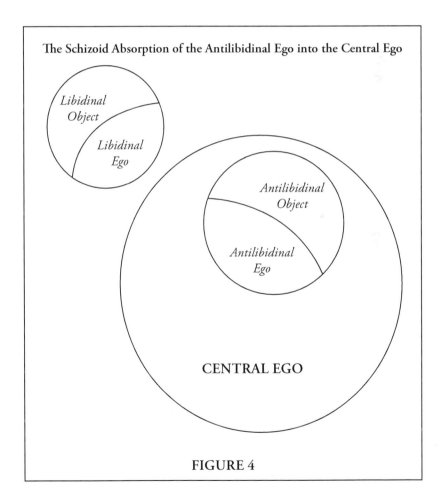

The Schizoid Absorption of the Antilibidinal Ego into the Central Ego

Libidinal Object

Libidinal Ego

Antilibidinal Object

Antilibidinal Ego

CENTRAL EGO

FIGURE 4

Reflections and Conclusions

In closing, what might we say about Harry S. Guntrip as a psychoanalyst and a theological philosopher?

Guntrip described the *schizoid phenomena* in intricate detail and with colorful clinical examples. He articulated a clear metapsychological model, following Fairbairn, of the internal world of psychic reality and how it makes sense of many clinical phenomena. He charted a course of psychoanalytic treatment that was characterized by the transference paradigm of Winnicott's notion of *regression to dependence* upon the analyst. He cited a central goal as the evocation of the patient's *regressed ego,* the *weak* self that ultimately must *come home* to relationships with others by embracing its own vulnerability. This was Guntrip's implicit *theology within* his psychoanalytic psychology. The experience of *grace* (embracing the *bad*), is made "perfect" (*telios:* Greek for "mature"), through the dependency of this *weakness.*

Guntrip's legacy to the psychoanalytic community was ultimately his autobiography of *schizoid phenomena,* punctuated with the literal autobiographical article about his analyses with Fairbairn and Winnicott. The nature of that self-disclosure has been controversial. The outcome for his own life, I propose, was the *paradox* of finding life by losing it, where his loss of Winnicott facilitated finding his unconscious, despairing *weak ego* in the presence of a faceless and armless mother. This, I believe, was also followed by the *schizoid tragedy* of being *alone* in his discovery of himself; essentially orphaned by the death of Winnicott. He was unable to go to another session with his "analytic mother" and share these dreams within the context of a living, dependent relationship. The question within Guntrip's title for his reflection on this experience, "How complete a result can psychoanalysis offer?" captions this picture of both triumph and tragedy.

Glossary

Classicalism. Aesthetic attitudes and principles manifested in the art, architecture, and literature of ancient Greece and Rome and characterized by emphasis on form, simplicity, proportion, and restraint.

Congregationalism. The system of government and religious beliefs of a Protestant denomination in which each member church is self-governing, such as the Congregational Church of England. The adult church affiliation of Harry S. Guntrip.

Deism. The belief, based solely on reason, in a God who created the universe and then abandoned it, assuming no control over life, exerting no influence on natural phenomena, and giving no supernatural revelation.

Demythologizing. An application of form criticism that employs a literary and rationalistic assumption that reported events which do not conform to the presuppositions of scientific materialism and are seen as "miraculous" are therefore mythical or fantasy creations that do not reflect, or distort, actual historical events.

Exegesis. An application of literary study where the meaning of a text is determined by grammatical and linguistic study.

Existentialism. A philosophy that emphasizes the uniqueness and isolation of the individual experience in a hostile or indifferent universe, regards human existence as unexplainable, and stresses freedom of choice and responsibility for the consequences of one's acts.

Form criticism. A method of textual analysis, applied especially to the Bible, for tracing the origin and history of certain passages through systematic study of the writings in terms of conventional literary forms, such as parables, proverbs, and love poems.

Hermeneutics. A literary study of a text that establishes its "meaning" based upon its exegetical, or, grammatical study, as well as upon the historical situation of the author, and the author's personal intent to communicate a certain message to a particular audience.

Methodism. An evangelical Protestant church founded on the principles of John and Charles Wesley in England in the early eighteenth century and characterized by active concern with social welfare and public morals. A revivalist tradition originating within the English state church of Anglicanism, emphasizing affective experience as a sign of spiritual renewal. The childhood church tradition of D. W. Winnicott.

Orthodoxy. Representative of non-revisable concepts and beliefs that are held as foundational to a belief system and worldview.

Presbyterian. The national church of Scotland reflecting the theological and psychological determinism of the Calvinistic tradition. The childhood church tradition of Ronald Fairbairn.

Projection. In the properly psycho-analytic sense: operation whereby qualities, feelings, wishes or even 'objects,' which the subject refuses to recognize or rejects in him or herself, are expelled from the self and located in another person or thing.

Projective Identification. Term introduced by Melanie Klein: a mechanism revealed in phantasies in which the subject inserts his self—in whole or in part—into the object (other person) in order to harm, possess, or control it.

Psychotherapy. In a broad sense, any method of treating psychic or somatic disorders which utilizes psychological means–or, more specifically, the therapist–patient relationship: hypnosis, suggestion, psychological re-education, persuasion, etc. In this sense psycho-analysis is a variety of psychotherapy.

Rationalism. The theory that the exercise of reason, rather than the acceptance of empiricism, authority, or spiritual revelation, provides the only valid basis for action or belief and that reason is the prime source of knowledge and of spiritual truth.

Regression. Applied to a psychical process, 'regression' means a return from a point already reached to an earlier one. In temporal terms, regression implies the existence of a genetic succession and denotes the subject's reversion to past phases of his/her development (libidinal stages, object-relationships, identifications, etc.).

Romanticism. An artistic and intellectual movement originating in Europe in the late eighteenth century and characterized by a heightened interest in nature, emphasis on the individual's expression of emotion and imagination, departure from the attitudes and forms of classicism, and rebellion against established social rules and conventions.

Sitz Im Leben. An aspect of the hermeneutical study of a text that establishes the historical "settings in life" of the author as well as the author's intended audience.

Splitting of the Object. Mechanism described by Melanie Klein and considered by her to be the most primitive kind of defense against anxiety: the object, with both erotic and destructive instincts directed towards it, splits into a 'good' and a 'bad' object.

Stoicism. A Greek school of philosophy, founded by Zeno about 308 B.C., believing that human beings should be free from passion and should calmly accept all occurrences as the unavoidable result of divine will or of the natural order.

Weltanschauung. The German word for "worldview," which constitutes the presuppositions of one's psychological, theological, and philosophical descriptions of reality. A comprehensive philosophy of the world or of human life.

Bibliography

American Psychiatric Association. *Diagnostic and Statistical Manual of Mental Disorders.* 4th ed. Washington, DC: APA Press, 1994.

Anderson, Ray S. *Historical Transcendence and the Reality of God: A Christological Critique.* Grand Rapids: Eerdmans, 1975.

Bacal, Howard A. and Newman, Kenneth M. *Theories of Object Relations: Bridges to Self Psychology.* New York: Columbia University Press, 1990.

Balint, Michael. *Primary Love and Psychoanalytic Technique.* London: Tavistock, 1965.

Bauer, Walter, et al. *A Greek-English Lexicon of the New Testament and Other Early Christian Literature.* 3d ed. Revised by Frederick W. Danker. Chicago: University of Chicago, 2000.

Bettelheim, Bruno. *Freud and Man's Soul.* New York: Vintage, 1984.

Bion, Wilfred. *Learning From Experience.* New York: Basic Books, 1962; Karnac, 1984.

Bollas, Christopher. *Winnicott Lectures* (Cassette Recording). Tustin, CA: Newport Psychoanalytic Institute, 1982.

Bonhoeffer, Dietrich. *Letters and Papers From Prison.* Edited by Eberhard Bethge. Translated by Reginald H. Fuller. New York: Macmillan, 1953.

———. *Creation and Fall.* Translated by John C. Fletcher. New York: Harper & Row, 1959.

———. *Life Together.* Translated by John W. Doberstein. New York: Harper & Row, 1954.

Bowlby, John. *Attachment and Loss.* 2d ed. New York: Basic Books, 1982.

Brandshaft, Bernard. "The Negativism of the Negative Therapeutic Reaction and the Psychology of the Self." In *The Future of Psychoanalysis,* edited by A. Goldberg, 327–59. New York: International Universities Press, 1983.

Browning, Don S. *Religious Thought and the Modern Psychologies: A Critical Conversation in the Theology of Culture.* Philadelphia: Fortress, 1987.

Coles, Robert. *The Spiritual Life of Children.* New York: Houghton Mifflin, 1990.

Davis, Madeleine, and David Wallbridge. *Boundary and Space: An Introduction to the Work of D. W. Winnicott.* New York: Brunner/Mazel, 1981.

Dicks, H. V. "Object Relations Theory and Marital Studies." *British Journal of Medical Psychology* 36 (1963) 1–12.

Eigen, Michael. "Guntrip's Analysis with Winnicott: A Critique of Glatzer and Evans." *Contemporary Psychoanalysis* 17 (1981) 103–12.

———. *The Psychotic Core.* Northvale, NJ: Aronson, 1986.

Eishold, Kenneth. "The Intolerance of Diversity in Psychoanalytic Institutes." *International Journal of Psychoanalysis* 75 (1994) 785–800.

Ellul, Jacques. *The Subversion of Christianity.* Translated by Geoffrey W. Bromiley. Grand Rapids: Eerdmans, 1986.

Engler, Barbara. *Personality Theories.* Boston: Houghton Mifflin, 1993.

Erikson, Erik. *Childhood and Society.* New York: Norton, 1993.

Fairbairn, Ronald. *Psychoanalytic Studies of the Personality.* London: Routledge, Kegan Paul, 1952.

Freud, Ernst, et. al., editors. *Sigmund Freud: His Life in Pictures and Words.* New York: Norton, 1985.

Freud, Sigmund. *The Interpretation of Dreams.* New York: Norton, 1985. Orig. pub. 1900.

—————. *The Psychopathology of Everyday Life.* In Standard Edition of the Complete Psychological Works 6. London: Hogarth, 1953–74. Orig. pub. 1901.

—————. *Introductory Lectures on Psychoanalysis.* New York: Norton, 1985. Orig. pub. 1916.

—————. *Anxiety and Its Vicissitudes.* New York: Norton, 1985. Orig. pub. 1921.

Gay, Peter. *Freud: A Life For Our Time.* New York: Norton, 1988.

—————, editor. *The Freud Reader,* New York: Norton, 1989.

Giovacchini, Peter L. *Tactics and Techniques in Psychoanalytic Therapy III: The Implications of Winnicott's Contributions.* Northvale, NJ: Aronson, 1990.

Glatzer, H. T., and W. N. Evans. "Guntrip's Analysis with Fairbairn and Winnicott." *International Journal of Psychoanalytic Psychotherapy* 6 (1977) 81–98.

Goldman, Dodi. *In Search of The Real: The Origins and Originality of D. W. Winnicott.* New York: Aronson, 1993.

Gomez, Lavinia. *An Introduction to Object Relations.* New York: New York University Press, 1997.

Grosskurth, Phyllis. *Melanie Klein: Her World and Her Work.* New York: Knopf, 1996.

Grotstein, James R., and Donald B. Rinsley, editors. *Fairbairn and the Origins of Object Relations.* New York: Guilford, 1994.

Guntrip, H. S. "A Study of Fairbairn's Theory of Schizoid Reactions." *British Journal of Medical Psychology* 25 (1952) 86–103.

—————. "Can the Therapist Love The Patient?" In *Personal Relations Therapy: The Collected Papers of H. J. S. Guntrip,* edited by Jeremy Hazell, 399. Northvale, NJ: Aronson, 1994, Orig. pub. 1958.

—————. *Personality Structure And Human Interaction.* New York: International Universities Press, 1961.

—————. "The Manic-Depressive Problem in the Light of the Schizoid Process." *International Journal of Psycho-Analysis* 43 (1962a) 98–112.

—————. "The Schizoid Compromise and Psychotherapeutic Stalemate." *British Journal of Medical Psychology* 35 (1962b) 273–87.

—————. *Schizoid Phenomena, Object Relations and the Self.* New York: International Universities Press, 1968.

—————. *Psychoanalytic Theory, Therapy, and the Self,* New York: Basic Books, 1971.

—————. "My Experience of Analysis with Fairbairn and Winnicott." *International Review of Psychoanalysis* 2 (1975) 145–56.

Hamilton, Victoria. *The Analyst's Preconscious.* Hillsdale, NJ: Analytic Press, 1996.

Hartmann, Heinz. *Ego Psychology and the Problem of Adaptation.* New York: International Universities Press, 1958. Orig. pub. 1939.

Hazell, Jeremy. "Reflections on My Experience of Psychoanalysis with Guntrip." *Contemporary Psychoanalysis* 27 (1991) 148–66.

—————, editor. *Personal Relations Therapy: The Collected Papers of H. J. S. Guntrip.* Northvale, NJ: Aronson, 1994.

———. *H. J. S. Guntrip: A Psychoanalytic Biography.* New York: Free Association Books, 1996.

Hale, Nathan G. *The Rise and Crisis of Psychoanalysis in the United States.* New York: Oxford University Press, 1995.

Heimann, Paula. "Counter-transference." *British Journal of Medical Psychology* 33 (1960) 9–15.

Hughes, Judith M. *Reshaping the Psychoanalytic Domain: The Work of Melanie Klein, W. R. D. Fairbairn, and D. W. Winnicott.* Berkeley: University of California Press, 1989.

Jones, E. *The Life and Work of Sigmund Freud.* Vol. 3. New York: Basic Books, 1957.

Jones, R. Tudor. *Congregationalism in England: 1662–1962.* Boston: Independent, 1962.

Jung, C. G. *Psychological Types.* The Collected Works of C. G. Jung 6. Translated by R. F. C. Hull. Princeton: Princeton University Press, 1971. Orig. pub. 1921.

Kohon, Gregorio. *The British School of Psychoanalysis: The Independent Tradition.* New Haven: Yale University Press, 1986.

Klein, Melanie. *The Psychoanalysis of Children.* London: Hogarth, 1932.

———. *Envy and Gratitude.* London: Tavistock, 1957.

Kiersey, David and Marilyn Bates. *Please Understand Me: Character and Temperament Types.* Corona Del Mar, CA: Prometheus Nemesis, 1978.

Laplanche, J., and J.-B. Pontalis. *The Language of Psychoanalysis.* New York: Norton, 1967.

LeBreque, Alexander. "The Cross in Perspective." *Evangelica* 7.4 (1987) 1–4.

Little, Margaret. *Psychotic Anxieties and Containment: A Personal Record of an Analysis with Winnicott.* Northvale, NJ: Aronson, 1990.

Livingston, James C. *Modern Christian Thought: From the Enlightenment to Vatican II.* New York: Macmillan, 1971.

Macmurray, John. *Interpreting the Universe.* New York: Humanities, 1933.

———. *Reason And Emotion.* London: Faber & Faber, 1935.

———. *The Self as Agent.* New York: Harper & Brothers, 1953.

———. *Persons In Relation.* New York: Harper & Brothers, 1954.

Mahler, Margaret. *The Psychological Birth of the Infant: Symbiosis and Individuation.* New York: Basic Books, 1975.

Markillie, Ronald. "Some Personal Reflections and Impressions of Harry Guntrip." *International Journal of Psychoanalysis* 77 (1996) 763.

Meissner, W. W. *The Paranoid Process: Classical Psychoanalysis and Its Applications.* Northvale, NJ: Aronson, 1978.

———. *The Borderline Spectrum: Differential Diagnosis and Developmental Issues.* Northvale, NJ: Aronson, 1984.

———. *Psychoanalysis and Religious Experience.* New Haven: Yale University Press, 1984.

———. *Psychotherapy of the Paranoid Process.* Northvale, NJ: Aronson, 1986.

———. *Treatment of Patients in the Borderline Spectrum.* Northvale, NJ: Aronson, 1988.

Meltzer, Donald. *Dream Life.* London: Clunie, 1978.

———. *The Kleinian Development, Part II: Richard Week by Week.* London: Clunie, 1989.

Meng, H., and E. L. Freud, editors. *Psychoanalysis and Faith: The Letters of Sigmund Freud and Oskar Pfister.* New York: Basic Books, 1963.

Miller, Alice. *Banished Knowledge: Facing Childhood Injuries.* New York: Doubleday, 1990.

Monte, Christopher F. *Beneath the Mask: An Introduction to Theories of Personality.* 4th ed. New York: Holt, Rinehart & Winston, 1991.

Padel, John. "The Case of Harry Guntrip." *International Journal of Psychoanalysis* 77 (1996) 755.

Polanyi, Michael. *Personal Knowledge: Towards a Post-Critical Philosophy.* Chicago: University of Chicago Press, 1958.

Pontalis, J. B., et al. "A propos du teste de Guntrip." *Nouvelle Revue de Psychoanalyse* 16 (1977) 29–37.

Rayner, Eric. *The Independent Mind in British Psychoanalysis.* New York: Aronson, 1991.

Richardson, Alan. *A Theological Word Book of the Bible.* New York: Macmillan, 1950.

Rizzuto, Ana-Maria. *The Birth of the Living God: A Psychoanalytic Study.* Chicago: University of Chicago Press, 1979.

Rodman, F. Robert, editor. *The Spontaneous Gesture.* Cambridge: Harvard University Press, 1987.

Schore, Allan N. *Affect Regulation and the Origin of the Self: The Neurobiology of Emotional Development.* New York: Erlbaum, 1994.

———. *Affect Regulation and the Repair of the Self.* New York: Norton, 2003.

Seinfeld, Jeffrey. *The Empty Core: An Object Relations Approach to Psychotherapy of the Schizoid Personality.* New York: Aronson, 1991.

Shur, M. *Freud: Living and dying.* New York: International Universities Press, 1972.

Spero, Moshe Halevi, editor. *Psychotherapy of the Religious Patient.* New York: Aronson, 1996.

Strenger, Carlo. "The Classic And The Romantic Vision In Psychoanalysis." *International Journal of Psychoanalysis* 70 (1989) 593.

———. *Between Hermeneutics and Science: An Essay on the Epistemology of Psychoanalysis.* New York: International Universities Press, 1991.

Stolorrow, R., and G. Atwood. *Faces in a Cloud: Subjectivity in Personality Theory.* New York: Aronson, 1979.

Summitt, Roland. *The Accomodation Syndrome.* Los Angeles: University of California Press, 1980.

Sutherland, John. *Fairbairn's Journey into the Interior.* London: Free Association, 1989.

Symington, Neville. *Emotion & Spirit: Questioning the Claims of Psychoanalysis and Religion.* New York: MacMillan,1994.

Waring, E. Graham, editor. *Deism and Natural Religion.* New York: Ungar, 1967.

Watzlawick, Paul. *The Language of Change.* New York: Basic Books, 1978.

Winnicott, C., R. Shepherd, and M. Davis, editors. *D. W. Winnicott: Psycho-Analytic Explorations.* Cambridge: Harvard University Press, 1989.

Winnicott, D. W. *Collected Papers: Through Paediatrics to Psycho-analysis.* New York: Basic Books, 1958.

———. *The Maturational Processes and the Facilitating Environment.* New York: International Universities Press, 1965.

———. *Babies and Their Mothers.* Reading, PA: Addison-Wesley, 1987.

Wolff, Hans Walter. *Anthropology of the Old Testament.* Translated by Margaret Kohl. Philadelphia: Fortress, 1972.

Young-Bruehl, Elizabeth. *Anna Freud: A Biography.* New York: Summit, 1988.